T0332030

BUILDING A RESILIENT ORGANISATION

In this book, John Arthur and Louise Moody introduce the concept of the reasoning chain, a new approach to risk-based reasoning systems in large, complex and distributed organisations. Arguing that these types of organisations are particularly focussed on a triple-helix of chain metaphors – supply, value and reputation chains – the authors propose that there is overwhelming evidence that the accepted approaches to risk and resilience do not complement this architecture. This is extremely problematic because risk and resilience constructs have been formally and informally regulated for these industries.

Building a Resilient Organisation proposes and illustrates a holistic solution to the problems thrown up by existing norms. The resultant reasoning chain can be intentionally designed on an equal footing with supply, value and reputation; a quadruple helix. Through challenge of best practice, an argument unfolds to outline a completely novel approach for risk based resilience reasoning in large distributed organisations. This is illustrated through a series of case studies and guidance to implementation.

This book is an accessible and valuable resource for two key groups. Policy makers, risk managers and operational decision makers – those responsible for large complex businesses. Students – those focussing on governmental, social and industrial applications for resilience and risk.

JOHN ARTHUR has a background in Psychology and Human Factors and blends multi-sector academic and industry interests. Initially focused on researching expert reasoning for high risk professions (e.g. air traffic control), he has held international roles in Unilever, (e.g. Resilience Director) before directing his freelance Organisational Psychology consultancy.

LOUISE MOODY has a background in Psychology and Human Factors predominantly applied in a design context. As an academic consultant she has worked globally in the areas of crisis, risk and resilience. She is currently Professor of Health, Design and Human Factors at Coventry University.

BUILDING A RESILIENT ORGANISATION

THE DESIGN OF RISK-BASED REASONING CHAINS IN LARGE DISTRIBUTED ORGANISATIONS

John Arthur and Louise Moody

Routledge
Taylor & Francis Group

LONDON AND NEW YORK

First published 2019
by Routledge
2 Park Square, Milton Park, Abingdon, Oxon OX14 4RN

and by Routledge
711 Third Avenue, New York, NY 10017

Routledge is an imprint of the Taylor & Francis Group, an informa business

British Library Cataloguing-in-Publication Data
A catalogue record for this book is available from the British Library

Library of Congress Cataloging-in-Publication Data
A catalog record has been requested for this book

ISBN: 978-1-472-48235-8 (hbk)
ISBN: 978-1-315-60571-5 (ebk)

Typeset in Minion Pro and Helvetica Neue
by Florence Production Ltd, Stoodleigh, Devon, UK

CONTENTS

CONTENTS

CONTENTS

FIGURES

PREFACE

THE BASKET CASE

A man in a hot air balloon realised he was lost. He reduced altitude until he spotted a man below. He descended a bit more and shouted. "Excuse me, can you help me? I promised a friend I would meet him an hour ago, but I don't know where I am."

The man below replied. "You are in a hot air balloon hovering approximately 15 metres above the ground. You're between 40 and 41 degrees north latitude and between 59 and 60 degrees west longitude drifting with the wind at about 0.5 metres per second on a heading of 036 degrees."

"You must be an Engineer," said the balloonist.

"I am," replied the man, "How did you know?"

"Well," answered the balloonist, "everything you told me is technically correct, but I've no idea what to make of your information and the fact is I'm still lost. Frankly, you've not been much help at all. If anything, you've delayed my trip."

The man below responded, "You must be in Management."

"I am," replied the balloonist, "but how did you know?"

"Well," said the man, "you don't know where you are or where you're going. You have risen to where you are due to a large quantity of hot air.

You made a promise, which you've no idea how to keep, and you expect people beneath you to solve your problems. The fact is you are in exactly the same position you were in before we met, but now, somehow, it's my fault."

Just then a third person came along and said:

"You know having heard your conversation I think there is a way out of this impasse. Why don't you lower a rope ladder and take this person into the balloon to advise you from up there? I think with a shared perspective the combination of your ability to drive the balloon in practice with their pragmatic knowledge of the physics of the situation means that working together gives you a higher probability of a favourable outcome. Not only that but if you can use your skills collaboratively then you will be making progress and the journey will become enjoyable for you both, at the moment you are both fixated on describing the problem only from within your own worldviews."

The two people looked at each other and said "you must be a Psychologist".

"I am" she said, "how did you know?"

"Because we are intimidated by the idea that you can understand something about this situation that we do not, and we haven't got the time to listen to you because we are much too busy being effective."

PART 1

A journey of design

CHAPTER 1

Introduction – landscape and journey

This book has been written to take you, the readers, on a journey of design. This is a journey which has itself been designed to critically examine two of the most important performance-shaping disciplines for modern business: those of risk management and organisational resilience. As the journey we set out traverses their varied and often quite challenging landscapes we will find ourselves constantly crossing the hidden valley which joins these two disciplines with a third – that of human reasoning.

You should know from the outset that this is not a journey which attempts to introduce new fads or denigrate existing hard-working systems or groups. Rather, it is one which seeks to examine, at the DNA level, the integrity of the decision-making processes found in relation to risk and resilience in the complex and dispersed systems of modern large distributed organisations. This is a DNA which we will come to argue ought to be made up in equal parts from operational logic, organisational psychology and statistical technique.

As we go, we will examine how typical governance, process design, operational success (and failure) factors, measurement approaches and management systems are not, on the whole, designed with these three (performance-shaping) elements in mind. Rather, they are almost always typified by powerful trade-offs based around, just to mention three: the complicated allocation of responsibility for risk and resilience in any business; their perception as credible disciplines to add business value; and the appetite for complexity of the organisation to deliver systems in support of them.

These and other trade-offs, we will argue, are the decisions which, under scrutiny, can be shown to dramatically weaken the value proposition for mainstream risk management and operational resilience. In some cases, they can even turn this into a negative proposition.

NATIVE FORMS OF RISK REASONING – SOME EXAMPLES

Imagine, if you will, just the following six scenarios:

SCENARIO 1: TRANSFORMATION

In a major transformation project for your business the team is tasked with coming up with a formal risk register. Using a group brainstorming exercise, a large list of potential risks is drawn up. Next these are transferred onto post-it pads and, again in a group exercise, the post-it pads are positioned on a makeshift Cartesian graph hand-drawn on a flip-chart. This graph has been split into four equal-sized quadrants. Its two axes are labelled, the first probability and the second impact. The risk events which position high on both axes are considered the priorities. This information is later transferred to a spreadsheet where actions are added and responsible persons identified. This spreadsheet is reviewed at each subsequent project meeting (if there is time).

SCENARIO 2: ENTERPRISE RISK MANAGEMENT

Your Corporate Risk Department has contacted your department requesting a contribution to its Enterprise Risk Management exercise. You have been allocated as the responsible person for: "Availability of production – ensuring a responsive, resilient, continuous and profitable operation". You are required to fill in a template which they have designed asking you for the following data:

- risk attitude;
- risk appetite;
- key activities;
- key Performance Indicators (including metrics and targets).

SCENARIO 3: BUSINESS CONTINUITY MANAGEMENT

The team responsible for Business Continuity Management has identified your function as business critical. In consequence they have asked you to use their template to provide a detailed business continuity risk assessment and mitigation plan. This must outline how you will ensure continued operation of your unit in the event of the loss of the use of the building. This is to include the steps you have taken to ensure:

- continuity of business;
- protection of staff;
- protection of reputation;
- protection of shareholder value;
- acceleration of effective decision making during serious incident or crisis.

SCENARIO 4: CYBER-RISK

The new team tasked with cyber-security in your organisation is drafting a cyber resilience strategy. They have contacted your team to inform them that all staff are required to sign off compliance with a newly drafted digital and computer hygiene policy. Furthermore, they want you to provide evidence that all staff have completed a basic on-line training package on cyber-security.

SCENARIO 5: EMERGENCY AND DISASTER RECOVERY

Following a recent corporate audit policy review your division has scored a level 2. This means that improvements are required. The Chief Operating Officer has therefore tasked you with an immediate update of:

- The Emergency Response Plan for your facility;
- The Disaster Recovery Plan for the IT hub you are responsible for;
- The Avian Flu Pandemic Preparedness Plan for your international team.

SCENARIO 6: SUPPLY CHAIN ANTI-CORRUPTION

As global Supply Chain Director for your organisation you have been tasked by the Corporate Secretaries Department to conduct a risk assessment exercise. This is to focus on the organisation's ability to satisfy OECD guidelines on: "Ensuring integrity and transparency in the international economy . . . in particular in such areas as transparency and anti-corruption."

THE NEED FOR A JOURNEY OF DESIGN

Why would you want to come on a journey of design which seeks to examine the integrity of the strategic and tactical decision making processes found in relation to risk and resilience in large, complex and dispersed systems? Well, these six scenarios will be familiar to a greater or lesser degree to anyone working in such an organisation. Each exemplifies ways in which the current industry standard approaches to risk and resilience, when viewed back to back like this, may be considered somewhat less than coherent.

More than this, much of the applied reasoning found within the processes which surround these typical, and very different, approaches to risk can be shown to be fallacious. Chiefly this is because such reasoning is constrained, almost from the outset, by a competing set of desires which are: coming from fundamentally different processes; requiring wholly different data types; supporting a completely different narrative for different parts of the business; and addressing wholly separate internal and external audiences.

The time and workload pressures alone these combined processes create for a large business build up natural constraints which tend to resist them. These amass to prejudice expedient, unsophisticated risk systems with a low tolerance for complexity. These are just some of the reasons which will predict a failure of these systems to add value and indeed a potential for these systems to strip it out. This is not least just in an inappropriate channelling of resource.

FACTORS WHICH SHAPE EXPECTATION

Resistance and expedience conspire in the face of a larger frustration still. The need for these plural forms of risk and resilience systems, like those shown above, has become a given in today's industry. Performance in this area, in a variety of guises, is therefore expected to be reported. That expectation may even, in certain quarters, be a regulatory requirement of the licence to operate. Perhaps because of that regulatory context, organisations often become heavily committed to a narrative of demonstrating outward compliance with policy and or industry standard. This is rather than analysing the operational effectiveness and value creation potential of risk and resilience systems for their own particular context(s).

This is a state of affairs not helped by the fact that both internal and external audit processes will tend to reinforce the expedience of measuring episodic performance indicators over measuring long-term business performance itself – a situation which is not helped by the shifting tides of British, European and International Standards. These are constantly co-evolving alongside a rather more robust kind of marketplace application of the concepts of risk and resilience by those tasked, but not necessarily formally equipped, to deliver them.

To all of these challenges you have to add two other observable performance factors. First, the professionalisation of the risk and resilience disciplines remains falteringly slow. The person given management responsibility to deliver a monitoring system in these areas is usually a manager of a different expertise who may have many other roles. This explains why it is easily observable that the design of systems remains so derivative. It tends to rest on the received wisdoms of accepted long-term practices, rather than benefitting from the many decades of formal research evidence on this subject.

Second, and lastly for now, it is important to note in consequence that many practice enablers, such as policy, processes and tools, can be shown to contain significant flaws. These continue to enshrine failures of logic and of definition, prominent reasoning pathologies and suboptimal, or even completely invalid, approaches to measurement and therefore deduction. This is a state of affairs which may, in private, be attested to by their responsible agents. However, it is justified by a cardinal set of fears around available time and tolerance for complexity.

Seen as a whole problem set, rather than traded off in private isolation against the wider aims of any given set of business priorities at any time, we would argue that these and other factors strain the strategic credibility of most risk and resilience systems well past breaking point. The received wisdom might be that such lowered strategic credibility will leave organisations more exposed to threats, crises and reputation losses. However, we argue that organisations are simply being rendered less effective in meeting their primary business objectives.

The solution to all of these challenges is a journey of design. One that tries to critically re-establish, perhaps from first principles for some, the purpose and the utility of risk and resilience reasoning for complex industries. A journey that suggests how risk and resilience systems might be purposely designed to deliver context-specific and strategically effective business value as a primary objective and compliance and reassurance as a side effect.

A MAP FOR OUR JOURNEY

So, as this book has been written to take you on that journey of design – to critically examine risk management and organisational resilience – we may benefit from stopping a moment to look at the map. The book will be split into four roughly equal parts as follows:

PART 1: ON RISK-BASED

Part 1 begins by examining how risk is currently constructed in industry (Chapter 2). Risk, we shall see from these arguments, cannot be thought of as having any agreed single definition. Its definition is therefore a case of choosing to speak of it by making a range of appropriate selections from the available dialects – for example, by comparing the language of ethics and diligence with the language of pragmatic events.

Continuing this discussion (Chapter 3), we examine some of the key design features that would enhance the definition and application of the risk construct in general. What becomes clear is that several critical reasoning problems stand in the way of the utility of the current end product – for example, the semantics of which risk terminology (agreed or otherwise) to apply and the use of measurement science to quantify business materiality. Negotiating these challenges early, and somewhat head-on, clears the space to talk about how a risk system might be designed and used.

To begin addressing some of the challenges raised by these early chapters, a detailed case study (Chapter 4) examines one applied solution which tackled them. This is a comprehensive risk methodology designed in a fast-moving consumer goods company. This chapter goes on to examine the benefit of accepting an appropriately complex formulation of risk. This is in order to reason effectively about the performance-shaping factors of its strategic decisions and business outcomes.

It is the (very thorny) issue – of the meaning of probability within the risk construct – which offers the first and the greatest challenge when we critically consider the measurement of risk (Chapter 5). The tensions within statistical science, which cannot agree on how probability should be constructed or applied even today, do not bode well for a pragmatic cut-and-paste of methods. Within any pragmatic application of probability reasoning, the correct method for which remains enormously disputed among different sectors, this tension cannot be considered at all insignificant. That problem will not be easily solved.

PART 2 – ON RISK-BASED RESILIENCE

Having laid these foundations for the emerging risk rationality of the book, Part 2 turns to address the question of the meaning and the function of the concept of organisational, or business, resilience. Resilience, it can be shown, is also beset with definition challenges (Chapter 6). Whether these are examined from the extant use of the concept in industry, in British or European standards, or in academic science, time and again it is the lack of agreement which becomes apparent. The chapter concludes by proposing a road map of five definition principles. These might act as a template to design a useful construct from the available architecture.

Crossing the valley between the risk and the resilience landscapes at this point, we take a first look at the contribution that some of the relevant theories human reasoning in the presence of uncertainty should perhaps have on our design (Chapter 7). Here, once again, the subject matter is typified by wide-ranging disagreement. Also, some highly counter-intuitive principles begin to emerge. These highlight research evidence which points to the need for a more naturalistic, human-centred and therefore more intellectually involved method as the most rational form of risk reasoning.

Leaving these debates to one side for a moment, we consider the ways in which industry conventionally measures risk today (Chapter 8). We note the highly flawed nature of the common assumptions found in these approaches. One particular assumption is that the choice of scales to measure risk (and therefore resilience) is somewhat of a simple matter of preference given the available time. This expediency reveals some of the deep cracks resultant in the statistical logic of mainstream practice. The conclusion here is as simple as it is challenging. Real expertise (statistical and mathematical) is needed to reason sensibly with these two constructs.

We close this part of the book with another case study, this time in risk measurement. This highlights an alternative method, and tool, to measure risk. This alternative applies best when the appetite for complexity within the organisation remains very low. When the expectation is that the accepted practices should continue, we predict that there is still room for reform (Chapter 9) that practitioners would support. The tool in question offers an enhanced method of scoring as a direct benefit from a software approach. This is designed to cater for the conventional appetite. This Trojan horse effect is seen as an important way to subvert suboptimal systems by initially supporting them.

PART 3 - ON RISK-BASED RESILIENCE REASONING SYSTEMS

As this is a journey to examine large, complex, distributed systems using the concepts discussed so far, Part 3 addresses some of the pressing applied challenges brought by such large systems. This discussion segues into a detailed examination of the nature, and the likely effectiveness, of a common solution, the practice of using British and International Standards Organisation Standards for risk and resilience constructs in this environment (Chapter 10).

The first part of this case study demonstrates, contrary to what may be commonly believed, that there is a lack of validated evidence to support the efficacy of the methods found in industry standards. Rather, they best represent a collected wisdom approach. The second part of the chapter takes licence therefore to perform a behavioural content analysis to ascertain what a large organisation would be required to do to meet just the top eight of these standards. This acts as a sobering organisational impact assessment for their rational (rather than nominal) deployment.

Moving on from this more academic treatment of these subjects we begin to ask, notwithstanding the many problems and hurdles these constructs propose, how they are used in industry today. An ethnographic look as some of the key organisational factors (Chapter 11) that shaped the success and failure of their legacy systems, like Business Continuity Management, begins to pave the way.

From this consideration we then examine the design constraints of a more effective system. A second case study (Chapter 12) from Consumer Goods addresses the critical question of where a (better-designed) resilience system might still struggle to find a place within the existing landscape of ideas – for example, with reference to emergency planning and crisis response.

As we round off this argument, the heavy work of actually implanting such a system within the existing reasoning infrastructure of an organisation (Chapter 13) presents a final volley of success critical questions. These must be addressed if the system is to meet the standards laid down in the journey so far. Part 3 of the book concludes with an advisory template for a minimum rationality in embedding a risk and resilience reasoning system – for example, the necessity to consider appetite for complexity and the pre-existing culture of decision making in the industry in question.

PART 4 – ON A RISK-BASED RESILIENCE REASONING CHAIN

Having systematically examined the pertinent landscapes of risk, resilience and reasoning from an applied academic and a practical reference point, our journey of design needs to finish with a commitment to the most valued performance-shaping factor for all industrial users of risk-based resilience, that of pragmatism. Part 4 seeks to rationally combine the findings of parts 1–3 into a chain of (better) reasoning for any large, complex organisation.

To begin this part of the journey we look backwards momentarily to summarise the principles we have already discerned, such as the need for a design-led analysis, the imperative to think in holistic systems and the need to engage deeply with the experienced reality of practitioners on the ground.

From this starting point we launch into a two-part consideration of the closing case study of the book. This is a larger-scale, risk-based resilience reasoning system in a VUCA (volatile, uncertain, complex and ambiguous) context. The first part of the case study (Chapter 14) describes the process, metrics, outcomes and software of this approach in a stylised Q&A. This concludes that a more complex system speaking many dialects of risk and holding these in tension with business outcomes is not only feasible – as is evident from the system in question – but it is desirable.

A second part to this case study considers something we have termed the 'so what' moment. This addresses (Chapter 15) how the outcomes of a risk-based resilience reasoning system can be used to design resilience countermeasures, or business interventions, that have been successfully translated back into the strategic reference grammar of the business – that is to say, proposed as a business case for an investment decision. This completes the case for the necessary business materiality of risk and resilience.

Beginning to close out the argument of the book we come full circle. We address why organisations want to use risk and resilience systems. Knowing what we now know, there remains an imperative to deconstruct the rationality of the high-level and lower-lying goals any organisation has in using risk and resilience intentionally and meaningfully (Chapter 16).

We conclude that the use of these constructs only gains traction when they become what we call business engines. That is to say, they are not an analysis or a regulatory end in themselves. It is imperative that organisations make a step change in their maturity of approach to these reasoning challenges in order to design these to support the material goals of the business concerned.

The final critical challenge of this enhanced reasoning must always be one of a translation back to an agreed utility for the host organisation. The supply chain, the value chain and the reputation chain of any business all have a palpable contribution to business value. So we argue that this new chain, the risk-based resilience reasoning chain, must be able to perform on exactly the same playing field.

To bring our whole journey to an end we look back to survey the features of the landscape we have crossed. Thus, we consider the unifying arguments for the reasoning chain. In Chapter 17 we review the necessary journey that serious professionals need to take in order for risk-based resilience systems design to be efficacious:

- the necessity to overcome ineffective definitions and reject flawed logic;
- the necessity of a systematic approach to purposely design an effective and pragmatic system that fits the appetite for complexity of your context;
- the necessity to take a mature approach to fashion validated tools that are highly aligned to the organisation's goals;
- the necessity to design in an accountable business materiality to the use of these constructs, rather than one which merely orbits an agreeable fallacy of illogical (re)assurance.

These are the necessary conditions, we argue, to create a reasoning chain for a business which adds a new strand to the existing DNA triple helix of the value, supply and reputation chains already in use.

Only then can risk and resilience take their place as performance optimisers which add value.

CHAPTER 2

Risk as a construct

Throughout this book we will come to speak of organisational risk not as one unitary thing – the fallacy of an agreed definition for risk – but as a range of discrete and observably different things arranged into observably different systems. The collective term we will use to describe these systems is dialectic. In essence what we would like you to accept is that the world of risk reasoning as fundamentally a dialectical exercise. By that we mean that it is possible to observe that different groups, even in the same organisation, will use a common language of risk but they are, in fact, speaking very different dialects of that language.

To better introduce this idea, let's proceed by way of analogy. With it we can bat away, for now, a lot of the traditional and contradicting preconceptions that tend to orbit use of this simple four-letter word – risk. What we will come to see is that these are the unfortunate standard baggage created by the assumption that all risk language is in fact relating to the same construct. To illustrate this, we will swap out that contentious word "risk" for another similar, but less hotly contested, word. That word is "Law".

THE ARCHITECTURE OF THE BRITISH LEGAL SYSTEM

Now let's be clear at the outset that this is purely an analogy. It is designed not for accuracy therefore but for applicability. If we ask, in Britain, *what is the law*, people might respond in a number of ways. You can try answering it in your head just now, if you want to play along at home.

Once the initial responses about civil society, or the role of police enforcement, are out of the way, people tend to step back and quickly realise something quite fundamental. Law is actually a complex construct. Thus, to use the word is to denote *a system of things not a unitary thing.* Law is a complex and multi-tiered system, yes, but also a very logical one. Here is a, very rough, outline of six of its major parts.

JURISPRUDENCE

Sometimes just called the philosophy of law, jurisprudence is the moral and philosophical basis for what we have as law, and also why we have it. It is always a societally reasoned artifice (which is why we can talk about British law). It is an argument or justification for the very nature of the thing, or things, we call law. In and of itself therefore, it is not the law.

THE RULE OF LAW

At the societal level this is an essential representation of what has been agreed and will be enforced as law. Despite the name it does not contain the rules, so to speak, upon which law enforcement will be based. It contains a sociological consent that, once any and all of those rules are laid down, they will be binding in total on everyone in a society. The rule of law agreement functions like a sort of social mandate. In and of itself, it is not the law.

LEGISLATION

This, arguably, is what most people would see as the recognisable substance of the law. It is the stuff that expresses the specific rules, and any ongoing changes to them. To sacrifice complete accuracy for the benefit of this analogy, let's say that in Britain there is no law that is not traceable to an act of Parliament. The democratic processes of this law-making ensures fairness, representativeness and so on. Legislation creates the acts and statutes that are definitely the substance of the law. In and of themselves however, they are not the law.

JUDICIAL SYSTEM

Again to keep things simple, let's recognise that where the law happens is, in fact, in a court. Each type of court has judges who examine real cases of suspected law breaking, or legal disputation, and pass judgement. These collective judgements are known as precedents (or case law). Future judges in similar situations can rest on these precedents or challenge them. In this form the law self-regulates, and indeed updates at a pace with culture and technology. In the judicial system the law becomes personal, it applies to real persons but in and of itself, however, it is not the law.

THE LEGAL SYSTEM

A group of professionals, usually barristers, solicitors and legal executives, make up a body in society who represent the law to the people and the people to the law. These lawyers expect client treatment to rest on legal precedents and will base their advice upon it. Of course, from time to time, the uniqueness of the situation means that they will also be responsible for creating precedents. In and of itself, the legal system administers the law but it is not the law.

PROSECUTION AGENCIES

Various police forces are agents who put the law into effect by preventing or apprehending lawbreakers. In so doing, however, they do not need a full and accurate knowledge of the law in the way lawyers or judges might. Rather, they have a rule set as their basis for apprehending and detaining potential lawbreakers. That full appreciation of the law is enshrined in the work of other prosecuting agencies, such as the Crown Prosecution Service. It is they who arbitrate, on the basis of evidence, which lawbreakers will face the judicial system (assisted of course by the legal system). The Police, the Crown Prosecution Service and other prosecuting agencies bring the law to bear. In and of themselves, they are not the law.

The law as system

Now you might be thinking, what has any of this got to do with the construct of risk? The answer is actually very much in every way. When we represent the construct of the law as we have, it becomes possible to see how, although it is a causal behaviour chain, each link in the chain requires a different dialect to be spoken. Notice that however we look at the system and its dialects we are drawn to a kind of fulcrum point where we can speak of the law as experienced. Figure 2.1 represents this.

Adding two more labels makes the diagram a little clearer. Figure 2.2 shows that there are five dialects being spoken here, two pertaining to what we can agree the law means and the other two on how we agree the law applies to experience. The fifth is the balance-point dialect, i.e. where these others meet in decision making.

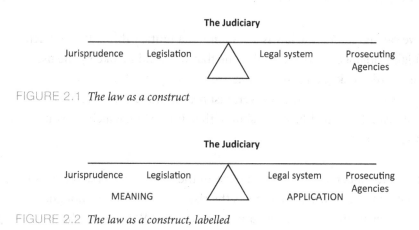

FIGURE 2.1 *The law as a construct*

FIGURE 2.2 *The law as a construct, labelled*

If, when you were talking about the law, it became clear that you really only mean to discuss the left-hand side of this diagram, the meaning part that relates to law as it is interpreted philosophically and socially, would you still be talking about the law? The answer is yes, but your focus would clearly be speaking more about its meaning than its application. You are essentially speaking only some of the available dialects of the law.

Conversely, if you sought to really focus on the application part of the law, you would have to speak very differently. This could be thought of as different dialects within that same language. Neither the meaning nor the application dialect would in any way be inaccurate, even though they would be speaking about very different things. They are simply at ends of a unified definitional spectrum.

Notice too, which is why we have drawn the diagram the way we have, that there is a fulcrum point. The judiciary is where these different dialects of law result in critical and meaningful causal behavioural chains – chains that come into effect whichever starting point you choose. The judiciary is the key inflection point – it is the place where what the law means and how it applies are judged in real-time decisions and their implications.

TOWARDS THE ARCHITECTURE OF A RISK SYSTEM

So we can agree that the law is a system not a unitary thing. It is, in fact, a highly analogous system to the one that we could invoke by the use of another word – risk. To illustrate that, we will keep the definitional wrangles to a neat shortlist. However, just bear in mind there is nothing in the least neat about the longer version of this discussion, which we will have to come to later.

What would happen if we invited the use of the word risk to reference not a unitary thing but a whole system? Is the risk construct better thought of in systems terms than as a single, unified definition? Well, as you have

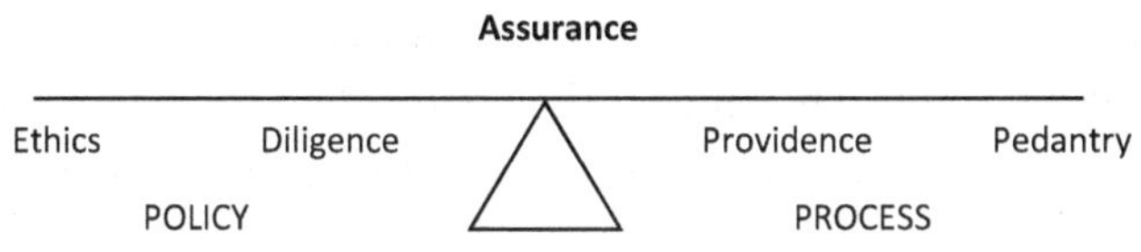

Assurance

Ethics	Diligence		Providence	Pedantry
	POLICY		PROCESS	

FIGURE 2.3 *Risk as a construct*

surely guessed, we feel that risk is only meaningful when it is thought about in systems terms. Using that same diagram approach, Figure 2.3 illustrates how that could work.

ETHICS

Risk can connote the imperative to do the right thing. Ethics can be societal: for example, where the acceptability or tolerability of risk(s) is a group judgement of a balanced equation around some greater good. In fields such as nuclear power, the ethics of societal risk shapes (almost) all of the main decisions and trade-offs.

Ethics can, of course, be personal too. In fields such as medicine, or aviation safety, the formal consent to a level of personal responsibility for accepting (inherent) risk actually forms a binding part of the social contract.

The wider ethics of risk are usually judged by an externalised court of opinion. An easy spot for why this sort of risk is important can be made by referencing the woes of the Volkswagen Audi Group over their now infamous emissions fixing scandal in 2016. The case is very complicated, but the company (corporately) clearly suffered an ethical lapse, or took an ethical risk. Society at large did not like it one bit and punishment was swift and commercially severe. All similar companies in the sector will have a heightened awareness of their own vulnerability to ethical shock.

DILIGENCE

Risk language can be used to refer to the mechanics of empowerment – the sort of mechanics which allow operatives (such as risk managers, regulators, auditors) to enforce a path of commonly agreed assessment for organisational risks. Diligence is the justification force for systematic behaviour patterns based around forms of risk, such as industrial safety.

The diligence (sometimes called due diligence) of risk practice is also judged by an externalised court of opinion. Regulators, key stakeholders and shareholders are the judges of the fitness of the resulting systems and controls. The diligence approach of an organisation is often historically founded. When a system has gone wrong in the past, corrective, preventative or even punitive measures are built into the future "due diligence" assessment of continued behaviour.

ASSURANCE

Risk is often an internal mechanism of self-explanation for an industry, particularly in corporate settings. One function of risk assessment is always to give licence to operate. Corporations use risk assurance behaviour to convince themselves, and significant franchised others such as audit, of the legitimacy of a pursuit: for example, the management of physically dangerous or commercially uncertain exploration behaviour.

Assurance is mainly judged by an internal court of opinion. Although often guided by external standards setting, it comes to be enshrined in internal policy. Indeed, the integrity of the policy requires it to be routinely tested (sometimes called a positive assurance exercise) for its impact on real-time decisions and behaviours.

The corporate world (and sometimes corporate law) internally judges the fitness of risk assurance. Sometimes those judgements can be up-scaled to more sophisticated constructs such as those of appetite and culture (see the emergence of the Safety Culture arguments in the late 1990s).

PROVIDENCE

Risk can be defined as the use of reasoned decision making to meet the challenges of a set of objectives. Often called risk management, this conveys benefits and offsets threats. This is mainly because the presence of internal risk-based reasoning often enhances the defensibility of action and investment. In a mature risk approach, those benefits come from trusting that analytical rigour has protected against a negative behaviour set and/or promoted a positive alternative.

Providence is less easily judged. Here risk is an internal tool within the purview of project management. As such, it is a good practice and suffers very few genuine checks and balances as to its quality or effectiveness. The actual judge of the fitness of a providential risk system is really business success or failure data. This creates an uneasy relationship between the idea of calculated risk and merely identified risk.

PEDANTRY

Risk can, of course, just be the following of rules and regulations surrounding the collapsing of its definition onto a routine audit of threats and hazards: risk here operating as a sort of collective noun. Its use can even be just an innate conservativism for its own sake. In the early history of risk, it is arguable that this was a primary use of the concept. Risk checklists proliferated and risk language was always pejorative.

Pedantry is perhaps the most culturally and internally judged form of risk reasoning, as well as the oldest. Risk used as a weapon of reproach like this can lead to idioms such as *health and safety gone mad*. Pedantic risk systems are inherently self-validating, and the danger of tokenism looms increasingly as responsibility for these approaches is sublimated down to the coalface and away from the strategic decision-making reality of business controls.

Risk as system

So, as with the law example, it is easily defensible to think of risk as having multiple discernible dialects. The five that we have here would not even be considered exhaustive, since they do not begin to break into the psychological, emotional or postmodern spaces of the debate. Limited as this group is, however, it does convey that same sense of gradation from meaning-setting to principles to practice.

The questions that flow from this dialect model are interesting ones. Considered in relative isolation, each dialect can highlight systemic decisions that have to be made. The choice of the primary dialect in a business would certainly be instrumental in the design of the resultant risk system and risk mechanism beliefs. It would certainly also be instrumental in setting the subsequent measurement foci and behaviours.

It is tempting, even at this early stage, to introduce the idea of the need to design a balanced risk system, i.e. one that speaks an appropriate range of these dialects. The range would be purposely tailored to appropriate times and demands predicated on the supply chain of decisions and permissions needed. For now, let's just note that this is a good idea which we will come to in more detail later as we propose a systems-led approach.

Accepting something like the discrete dialects in this rough model, the key question can clearly no longer be: what is risk? Instead, that question ought to be: which dialect of risk is the appropriate one to be speaking in which circumstances? If you call to mind the six risk scenarios at the head of the previous chapter, it might strike you that we could now revisit these and fit them to this dialectic schema. To ask, in essence, what is each of them actually talking about?

- Transformation risk register – providence/pedantry
- Enterprise risk management – diligence/assurance
- Business continuity plan – diligence/assurance
- Cyber-security – diligence/assurance
- Corporate audit – diligence/assurance
- Anti-corruption – ethics/diligence

What that would show is that these six challenges, all ostensibly calling themselves a risk assessment, can span four of the available dialects of risk in our basic model. Notice a problem here, however: the majority of them (four from six) are only actually attempting to speak two dialects. Furthermore, it is the two which lend themselves to being formalised in policy and not, as one might have expected from the description of the analyses, in process. This does give us a bit of a problem to face, but it is as well that we talk about it now.

THE SPECIAL CASE OF RISK AS PROVIDENCE

Our problem can best be illustrated if we re-work our diagram as shown in Figure 2.4.

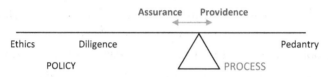

FIGURE 2.4 *Risk as a resolved construct*

Risk systems have always benefitted emotionally, if that is the right word, from too much policy compliance, too much reassurance-seeking behaviour and not enough pragmatic decision making. They have always favoured assessment over action. What we have called providence here is the only dialect that has a pure process outcome. Clearly pedantry is very process driven too, but we do not consider this dialect to be operationally helpful at all.

For reasons we will go on to discuss in later chapters, it is the process element of the risk dialects that deserves to be their fulcrum. Providential risk, in company terms, is the one dialect that impacts the way agents and systems can experience risk as cognition and behaviours. It is the one dialect of risk that describes something phenomenological, something in real time and space. The one that most easily links it to other behaviours, such as decision making. This is as opposed to those three very stylised dialects which really only connote believing something which is largely suspended in theory. We might note that is why it is the corporate reporting jargon of risk assurance.

Providential risk, which we will later come to consider as events-based risk, has to be the fulcrum dialect. It describes the operational interface with real matter, or, because we are in the digital age, with real matter and real data. Decisions based on, or ignoring, providential risk are going to move that matter or data around meaningfully in a universe of results. Decision making around real material cause and effect is what gives risk any meaning.

If you do examine the body of work around risk in your organisation, it is a critical and easy step to ask whether you are using a dialect of phenomenology. What is being measured, reported, controlled and influenced ought to be real, not just perception. This means is that our reasoning object (and of course what and how we might measure) must cross over from the politics of intention to the pragmatism of decision making.

Risk, emotionally in large, complex, distributed organisations, once it moves away from safety as a working concept, has always, to its discredit, tended towards a policy dialect. This is despite the fact, useful as it may be for a corporate language of reassurance, that the utility of the risk construct remains at its most effective at the process end of the spectrum. This is assuming that it avoids a descent into pedantry.

CONCLUSION FROM THIS CHAPTER

Only two main points, by way of closing this initial discussion on the risk construct being dialectic in nature, are really needed thus far.

First, we believe that it is a quality check on the effectiveness of industrial risk systems that they are designed to be (at the operational or enterprise level) at this providential end of the spectrum.

What this does not mean, however, is that the definition of risk fuelling that design can be understood in isolation to these other dialects we have discerned. That would be a profound weakening of the construct. Rather, the definition should emanate from and return to the three elements above it (ethics, diligence, assurance). The result will be a utilitarian and, importantly, externally validated and multi-audience system.

Second, the deliberate application of risk in these dialectical forms can only evolve actively within the consciousness of a company if it helps it pursue its core material purpose.

The name many commentators are now giving to this process is understanding *appetite for risk*. Risk systems must be operationally valid realities predicated on an appetite that can be satisfied through expressing business value in the context of social value.

To put that in a much shorter sentence, risk for any company should be considered:

The optimisation of profit within ethical parameters.

CHAPTER 3

Designing a risk system – some key early challenges

In this chapter we will simply address four key early challenges around the intentional design of a risk system for any large organisation. We will see that these surround the pressing high-level questions of the acuity of the risk definition and the accuracy and effectiveness of the measurement system which assesses it. Accepting a poorly-defined risk construct as the starting point for the design of this system is a choice that very quickly backfires. This can only lead to one of two further propositions. One, the slightly absurd and reductionist position, that the risk measurement predicated on this definition can also afford to be almost completely abstract in that case, and yet somehow still be meaningful. Two, the challenge to immediately expand the attribute set of this risk construct to make it amenable to an organisationally pertinent measurement.

Favouring the latter solution to poorly defined risk (as construct and measurement), we will propose a four-fold master schema. This will help us arrive at a first pass for a credible definition of a meaningful risk system, i.e. one which defines a clear construct and its measurement. This insists that risk definition is an involved process of the semantically accurate objectification of a measurably material outcome. The test for the authenticity of this definition and its measurement is that they evidently can go on to support strategic business decision making. To do this they must be accepted within the main reference grammar of the organisation.

Having reached this first pass of, relatively straightforward, scientific conclusions about the necessary framing of risk definition and measurement in a business logical and systemic approach, we encounter a further challenge. We consider why, although many risk systems could benefit from this rationality, organisations would still appear to be confused about how to design and deploy them.

CURRENT DEFINITION AND MEASUREMENT

So far we have said that risk, for large, complex, distributed organisations, needs to be understood as an interwoven series of appropriate dialects. Each of these is facing different objects and is designed to speak to different audiences. We have also concluded that the outcome of reasoning with risk like this should be seen as: the optimisation of profit within ethical parameters. Although we haven't yet fully expanded on what this means in practice, two things become clear if we accept it for now.

First, when it comes to the measurement activity that would support a sophisticated model of risk like this, we would expect to see something suitably complex. Certainly something more complex than the widely accepted and reported "formula" which uses probability and impact to create a set of Cartesian coordinates or multiplies them to form the single statistic:

$$R = P \times I$$

Second, when it comes to the support of business decision making based on risk analysis, we would expect to see something that applied itself directly to the question of business value. This would support operational decision making in a similar way to the way that the supply, value and reputation constructs do. That is to say, from within a systems approach. Such a system would be designed to produce (decision making) behaviour not just information.

If we accept the need to do these two things – to purposely design this behaviour-based form of risk measurement and to purposely design its subsequent interface with business decision making – this begins to expose a very real tension. It comes in the form of a further key challenge. Will our risk construct be measured by objective facts or subjective beliefs?

The route that most industry risk measurement systems appear to take to navigate these challenges is basically to ignore them. These, wholly scientific, tensions are batted away by busy managers as an inconvenience of philosophy. Instead, risk assessment agents are expected to present people with the widely accepted and endorsed norm: a form of the probability/impact formula and a spreadsheet upon which to record, and sometimes annotate, their results.

Thus, simplified and apparently practical questions and robust (easy to use) scales take the place of any real measurement science. The use of attractive verbal and numerical surrogates allows users to generate quasi-statistical judgements believing them to be good measurement and, importantly, best available practice.

Typically, this expedient approach is a question of outcome at the cost of process on the basis of available time. This is something we will go on to discuss as an appetite for complexity. So, when the appetite is low, we produce these hastily generated measurements and practice a naïve Mathematics on them. For example, we can comparatively prioritise discrete probability impact assessments for risk as if the risks themselves really were independent and had been measured as like for like.

When we later examine the outcomes of this process – our resultant priority list – we can also practice a naïve type of factor analysis. We can aggregate what now appear to be highly similar risks into larger groupings. This means we don't end up with too many results to be communicated to busy audiences who are perhaps looking, in any case, for that very popular "top ten risks" type of judgement from us.

THE COST OF CHALLENGING THE STATUS QUO

It does not require close examination to demonstrate that, without some significant scientific buttressing, these heuristic shortcuts are fallacious. They are not, as they pertain to be, a simplification of a complex set of constructs driven by the need for pragmatism. They are just simple and, with that, virtually meaningless. To reason in these ways is to fail to accept that risk is innately a socially constructed metaphysic, one which lies completely at odds with an oversimplified heuristic that imagines it to be reducible to the product of set of probability and impact scores (really judgements) given to a discretised list of events.

This tension, in our view, can only be consciously bridged by interrogating the integrity of your working definition for risk in tandem with the validity of your measurement system. This integrity and validity must be expressed in how the system's designers have chosen to embrace appropriate complexity in the interests of system utility – or, to put that another way, to design something which works, which is actually fit for purpose.

To do this well requires the risk system designer overcome at least a quartet of meta-level challenges common to any credible (scientific) use of the construct of 'risk'. These are: semantics; abstraction; measurement; and materiality. Together they provide us with an initial framework for the design of a meaningful risk system.

THE SEMANTIC CHALLENGE

Semantics relate to meaning or logic in a language. So, for example, words like education and medicine, although those convey quite complex and sometimes even abstract ideas, are semantically quite rich words. They can comfortably stand alone and still refer to something immediately meaningful and accessible to their user without qualification. Qualification can, of course, be added to sharpen their focus, e.g. further education, Third World medicine. However, words like these do not lack focus when they have no prefixes or suffixes.

Risk is not like that. It has something of a semantic problem therefore. It is comparatively poor at conveying any meaning *unless it is qualified* by suffixes or prefixes. Risk has varied and even contradictory meanings in its contemporary use, and the briefest look at the extant research makes this abundantly clear. Risk has a disputed meaning. This goes some way to explaining why, in industry, the word is almost never used by itself. Prefixes like financial, safety, supply-chain, and suffixes like evaluation, assessment and exposure, are commonplace. It is clear that these prefixes and suffixes do most of the semantic heavy lifting. It is these terms, more than the risk term, which tell you what you might actually be expected in terms of data, measurement and decisions.

Any genuine pluralities of terminology within an organisation's risk system are likely to be needed because there is actually a different referent, e.g. corporate risk compared to supply-chain risk compared to financial risk. This is, once again, our dialectic argument. It is easy to see that, as these are different things measured by different methods using different currencies, they should be consciously held in a semantic tension. People need to know that risk means something different in each case. Different decisions need to be informed by different forms of risk.

This is no more important than when large distributed organisations display the tendency to round up risks as their communication moves up the organisational hierarchy. Risks, of different kinds, are usually rolled together and re-prioritised in a simplified from in order to satisfy auditors, regulators and executives who may demand a depleted list. To place the pluriform concepts connoted by the meanings of risk discussed so far in these different contexts into a single semantic blender is hugely ill-advised.

Accepting the imperative to address the semantic challenge means that risk will not have a unitary meaning or measurement in any organisation. Instead the organisation can specify, diversify and enforce different meanings in different contexts and simply hold these in tension. The way to manage this tension is within a system of thinking with differential consequences for decision making. Appropriately sophisticated risk semantics are critical to diversify the effective reasoning appropriately.

THE ABSTRACTION CHALLENGE

Risk, in and of itself, presents us with a challenge because it is abstract. Any desire to use it to help an organisation must first decide what it is that a discourse on risk is "abstracting". That means to say, what sort of thing is it that is essentially being brought to light for the organisation? To make the meaning of risk come to life currently we usually denote it by narrative statements describing feared eventualities. This narrative abstraction is usually quantified by some kind of numerical referent, such as an assessment of likelihood.

Often the numerical representations of the risk object go on to be displayed diagrammatically in order to communicate relative severity. A Cartesian plot or similar is the preferred choice, although sometimes a simple colour ranking (so-called traffic lights) does suffice. Here the temptation to add a new summary narrative element is high: for example, when the plot is split into quadrants each quadrant is given an actionable description, a hugely common practice. Taking another example, when colour ranking is used, a trend indicator is sometimes added to denote increasing or decreasing "severity".

These standard sorts of practices, however commonly accepted, are surrogates. They are actually a long way from being real modelling. To use them as they are to inform decision support is expedient, based on appetite for complexity, but premature based on any measure of efficacy. Something much more effective is needed.

VALIDITY, VERACITY, VERISIMILITUDE

To build an effective model, any model, and particularly one in an industrial psychology space like risk reasoning, three logical criteria must be satisfied early on. If the variables, scores, colours, shapes and other representations within a risk model claim to support effective reasoning, the whole system should satisfy three core criteria: validity; veracity and verisimilitude.

Validity

In psychology whenever a measurement instrument, such as a questionnaire, is designed it is assessed on validity. If the instrument does appear to be asking the right things, from an intuitive perspective, then it is said to have face validity. However, effectiveness is predicated upon construct validity. That is to say, there has to be further research evidence that the underlying constructs (belief, attitude, intention to behave, etc.) can actually be differentiated in a population by this instrument. Only when this is the case do we say that the instrument is validated.

The validation of a risk measurement system should be treated in exactly the same way. Do the things it measures and the way they are to be measured make enough sense in the culture of the organisation? Are the things that have been chosen to be measured drawn from sound and applicable evidence that these are in a direct relationship with real and relevant behaviours in this context? Do the measurement outcomes and the way they are reported appear similar to the other outcomes that support decision making in your organisation?

In short, a risk measurement system is valid when it is sensible, representative and informative of decision making in ways that already

have a track record of being appropriate in the receiving culture.
This is not at all an easy process to get right. Typically, it is easier to spot invalidity. So, for example, if your system is called a "tick-box exercise" it is generally considered invalid by someone.

Veracity

The risk reasoning system's process, inputs, outputs and algorithms are its critical performance-shaping factors. Whether these are adopted from another discipline, or copied from a British Standard, organisations must stop and consider the question of veracity. That is to say, is this best practice, tool or advice linked to decades of rock-solid research evidence? Do organisations who apply this discipline have evidence of fewer negative incidents or much better business results as a direct consequence?

The flipside of that argument, uncomfortable as it will be for some disciplines, is to ask another simpler question: is this just untested good advice? Has it been arrived at by way of practitioner commentary? Likewise, it is important to ascertain the veracity of the statistics that are performed on risk measures. Would a statistician actually support the approach as being meaningful reasoning?

In short, a risk measurement system has high levels of veracity when its methodology, guidance and statistical components are founded upon sound and applicable evidence that they perform as intended. As intended, to be absolutely clear, must refer to an enhancement of an organisation's value.

Verisimilitude

Although this is an old word, it remains quite a powerful concept. It refers to the degree to which any model can be considered a faithful copy of that which it represents. To put that in more accessible terms, model users should be able to ask the following. Is the model of organisational decision making this risk system supports adequately representative of what actually goes on in our organisation? Do the outputs of the system readily translate into the culture and the behaviours the organisation routinely displays?

In short, a risk system has verisimilitude when the model of your organisation, its operating world and its decision support needs are accurate enough. Typically risk models tend to sit at an abstract distance from the main business of the organisation and are sometimes only reviewed annually and for their own sake.

The abstraction challenge is these three exacting standards taken together. The more a risk/resilience system has low validity, arbitrary veracity and poor verisimilitude, the more likely it is to be a paper tiger – system for appearances sake. The more difficulty a system suffers in abstracting any practical utility for an operational system, the less likely its outputs will be respected enough to inform decisions to adjust course or modify behaviour.

THE MEASUREMENT CHALLENGE

When semantics are agreed, and there is a satisfactory level of abstraction in place, there is still work to do to create an effective risk system. Risk estimation will always need to be founded on some kind of scaled measurement. Normally, because of the demand characteristics of the existing culture, e.g. senior reporting conventions, this measurement will have to be one which subjects itself to later summary.

The dominant form of scaled measurement observable in risk systems reasoning is that of prioritisation, i.e. putting things in order using one or more importance variables. However, even with a measurement as self-evident as prioritisation, there are questions. Are the elements even comparable? Can two different types of risk be compared on one scale – the so-called 'apples and oranges' problem.

Furthermore, beyond the fruit there are bigger technical issues. Is the organisation interested in comparing state, trait or rate information? That is to say, do you want to measure the way things are, what their effect is likely to be or how much of something they relate to? The answer may be that you want to measure all three at different points. If so, the measurement scaling needs to be appropriately designed.

This measurement challenge has also to extend to asking how the risk measurements relate to all the other business measurements which are in play to support strategic decision making. For example, are they reduced to the same units and currencies (of cost, efficacy, value-add) or are they expected to be in some completely different language?

To social scientists the next question is obvious, but to practitioners in industry it is often completely overlooked: what kind of scaling is the appropriate kind? Leaving aside the question of objective versus subjective judgements for the moment, should risks be measured using categories, orders of magnitude, intervals of outcome or direct ratios? Should risk be measured by proxy indicators (like beliefs around probability) or by real business outcomes – such as cost, time, operability and productivity? After all, isn't monetising the best form of comparative clarity for a business?

What we find is that typically risk measurement systems have not been designed by social scientists. They have an altogether more 'copy-and-paste' feel. Often this is evidenced in a naïve approach to measurement (itself an effect of low tolerance for complexity). So, for example categorical data, such as the ubiquitous 'high – medium – low', are treated as if they had the same properties of interval or ratio data. So the measurements are blithely multiplied and averaged – naïve to the fact that these operations on this sort of data are a statistical *non sequitur*.

Also, the question of monetising risk is often considered too challenging. This is remarkable given that profit and loss, turnover and volume are the most attention grabbing of metrics to almost any large business. One has to enquire why risk data cannot be translated into such clear and attractive terms. Wouldn't it make more sense if they were measurable on the same scales as all the other business outcomes?

A final measurement question for now is that of representativeness. Everyone agrees that summary measurements are a boon for communication, especially senior escalation. The challenge here is to ask: when a measurement system has not, other than naively, answered any of the questions posed in this chapter so far, how much can the coloured summary diagrams it uses to report its results be considered anything more than a *reductio ad absurdum*?

THE MATERIALITY CHALLENGE

Business materiality is a critical currency in industrial planning and decision making. So, asking to what degree the precepts, perceptions, process and products of a risk system convey any *material significance* to a business is absolutely non-trivial.

Raw assessments of risk are fundamentally immaterial. They are equally at home in any dialect, from corporate ethics to coalface safety. They fit so easily anywhere that there is a danger of losing meaning everywhere. Risk reasoning systems are, in fact, purposefully immaterial. They are usually put in place to create necessary precaution, prevention, permission, legitimacy and even a certain reticence, or fear, in an organisation. Although these are valid emotions which do indirectly support sound business decision making, they are, first to last, fundamentally immaterial.

This is the challenge: risk is simply not like the real physical things of a business, such as cost or production rate. It is not a physical object at all, it is a metaphysical one. It's not a pre-existing object at all, it is a socially constructed one. A common solution to the challenge of the business materiality of risk is to attempt simple transliteration. Take supply chain stress testing as a good example. One of its purposes is to identify suppliers who may pose a risk to operations and take remedial action. A tempting proxy for supplier risk therefore is simply materiality, i.e. how much money is spent with the supplier. The greater the investment the greater the risk, this seems logical. You take one language and you move it to another.

This is tempting on at least three fronts. First, expenditure is always a key boardroom concern and in terms of validity this certainly scores well and creates traction. Second, expenditure data can be co-opted with no extra resource, so it is expedient. Third, using existing expenditure data over new risk measurements can greatly reduce data burden. Consider that in a large, complex, distributed organisation you may wish to risk assess twenty-five thousand suppliers. Even a ten-minute glance at each would be two years of a full time employee's effort.

So if expenditure data is material and it can also be a proxy for risk, why is this not the perfect solution? The reason is because this is flawed reasoning pretending to be good common sense. The materiality problem for risk is not about translating risk (completely) back into a raw materiality assessment that you already have to hand. It adds no new meaning for you do this.

So we have to avoid what seems a parsimonious solution and ask where exactly is the added value in giving the same data a second name? Second, and more importantly, we have to ask: what is it that is actually of interest in the culture and the observable behaviour of suppliers that is risk informative? What is it, after cost, that keeps supply-chain directors awake at night? The answer is that tests of supplier risk ask behavioural questions:

- Continuity: will supplier A always supply on time and in full?
- Critical dependency: is supplier B the only supplier for this raw material or service irrespective of how expensive?
- Common mode: does supplier C produce an ingredient that is common to most, or all, of the portfolio?

Any seasoned supply chain expert will tell you that not all inexpensive things are immaterial. When even a very small, cheaply sourced amount of material finds its way into an entire range of functional products, then disruption of supply can be catastrophic and, in consequence, highly material to the business. These are behavioural cause-and-effect sequences. They need a system of monitoring to understand them. Using expenditure as a proxy for risk materiality is a fallacy, because risk materiality has to deliver another source of benefit to be worth the effort.

This is the real challenge of the science behind designing a materiality component to a risk system. Whilst risk processes must try to utilise available and coherent real-world material measurements, the measurement of risk itself must remain distinguishable from them. Risk measurements are a bespoke and stand-alone exercise aimed at understanding not quantity but causality.

The challenge of materiality therefore becomes the need to accept only a partial translation. The function of risk is to act as a bridge between business materiality and lucid phenomenology. Its logic must neither be allowed to be purely immaterial nor totally material – it must be trans-material.

WHY DO ORGANISATIONS SEEM CONFUSED ABOUT THE MEANING OF RISK?

It is a safe bet that many practitioners reading this chapter may not recognise the standards it is calling for, so far are these from the mainstream pragmatism that typifies this discipline. It is also a reasonably safe bet that many practitioners will also be getting that prickly feeling that comes when something that is supposed to be quite utilitarian is made more complicated. More complicated, we dare say, than many organisations using the current practices would be comfortable to accept. Yet, we would say this, you should accept it.

If you actually want your risk system to be the best practice and not 'a' best practice, you need to begin to challenge the reasons behind that prickly feeling. To conclude this chapter, let's ask some open questions about why organisations seem so confused about the meaning of risk.

NAIVE REALISM

The first explanation as to why organisations seem confused about the overall meaning of risk, or at least seem to be using multiple and overlapping definitions, is to concede that there might not be an explanation. Their use of the risk concept in plural, and even postmodern, ways could just be wholly naïve. This naïvety could be a function, in fact, of an informally articulated distributed reasoning system.

Simply put, because very different parts of the organisation are all actually dealing with completely different *risk scenarios*, they need to operate almost unique sets of *risk constructs* to describe them. This is done at a certain intellectual distance from each other. In this way the most suitable definitions of risk and of resilience would simply need to be determined rather independently at a local point of need.

Furthermore, as the people determining these definitions are not likely to be trained in organisational psychology or statistical methods, they will most likely draw on the received wisdom of industry standard thinking around the definition and measurement of risk. In this way the different definitions will probably still be measured and reported using very similar methods.

Accepting that, a further question is key. What does your organisation do upstream when it wants to meaningfully collect such, very different, definitions to express a logically corporate view? How do these contribute to an overall risk burden and/or resilience benefit? For example, how would these many differing definitions work in an annual report to shareholders?

As a further observation, the different people responsible for this process are no more likely to be trained in organisational psychology or statistics themselves. They remain equally likely to use the industry standard thinking, albeit at a higher level of aggregation.

The evident response from observing the corporate risk registers in many different organisations tends to show one key thing. This overall risk burden exercise does not become a question of meaning or definition as such, but a question of editing. The task to edit a corporate risk position often falls to this separate professional group. Their forte can best be described as rolling up of data and information into bytes of meta-knowledge. This task is not driven by attention to the complexity. The detailed factual and interdependent causality presented in the multiple risk landscapes of the business is not the focus. Rather it is driven by the need to surmise these, mainly through simplified colour rankings, supposed key performance indicators and rating trends. This is done in the pursuit of what we might call an interacting generality. Thus the result is not so much informative as reassuring.

REPORTING LED RISK

An alternative, potentially more naturalistic, explanation as to why some organisations are operating multiple and distinct definitions for risk (and resilience) could be a common consent argument. That is to say, that different parts of the organisation are consciously trying to work towards a largely agreed, but nonetheless highly generalised, framework for risk and resilience reporting. This is driven by the fact that it is necessary to report on risk and resilience in an annual exercise. The mandate for this exercise is often what sets the corporate arms of an organisation off on their risk journey in the first place. Thus it also sets their demand characteristics of the exercise, a demand that what is needed is a summary report.

The discrete bits of the organisation – external affairs, supply chain, legal, sustainability, marketing, etc. – are expected to explore their unique concerns. What results is differentially perceived threats to operation. As long as the parts of the business are kept apart for this exercise, this naturally leads to distinct risk and resilience definitions in localised points of reference – different points of organisational culture in fact.

As this case is not so very different to the naïve realism case it tends to go in the same direction in the end. The organisation still aggregates these highly localised risk and resilience formats into a single corporate expression. Rather than being a slightly unconscious redaction process that strips out meaning, it is the deliberate question of some sort of universal final translation into a new language of *tolerability*.

INCOMPREHENSION

There is a third, and potentially far cleaner, explanation for the observable confabulation of risk and resilience across the divisions of any large complex organisation. This might simply be that people don't understand the science behind these constructs at all, especially since it is outside of their formal disciplines – in particular since it is, as we have noted in detail, a highly diverse and disputed science in any case. In this case it is templates and a history of use which save the day. The central risk team, whatever form they take, essentially baby-sit the organisation into filling in *pro forma* to a satisfactory standard. The *pro forma* themselves become a proxy for the meaning of risk.

In dealing with the tension – between this lack of comprehension and a need to still use the constructs – organisations may have simply learned to use this distinct language (of risk and resilience) culturally. What we are seeing is not intentional industrial reasoning at all, it is a coping mechanism.

A PRAGMATIC STATE SPACE

Thus, whether it is naïvety, a desire for a common thread to report on, or a basic incomprehension that drives the illogical use of risk meaning, the concepts of risk and resilience ultimately become a matter of pragmatism. Risk concepts are used not to practise (decision) science, but to meet the demand characteristics of that recent cultural requirement in the modern industrial landscape – that we must all now be seen to assess risk and resilience.

To do this efficaciously – with a low level of disruption to normal operating – responsible managers design their approach based on a combination of external guidance and comparison to peers. This is phrased as a wish to mirror the "best practices". They become confident that these may be found in the generality of industry standards and in the specific advice of industry associations. They are further confident that the one-stop-shop approaches of consultancies use such proven principles, even when these tend to set the meaning of risk within the products that they sell. So these are usually where people turn to identify a suitable process and a set of *pro forma*.

It is this marketplace, rather than academic science, that informs industry on the meaning of risk. The pressing modern questions of organisational psychology, statistical logic and efficacy are supressed. What is interesting is that the people who buy off-the-shelf risk systems definition from this unambitious marketplace are copying rather than designing their approach. Moreover, they do not fully see that confidence this marketplace, because it starts from a point of trying to dispel their incomprehension, may be misplaced.

The industry standards are the work of wisdom sharing – they are not evidence-based tools tailored to the organisation in question. The industry associations are heavily represented in the authoring of such standards. The consultancies who create service models for the sale of risk and resilience products tailor them to meet these standards as a marketing tool. These are often the same consultancies who are the industry-accepted authorities when it comes to auditing wider corporate governance.

So, if the notion of independent expertise in risk is a fragile one, this should raise a little more concern than it sometimes does. For, if we were to take that observation just the one step further, we might stop and ask: where is the evidence that these (author and auditor) groups themselves have understood the (complex and disputed) science of risk and resilience? Is it a worry that they both stimulate and meet a simplified cultural demand characteristic for these?

CONCLUSIONS SO FAR

The conclusion from these first three chapters is rather straightforward. Defining the construct of risk, and the rationality which should determine its use to support industrial reasoning and strategic decision making, is a non-trivial problem. The widely observable industry norms seem to have largely evaded this problem within their current designs.

In terms of risk definition, we have set not one but several possible descriptions in place with our dialectic model (ethics to pedantry). This brings much-needed clarity for those charged with risk systems design. It also brings much-needed choice because risk definition is an obfuscated space which remains academically and pragmatically in terminal dispute.

In terms of a risk measurement system, we argue it will be nonsensical unless it is accompanied by a brutally clear set of applied semantics, a fundamental level of agreed abstraction, a cogent set of appropriately scientific – and therefore statistically accurate – measurements and a demonstrable link to business material outcomes. This it must achieve without losing its ability to explain causal phenomena, and therefore add value over and above conventional materiality measures – something which we have termed trans-material.

We have noted with interest that the arena for the definition of the best practice in risk systems design suffers from two searching problems. First, industry itself, for a host of good reasons, might just be historically confused about what this all means. Thus they presently lack the methodological rigour to design a system which is effective and pragmatic. Second, the academy is not the source of good practice advice – the marketplace is.

It is, frankly, difficult to understand what a business is referring to when it speaks of 'a risk', let alone when it pertains to have a system to measure and manage sets of them globally. What we can conclude from this preliminary discussion is that steps may need to be taken to redress the balance. Or to put that another way:

Risk should be semantically coherent, abstracting genuinely meaningful behaviours and measured within a scientifically valid system to generate outcomes which have a clear link to business materiality.

CHAPTER 4

Transformation risk – a case study

Although it may seem a little too early for a case study, we promised you a pragmatic journey of design. Having alluded to some of the challenges of applying standard risk assessment systems and the need for a more in-depth design and application, this is an appropriate point to take a brief leap forward and look at some principles in action.

The case we will examine you may recognise as one of the examples from Chapter 1. It considers the transformation of a large manufacturing operation. Transformation, in that context, can be thought of as synonymous with upgrading or modernising. This is one of the most common applied problems for large distributed organisations, and can take several forms: updating of the computer systems; the acquisition of another company; a reorganisation of the management structure; changes in legislation; and so on.

In 2013, whilst the Director of Resilience, I was approached by a team from one of Unilever's largest and most significant manufacturing facilities. Unilever was riding high at this point, just about to turn a landmark corner to become a 50 billion euro company. The category of manufacture, and the facility concerned, were globally pivotal to that value. This factory was about to undergo an unparalleled programme involving:

- five simultaneous hardware transformations;
- the installation of an entirely new production line;
- simultaneous global launch of the resulting innovation platforms for the entire brand.

The team, however, was worried. The source of their worry was, in a word, risk – a highly lucid worry, for two reasons. The first, and this is a picture of the centrality of this Sourcing Unit, was the performance target for the transformation period:

- 99% customer service;
- zero impact on quality;
- meet all stretching business growth targets;
- deliver the transformation in full and on time.

This is much more like the crucible for modern industrial risk. Risk has to function as an operational construct often within highly demanding business conditions. Nothing moves over to let risk in. It has to run at the same (high) pace as everything else.

The second reason the team was worried was, having examined the current risk assessment methods in the company, they knew instinctively that these were not at all fit for purpose for a programme of this importance. Their challenge to me was simple. Let's build a new one.

This case study concerns itself not so much with the content of what risks were discovered and how they were managed, rather it is interested in describing the architecture of this new methodology created with the team. As we briefly describe the process for this, an argument will be emerging. We will start to discuss the necessity of a more intentional form of risk systems design for large, complex, distributed organisations.

ASSESSING THE STANDARD APPROACH

In the interests of time, we have to leave out much of the story. The first issue we want to discuss should not surprise you. It was how to help the team address what we have called in the previous chapter the semantic challenge.

The risk assessment method the team had to hand was the "classical" model, i.e. listing discrete risks (events) on a spreadsheet and scoring those by probability and impact. A typical output of the classical system is shown in Figure 4.1.

Features vary slightly, but the standard approach generally contains common elements:

- a discrete longlist of (independently defined) risk events;
- a "scoring" methodology based on probability and impact of individual events;
- a red–amber–green colouring system;
- some kind of consequential allocation of task, action or responsibility.

By default, the semantic level the team would have chosen if they adopted this method would be technical. Each risk event would be a technical or project management eventuality or fear. This reasoning method will, in the main, therefore abstract problem statements in the form of unwanted events. We can already highlight four key problems that these (largely accidental) semantic and abstraction choices are going to bring:

- Independence: although attempts are often made to collect risk events under headings, they function as independent single cause-and-effect sequences and they do not interrelate to reflect a complex reality.

- Static scoring: the influence of time, and by definition any insight into volatility, is wholly absent. Single scores are assigned at a point in time with little representation of variance over time.
- Link to decision making: there is no positive feedback loop to the actual decision-making process in the programme to which these risks refer.
- Control: all controls identified are independent, risk-centric and based upon a single method, i.e. action planning. Given the priority risk registers like this maintain in complex projects, their effectiveness is questionable.

VALIDITY, VERACITY, VERISIMILITUDE

These four problems alone, despite their wholly normative status in a typical industrial risk assessment of this kind, cast significant doubt on the validity of this reasoning process. The exercise hasn't defined an adequate semantic to reason in or object to abstract. The efficacy of the methodology, other than the creation of these lists and colourful charts as an end in itself, remains untested. The resultant dialect is most likely to be assurance, which won't be valid for the transformation subject matter.

The veracity of the control features is in serious doubt. Even though there is an action plan attached to this ordered list of events, closer examination shows that this is really just a static list of actions. Stressful project meetings for a programme like this one will render this list-making and reviewing behaviour highly ineffective. Frequently, these lists are consigned to be monitored in an offline assessment, if they are assessed at all.

When risk outputs like this become swallowed up in their own imposing detail, they are not a model of the project's strategic decisions or critical pathways. They are a list of codified, isolated, worries. To discuss each worry for thirty seconds would take more than seventy-five minutes. Few teams will allocate even that sort of time to a risk register exercise.

Date of last update: 7th Dec 2011
Owner: Sebastian Latten

1	Business Case / Financial - P1
2	HR/ People / Unions - P2
3	Service / Quality / Supply Security - P4
4	Engineering / Plant Design - P5
5	R&D / Scale-up Innovation - P6
6	Factory Specific - P7
7	Project Mngm / Stakeholders - P3

1	Swift
2	Parking
3	Delegate
4	Duplicate
5	Remove

Marking if HIGH

ID	Initial risk	Post Mgt	Risk IP Order	Risk IP Group	Risk Filter	Risk Sub-Area	Risk Headline Impact: Cause(s):	Comment	Root Cause [Risk Impact - Column M] [Risk Input by - Column O]	Urgency of mitigation
					►		►	►	►	►
1	2	0	47	R & D	1	CTI	Insufficient budget o pay for consumer tests (BIC)		poor R&D budget planning. disagreement who pays	
2	4	0	139	Pr oc ur e m en t	1	Material Cost			Not all suppliers respectively materials will be harmonised / localised at go live in receiving SUs for	
3	6	0	140	Pr oc ur e m en t	1	3PM Back-up				

Impact >

5	Serious project delay [not able to compensate] or Unacceptable impact on quality/service/safety [high risk for incidents] or Will not meet business case at all [10% and higher overspend]
4	Significant delay [+4 weeks with some chance to compensate] or Impact on quality/service/safety [so that targets cannot be met] or Unlikely to meet business case [2-8% overspend]
3	Project delay [+2 weeks] or Impact on quality/service/safety or Risk to meet business case [up to 2% overspend]
2	Slight project delay but No impact on quality/service/safety but Business case in plan
1	No impact on project timing or business case

	0-20	20-40	40-60	60-80	80-100
CRITICAL	5	10	15	20	25
SEVERE	4	8	12	16	20
HIGH	3	6	9	12	15
MEDIUM	2	4	6	8	10
LOW	1	2	3	4	5

Likelihood >

FIGURE 4.1 *A conscientious application of the classic approach*

The route from a risk assessment (of more than one hundred and fifty colour-coded, isolated, scored events on a spreadsheet) to enhanced decision making for the transformation project is completely unclear. Certainly, if highly worrying features were observed, some actions would be taken. However, the holistic control of the portfolio of risks is always in grave doubt once the list expands beyond a certain size.

Expressing the transformation project team's worries in our terminology, we'd say the following. The dialect is diligence and assurance (where it should be providence). The semantic lacks integrated meaning. The abstraction leads to isolated events, scores, owners and actions. These have a low validity to the programme strategy, and low veracity in terms of evidence for control. The overall model has low verisimilitude when compared to the business benefit sought, the significance of failure, the strategic decision-making pathways, the project management effort and the costs of the programme.

DECIDING UPON A NEW APPROACH

There isn't space here for a blow-by-blow account of the process we used to design an alternative risk methodology. What we can highlight is that a great deal of effort was required to do this. A first key difference to the standard method was to significantly alter the semantic. The target was to be a representative set of interrelated meta-risks. A meta-risk, as the name suggests, is a higher order of description. Twenty-two such meta-risks were described in seven categories. Their interrelationship was described in terms of combined impacts that might generate risk scenarios and their associated programme controls.

Meta therefore, doesn't just connote some kind of lazy compression of risk events into larger categories – like the typical aggregation in the classical approach. Meta denotes influence, connectivity and control. This is the level of abstraction that the team felt was commensurate with the organisational burden of losing control of part, or all, of the transformation programme. In the fine detail therefore, the need to describe what any meta-risk or combination of impacts might mean in practice was left entirely to the professional knowledge of the team. It was a competency. It was not recorded.

To arrive at sensible and effective meta-risks which function like this, and to design a management programme for them did require considerable offline work. Once the necessary content had been identified, a facilitated risk and resilience workshop using a cross-functional team of leaders representing a full end-to-end supply chain of the brands was then needed.

A summary of the whole process is shown in Figure 4.2.

This process achieved seven objectives which would be transferable to any other large organisation facing a transformation process:

- Consider the transformation programme in totality: what is sometimes called making sure everyone is on the same page. The team needed a shared understanding of the transformation programme in a risk-independent form from the outset.
- Identify the key meta-risks for the programme: using a facilitated technique called Perfect Storm Analysis, the team (relying here on pre-work) developed a risk-and-time chart for the full programme. Using a series of mini-war game-type exercises, these discrete risks were collected into the eponymous "storms", i.e. concurrent, collected or connected risk pathways. Agreed storms become the meta-risks.
- Reality check – risk meaning and impact assessment: once meta-risks are refined, a number of reality checks are required. This is to suppress the tendency to focus on downside risk. An initial understanding of the impact of the meta-risks over time is derived. This includes positive impacts, working advantages and benefits (where found).

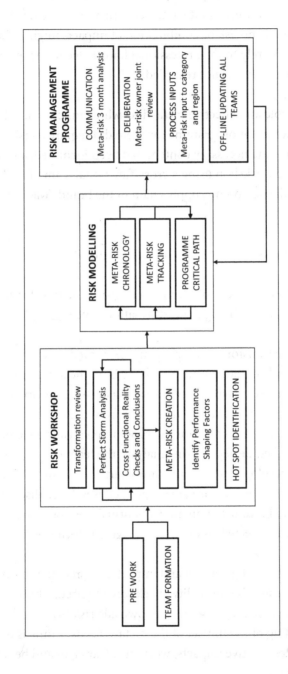

FIGURE 4.2 *An alternative methodology*

- Agree meta-risk ownership and management approach: this is a crucial feature. The right people (expertise and authority) are needed. They need the right tasks to do. They must not be allowed to be only expert assessors of risk. They must accept direct liability and responsibility.
- Understand the performance-shaping factors for control: this technique is an involved elicitation of expert judgement. What is being sought is not the typical action plan on a risk-by-risk basis, but a description of the efficacy of the existing business controls. This includes an examination of the external operating environment. The team is searching for the common control points to deal with meta-risk clusters.
- Identify hot spots: hot spot is shorthand for key decision points and critical future activities with potential to amplify programme risk in two forms. The simplest is time, or time pressure where any aberrant events – caused by uncontrolled risk – will interact with time criticality. The second is programme complexity, or criticality, at specific times. In short we are asking what is a really bad time for things to go wrong?
- Map the chronology of meta-risks: the team is now able to prepare two visualisations to be used in conjunction for decision making and communication. They are the meta-risk chronology and the hot spot evaluation.

Despite their humble appearance, these are powerful representations of the influence of a well-defined risk construct. Two further overlays onto this argument, used by the designated risk owners, demonstrate how that power works. First is the meta-risk tracker.

This tracker allows the individual meta-risk owner to predict the expected impact over time. Notice, although impact here is being reduced to high, medium and low, those are behaviourally anchored measures. The anchors are designed by experts in the team. Time is being projected in a dual detail: a half year-by month assessment; a summary, by quarter, for the following year.

Risk Owners		Calm before storm		Premium Action		Clarity with implications		
		March	April	May	Jun	Jul	Aug	Sep
	Project Management							
RCLT	Risk cluster 1							
RCLT	Risk cluster 2							
CLT	Risk cluster 3							
SCLT	Risk cluster 4							
Programme X LT	Risk cluster 5							
Programme Y LT	Risk cluster 6							
	Timing							
Team 1 lead	Risk Cluster 7							
Team 1 lead	Risk Cluster 8							
	Technical							
Team 2 lead	Risk Cluster 9							
Team 3 lead	Risk Cluster 10							
	Supply Chain							
Team 4 lead	Risk Cluster 11							
Team 5 lead	Risk Cluster 12							
Team 5 lead	Risk Cluster 13							
	Customer							
Team 6 lead	Risk Cluster 14							
Team 6 lead	Risk Cluster 15							
Team 6 lead	Risk Cluster 16							
	Supplier							
Team 7 lead	Risk cluster 17							
Team 7 lead	Risk cluster 18							
Team 7 lead	Risk cluster 19							
Team 7 lead	Risk cluster 20							
	Risk cluster 21							
	Reuglatory							
Team 8 lead	Risk cluster 20							
Team 8 lead	Risk cluster 21							

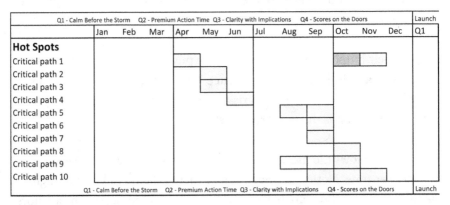

FIGURE 4.3 *Meta-risk chronology tracking*

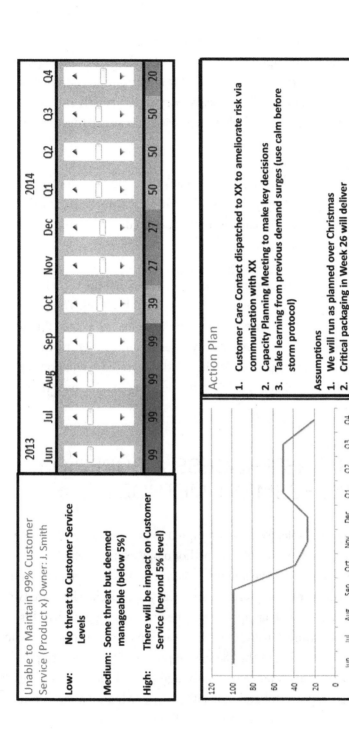

FIGURE 4.4 *Meta-risk tracker*

Every meta-risk now has a trajectory visible in summary overview (in the line graph) and updated in the light of real events. Action planning at the meta-risk level is not prohibited, if it is appropriate, although key assumptions are required. This transparency is particularly important for the collective risk analysis when meta-risks are added together in scenarios.

The final overlay not shown here is perhaps the easiest one for the business to find. It is simply the transformation programme critical pathway diagram. Key elements were mapped to the meta-risk exposure.

Although an involved description, what is clear is that the team have faced the challenge of risk definition and measurement head-on. The measurements being used are not anodyne free-floating probability and impact judgements. In fact, probability assessment is never used in this methodology. Instead, they are detailed and integrated evaluations of meaningful things which link back to the decision making over time in the programme.

WHY IS THIS PROCESS A SUPERIOR RISK ASSESSMENT METHOD?

In the space available, we have attempted to give you a snapshot of a very sophisticated and powerful risk methodology exercise which addressed all of the challenges we have laid out so far. It is clearly a detailed, time-consuming, content-rich and reasoning-heavy approach. There are two typical responses to such an approach. The first is to suggest that this is too complex and too time consuming. That reaction comes from those who have grown up on a diet of the classical approach. The second response is varying degrees of acceptance that, although more difficult, this is clearly a more intelligent, powerful and, crucially, business logical approach to the risk associated with protecting a multi-billion-euro brand.

This argument is fine as far as it goes, but can we be more precise about how this methodology improves on the far less complex and time-consuming classic approach to risk? We'll conclude with four main reasons:

- Dependence: the risks in this approach – the discrete technical and project feed-stock for the meta-risk creation and the meta-risks themselves – are never considered in isolation. They are not independent, rather they are always in causal relationships. This highlights two superior risk reasoning methods:
  - Volatility modelling: a risk (meta-risk or otherwise) always lives 'on a curve'. It is not a fixed entity but a dynamic one. Some have a more volatile nature and this is a key feature to capture in anticipating the cost of their control.
  - Amplification: risks act on the other risks in a system by being capable of amplifying or suppressing them. This is taken into account.
- Dynamic scoring: This system does not use repeated static scoring. The risks are always measured on a timeline to convey volatility. Each meta-risk timeline is overlaid onto the others, making the macro volatility of the whole system evident. The real time-line of the whole project is used as the true context for impact. The creation of hot spots, understanding at which key times the system is at its most (time or complexity) pressured, allows reasoning to be updated in real and project time.
- Link to decision making: this approach is business intentional, providing inputs to a pre-existing decision-making process and elevated to a decision critical role.
- Focus on control action: this assessment functions as a business control mechanism; it has efficacy because control, not assessment, of risk is the end-game. Those controls are designed by the team to be accepted seamlessly into the controls of business.

AND FINALLY – MATERIALITY

Classic risk analysis, especially in smaller and less complex settings, can add value to a business. We are not suggesting that it is completely bankrupt. However, when programmes are more complex and businesses larger, this methodology begins to struggle. Its results are often sold back to the business by aggressive aggregation of large arrays of risks into more acceptable shortlists. This is where, as the materiality of the argument suffers from too much translation into a dialect of assurance, the potential value is lost.

The design in this case approaches the materiality challenge from two perspectives. The first is effective communication. The ability to communicate the status of risks is a success criterion. This is the shop window for risk materiality. A risk assessment cannot be material to a business that is not willing to examine it.

This is where the power of the meta-risk approach – as a formal complexity reduction process – comes to the fore. The status of these risks could be sensibly communicated in a standard summary heuristic without fear of losing meaning. The team created a summary visualisation of all 22 meta-risks as the principle communication device for senior teams.

This is a three-month rolling visualisation of the predicted impact of the meta-risks on programme success. It contains the familiar red–amber–green motif, but this is not a judgement call on risk severity. It is a summary variable expressing all the metric data discussed so far. It is not a simplification of the risk assessment for ease of consumption. It is a complexity reduction of (all of) the data for ease of communication.

The second perspective on the materiality challenge is to ask what has happened. How have the decisions about intervention, cost, benefit, etc. been shaped as a result of this work?

Premium Action Setting Period				Clarity with implications		
Risk Owners		Jun	Jul	Aug	Sep	
	Project Management					
RCLT	Risk cluster 1					
RCLT	Risk cluster 2					
CLT	Risk cluster 3					
SCLT	Risk cluster 4					
Programme X LT	Risk cluster 5					
Programme Y LT	Risk cluster 6					
	Timing					
Team 1 lead	Risk Cluster 7					
Team 1 lead	Risk Cluster 8					
	Technical					
Team 2 lead	Risk Cluster 9					
Team 3 lead	Risk Cluster 10					
	Supply Chain					
Team 4 lead	Risk Cluster 11					
Team 5 lead	Risk Cluster 12					
Team 5 lead	Risk Cluster 13					
	Customer					
Team 6 lead	Risk Cluster 14					
Team 6 lead	Risk Cluster 15					
Team 6 lead	Risk Cluster 16					
	Supplier					
Team 7 lead	Risk cluster 17					
Team 7 lead	Risk cluster 18					
Team 7 lead	Risk cluster 19					
Team 7 lead	Risk cluster 20					
	Risk cluster 21					
	Reuglatory					
Team 8 lead	Risk cluster 20					
Team 8 lead	Risk cluster 21					

FIGURE 4.5 *Meta-risk summary prediction*

1 Management oversight (regional and category supply chain leadership team) insisted on a monthly meeting with the risk owners to ensure review and update of the meta-risks.
2 Leadership team meeting agendas were modified to add time to take a standardised presentation on the condition of the meta-risk and all key decision recommendations.
3 An offline updating process for all teams was also instituted with an escalation procedure in the light of the risk burden and the likelihood of volatile scenarios.

It is critical to understand that this is how you judge the materiality of a risk assessment in a large, complex and dispersed organisation. The programme that it analysed was materially changed through the existing business process and controls as a direct consequence of its reasoning.

CONCLUSIONS

Four key conclusions for you, the reader, operating in an analogous situation to the team in this case study, are listed below. Notice how they underscore that effective risk reasoning should be able to speak all of the right dialects at the right time.

1 Appetite for complexity should be determined by fitness for purpose

    a) Challenge the received wisdom that the classical approach to risk is always valid for your operational setting.

    b) A valid risk measurement and monitoring system should not cave in too early to the pressures of expedience.

    c) Complexity reduction is the key to effective outcomes. Allow professionals to do the right amount of work to validate methods and metrics.

2 Inter-connectivity is essential

    a) Assessing risks in a system which treats them as independent will not generate the required control.

    b) Any risk system you design should respect your operational context – particularly its speed of movement, pace of change and planning timetables.

    c) The experts in the operations of your business are the experts in the connections between its risks, their intelligence is the system

3 Modelling not measuring is the key

    a) Risk systems must model with the passage of, programme and real, time.

b) Enabling tools which help measurement and visualisation are the key to efficient use of professionals' time.

c) It is not always necessary to model with probability to model with risk.

4 Operational application is the true end-game

a) A risk assessment system cannot persist in an operational vacuum. It must affect the business processes it pertains to support.

b) The key to risk communication to senior leaders, to the wider affected organisation and to stakeholders is complexity reduction, not simplification.

This case study is real. It actually happened in one of the world's largest and most globally distributed manufacturing companies. It concerned one of its largest and most profitable brands. If we are honest, it probably did surprise the transformation team a little quite how involved the design process needed to become. However, they never for a moment doubted the importance of getting it right. The stakes were simply too high.

What that team also found, and this, we imagine, is what a lot of transformation programmes do discover. This is that some of the outcomes of reasoning about risks in this way were the key to both articulating and solving a number of other operational problems which had long been affecting the business as usual.

This case study shows that it is the integration of appropriately sophisticated risk reasoning with business decision making that was the eventual victory. The reasoning of competent professionals was enabled to support and improve decision-making processes and outcomes in a concrete way.

The success of this more involved, more analytical and more dialectic approach fights the tide of the received wisdom and prized expedience of most classical approaches to industrial risk. This is an expedience which is caused by organisations having learned to have a low appetite for complexity when it comes to risk – an expedience which borders on the absurd when you look at the compromises in the quality of reasoning this can cause.

Or to put that another way:

It is good reasoning itself which is the prize of risk-based resilience systems design.

CHAPTER 5

Beginning to measure risk

Seeing risk as the optimisation of profit within ethical parameters might be fine. However, the need to design a reasoning system around that definition that is as involved as the transformation risk example described in our last chapter is going to come as a bit of culture shock to a very large group of people. That is the people who are insisting that risk is not nearly as complex as all that, insisting, in fact, that risk is a rather simple business tool.

Risks, for this group it is agreed, are formed out of the probability of unwanted outcomes multiplied by their impacts. To state the naked reality of that assertion is to say that all necessary risk measurement is reducible to the following:

$$R = P \times I$$

This is to say that measuring it is as simple as tabulating this 'R-value' of each risk, prioritising them on the basis of magnitude and deciding what to do in response – just the combination of two simple everyday project-level tools. The universal application of this method enables any company to meet its objectives and satisfy its regulators and onlookers.

In this chapter let's leave behind the rarefied context of high stakes transformation projects and just unpack that simple and attractive worldview. Let's do that particularly with a view to looking at the implications for measurement. Let's see if it is the applicable all-round good common sense that it pertains to be. To do this we will want to ask two perfectly logical questions. When people say that risk is probability multiplied by impact, to what, precisely, do these probability and impact terms refer? In fact, let's just begin with the first term, because that is going to take a while on its own.

CAN PROBABILITY BE JUDGED?

To address the question of whether probability can be judged in the way the standard risk algorithm asks, we are going to attempt an extended thought exercise. This will be done using the uncommon juxtaposition of confectionery, sociological reasoning and geopolitics.

CONFECTIONERY: TESTING YOUR THOUGHT PROCESS

The age-old practice for explaining "the laws of probability" has always been to simplify them by example (flipping coins, rolling a die, etc.). At the outset we should note that the idea that these instructional examples simplify anything is a fallacious one. Not only is there no such thing as a fair coin, a fair die, but, even if we were able to manufacture such a thing, an entirely random method of tossing or rolling it would not be physically achievable.

We can and do, of course, accept that these are just informative classroom models to help us understand the concepts. Accepting this, we should perhaps pause and spend a bit more time in that classroom. For example, is it worth noticing the speed with which these simple examples become quite intensely complex? Would this serve as an early warning bell against their use?

So, supposing that you have had enough of coins and dice, let's take a foray into the world of the statistics of probability reasoning by a thought experiment with a different subject matter.

Let's buy a packet of sweets.

The confectioner Rowntrees makes a sweet called Randoms. Let's assume for now that you have never seen, or even heard of, a packet of Randoms. Here is our first probability reasoning question: what is the probability, that the first sweet drawn from a packet of Randoms will be red?

Here's the first answer you might give: "I don't know. Furthermore, I cannot know."

That is a good answer. You might have been tempted to say: "well, I've seen packets of sweets in general before, red is a popular colour for those, so I'm going to assume . . ."

To do this would be bad science. You don't know, you can't know and you cannot reasonably judge in a knowledge vacuum. So you really are on far safer ground to state the truth of this situation. It is impossible for you to make, at present, an assessment of that probability. So, to deal with that knowledge vacuum, we let you examine the packet, but we don't let you open it. As you do this, you see that "each pack" contains six natural fruit flavours: blackcurrant, cherry, strawberry, orange, lime and lemon. Each pack also contains an average of twelve sweets. Now what is the probability that the first sweet drawn from a packet of Randoms will be red?

Here is the answer you might give: "I think the probability of a red sweet being taken first is one third (you might also express that as 0.333 or 33.3%, and so on)."

How did you come by this increase in confidence? Well here is what you might have reasoned: two out of every six sweets will be a red flavour (strawberry and cherry), so I have a two in six chance of a red sweet and that collapses to one in three.

What happens if we do not accept your answer can be accurate? This is given that it is based on no actual measurements? So, to further help your analysis, we do let you open this packet. You can tip all the sweets out on the table and then the following will be knowable:

1 How many sweets are actually in this packet?
2 Exactly how many of them are red?

Now, once you have put the sweets back in the pack, we can restate the question. What is the probability that the first sweet drawn from a packet of Randoms will be red? Here is what you may now choose to reason: I've divided the number of sweets in the (sample) packet (total) by the number of red sweets (observed) and simplified this to a fraction. That result is the best way to express the probability that a red sweet could be drawn at random from this packet.

However, you notice a key flaw in your own methodology at this point. That is only the observed result from *this packet* and the question relates to "a packet" not this packet. So, you might, against your own best instinct, answer: "I do not know, furthermore I cannot know."

What you are more likely to answer is: "I think the probability is 'X' on the understanding that I consider this packet to be reasonably representative of all other packets that have been made or sold."

However, we are still unhappy with the accuracy of your answer. So we give you a little time to work on your method. In that time, you go off and buy a further 100 packets of Randoms and open 99 of them. Carefully, you build a spreadsheet where you record the frequency (green, amber, red, black) of the sweets you have found per packet. As you have the power of a spreadsheet to hand, you also codify mean, mode, min, max and standard deviation allowing yourself to create a frequency distribution of the sweets from which you can then sample the probability. Then you turn to an unopened packet and you are ready to assess the probability that the first sweet drawn from it will be red, job done.

And that, dear readers, is the problem. At no point in this problem-solving exercise did you ever reason about probability in the same way twice, or indeed did you reason in the same way twice.

1 You expressed only ignorance.
2 You provided a subjective probability (actually a belief).
3 You provided a subjective inference (which was still actually a belief).
4 You created a hybrid inference made of the measurement of a single-frequency observation (objective observation) and considered that it might reasonably be representative (subjective belief based on sampling).
5 You built a model based on a short-run frequency observation (finite objective observation).

What were you thinking? More importantly, how was what you were thinking interacting with what you *could, in fact, know*? Was your use of probability accurate and informative?

STATISTICAL SCIENCE: THE PROBLEM OF PROBABILITY INTERACTING WITH KNOWLEDGE

The first principle we are trying to get at here is this. Probability judgements interact with the quality and accuracy of the available knowledge. When you had never seen a packet of Randoms, you had no knowledge, nothing to go on, since you did not even know whether any of them could be red. You were ignorant of the facts. That ignorance was complete. To assess probability at all here would have been a pure guess. If you had given any kind of figure at all it would only relate to your subjective belief based on your, potentially spurious, experience.

This behaviour is called subjective probability. Not all statisticians would agree that this type of probability exists.

When you were allowed to gather some data, you could start doing some science: the packet has multi-coloured pictures of the sweets, including red ones; it gives you a clue by promising the presence of six flavours, two of which you know to be sourced from red fruits; and you become aware there are roughly twelve sweets to a pack. You conclude that the probability of a red sweet is one in three. For certain you are no longer guessing, but the probability judgement you have made, mainly because the evidence you are using is indirect, is now only marginally, if at all, improved.

This behaviour is called subjective inference. Not all statisticians would agree that this type of probability is valid.

When you were allowed to gather knowledge, to observe your first real (objective) data you were permitted to actually measure the frequency of red sweets in your pack. At this point there is no probability (a.k.a. uncertainty) around this particular pack, only facts. When the sweets are returned to the pack, *the probability under scrutiny* (of selecting a red one first) reasserts itself.

However, it now reasserts itself in an observed universe. It is in the presence of data (knowledge). Now you give an exact statistic (summary of your current knowledge state). This represents your probability (in this case) based on a single observation of all available facts, a pure deduction. This is the objective probability, right?

Well, of course, we are not trying to trick you but the question was not about your pack, the question was about "a pack". You have certainly made an observation of your pack and deduced a reasonable probability statistic from that. Whilst the observation (knowledge) was certainly accurate, you cannot know whether it is also representative. Did your data dispel *enough* of your ignorance?

So lastly, casting financial caution and tooth decay to the wind, you increase your sample 100-fold (increase the frequency of observation) and you not only observe the actual frequency of the red sweets, but you make some observations as to their distribution as well.

This behaviour is called science (measuring frequency distribution to be exact), and most statisticians would accept this kind of probability does exist.

TOWARDS OBJECTIVE PROBABILITY

Does doing this kind of more exhaustive measurement, at last, give us (a form of) objective probability? Well, the next time you open an entirely new packet of Randoms you can be in possession of a probability judgement which is sourced in objective observations. If, when tested in the fires of real experience, it proves "wrong" in any way you can easily update your statistics to include this new result. This is also a principle of empirical science. Your reasoning will then be *even better* next time. You reasoned about the probability of an event by building a statistically valid model of its occurrence. Furthermore, you may legitimately keep updating this model over time.

What should be clear is the thing that has improved, with each step forward in your methodology design, is not your judgement of the probability. Rather it is the *accuracy and reliability* of the knowledge you used to make that judgement. But you have done a bit more than that, haven't you? When you stop and think about it, you may have built a prototypical set of rules for yourself about how you might want to reason about the probability component of any risk construct you use. These could be applied to the risk construct used in your company, could they not?

- Probability judgements should be considered more accurate if they are based on observed data.

- Observed data, to be effectively deployed, must be both of an adequate quantity and quality.
- Probability judgements take both real time and real calculation efforts to be meaningful.
- A statistical model, and therefore a knowledge of statistics, is required to reason effectively about probable outcomes.

So here is an applied challenge of the measurement of risk: when you consider the probability judgements currently found in the risk assessments of your company's reasoning systems, which of these qualities would you say they display?

"FREQUENTLY ASKED" QUESTIONS

Alas, even if you were applying these four principles this will not assuage all of your probability-related woes. This is because, as you buttressed your reasoning system by adding knowledge and improving data quality, you also subtly changed its reference point and its rules. In changing these, you potentially changed the research question from being about a probability judgement (a.k.a. uncertainty) to being about a frequency prediction. Science calls people who practice this 'frequentists'. Should it be a worry that you have become one?

We wouldn't expect you to worry over much about what might appear on the face of things to be just a semantic shift, if anything. However, statistically speaking, that shift is a very real worry indeed. It raises an important question, which is this: is it true that probability, risk and frequency are effectively synonyms?

For example, if you were using a common probability scale such as the one in this figure, or something like it, to what, precisely, would you say "1 in 2 years" refers?

Does it refer to an expectation of likelihood, i.e. we will expect to see this sort of event once every 24 months or so? Or does it refer to a historical

Score	Likelihood Descriptors	Probability Intervals
1.	Remote	0 – 1% (1 in 100yrs)
2.	Very unlikely	1 – 5% (1 in 20 years)
3.	Low	5 – 15% (1 in 6/7 years)
4.	Possible	15 – 40% (1 in 2/3 years)
5.	Likely	40 – 75% (1 in 2 years)
6.	Almost certain	75 – 100% (1 in 2 years +)

FIGURE 5.1 *Likelihood and probability "reckoner"*

fact, i.e. we do see this sort of event every 24 months or so? The latter related to a question of record; the former is a question of predictive judgement in the absence of record. One is a statement of frequency using time as its scale; the other is a statement of uncertainty using time as its proxy. We shouldn't have to point out that these are very different forms of reasoning.

Whilst we can all agree that our reasoning *feels stronger* in the Randoms example when we build a model of the available data, what actually caused that increase in confidence was that we became frequentists. We developed the ability to plot a real frequency distribution. So what happens if the risk-modelling environment in your company doesn't allow – on time, complexity or ethical grounds – for the collection and analysis of real frequency data? Can you still measure probability there?

Unfortunately, we have to tumble a little further down the probable rabbit hole to answer that question because it concerns the applicable principles of measurement. These are also, as we will see, not as simple or as clear as one might suppose.

MEASUREMENT IS (SEMANTICALLY AND STATISTICALLY) DISPUTED

In any measurement system, for it to be a true system, it is incumbent on us to fit the right statistical algorithms. This we must do with something like the accuracy we desire to see in the outcome measure. When we try to search for these algorithms for a risk measurement system which owes half of its meaning to probability, what we will discover is that those scientists who might come to our aid have by no means finished their discussions.

In fact, they haven't even agreed on the semantics (the risk dialect) that might frame the discussion in the first place. What we will also find is that their view on this has a superlative bearing on the statistics that can be reasonably applied to support us in the effective measurement of our real-world risk construct. Indeed, on whether they can support us at all.

RISK OR PROBABILITY?

In the measurement disciplines this semantic problem remains compounded by the history of ownership. By far the largest claim, rightly or wrongly, on the definition and formal measurement of our construct 'risk' has come from the world of statistical science. Frank Knight, back in 1921, will perhaps serve us as an accessible entry point to that key debate, although we will note that it started many centuries earlier and continues unabated today. Without introducing any technical terms (or squiggles) at all, here is what Frank Knight thought about the relationship between risk and probability.

Knight, an objective scientist, understood things to be true or false. He believed therefore that there was a class of objects which had a "measurable uncertainty", e.g. the roll of a die, the proportions of red to black balls in a lottery bag and so on. The term he applied to his measurable uncertainty was, in fact, "risk".

For all other kinds of possible probability observations and associated inferences, e.g. business data (which were too unique and complex to be statistically tabulated), Knight stated that their uncertainty was *unmeasurable.*

Let's just allow the impact of that one assertion sink in. Statistics does have a school which has concluded that exactly the kind of probability inferences that are essential to our aim (assessing probabilities and multiplying them by impacts), those pertaining to business data, are not statistically measurable. So our quest to improve the quality and reliability of our risk measurement is entirely thwarted on the grounds of its unviability.

The term Knight wanted to use to describe our class of objects was simply "uncertainty". Risk, for Knight, was not, nor could it be, about such a thing. Risk, in essence, was really just a synonym for objective probability – a form of classical statistical reasoning based on knowable, observable, verifiable systems of truth:

> To preserve the distinction . . . between the measurable uncertainty and an unmeasurable one, we may use the term risk to designate the former and the term uncertainty for the latter.
>
> Cited in Holton, 2004

Already you can object that there are four subtle flaws in Knight's definition of risk.

First, restricting his use of risk to systems the properties of which are already known seems illogical. Someone – and it doesn't really matter who – does *already know* how many red balls and black balls are in that lottery bag, or has already verified that the die is a fair one – by rolling it over and over. You can see shades of this unreality in many of the archetypal probability problems. A judge, with perfect knowledge, presides over the admissible knowledge in the problem space in advance of your being invited to take part in it.

Of course, we might want to argue that reasoning about risk in the real world has a far greater utility to us if we can apply it to managing precisely the other kind of uncertainty – the kind where we are worried because no-one knows, with a fixed probability, what might happen.

Second, Knight is really channelling the most long-running debate since science began. He is pitching objectivity against subjectivity. Like a lot of scientists, he favours objectivity as the truth – a truth discoverable by science, and subjectivity as an expression of ignorance – ignorance that cannot be (easily) dispelled by science. The former, we are to embrace, the latter we must reject.

Of course, we might want to argue the validity of reasoning about risk in the real world comes from understanding risk from the point of view of human agents or cultures who want to use it to wrestle with their troubling ignorance – a kind of understanding that is informative of applied decisions and real behaviours in a real-world context.

Third, Knight has absolutely no use for the term risk. It is only logically equivalent, in his view, to a measurable uncertainty or a probability. Both are fundamentally conceptual and neither conveys any sense of consequence measure. So, for Knight the risk algorithm is even simpler than $P \times I$, it is simply $R = P$.

We might argue that the cultural validity of the term risk, and therefore the utility of the concept, lies in its ability to conceptualise a cause and effect hierarchy that assists, or informs, decision makers about real future consequences.

Fourth, Knight has absolutely no scientific basis imaginable for labelling his admissible kind of probability as "risk" and all the (inadmissible) others as "uncertainty". His view is that risk is essentially only a synonym for objective, factual, observable probability. Why should we believe him when that move is fundamentally semantic, not scientific? Also, whilst it might not be dishonest, it is highly arrogant.

We might argue however that the validity of our use of the term risk, and therefore the utility of our application of the concept, lies in our ability to deliver a compelling scientific, and not just semantic, argument about what it should mean and how it should be measured.

Even from this one example, four problems with any clumsy combination of the concept of probability with the construct of risk now hove into view:

- model-world reasoning vs real-world reasoning;
- subjective belief states vs objectively observable data;
- the existence of any true relationship between risk and probability;
- what we say we mean by words vs what they "do mean" to those who hear them.

A QUESTION OF EPISTEMOLOGY?

Our risk construct, or more importantly its meaningful use and measurement, is fast becoming a challenge of epistemology. Even if you contend, as many in industry do, that risk is immediately reducible to "probability multiplied by impact", numerous questions around just *the meaning of that 'probability' term* very quickly arise. If science refuses to legitimise that concept within its own boundaries, how can we, with all certainty, come to a common agreement what 'probability' should be referring to? One that means that when we judge, with certainty or otherwise, what we know about it we are being rational.

If it is not our (arguing) scientists then who is to be the arbiter, or the judge, of the accuracy or sagacity of our risk measurement? Who will support that what it is we claim to therefore know, with (probable) certainty, is actually good science? More than that, how can *what we believe we know* be used to make (rational) business decisions?

How can what we only believe we know lead us to draw conclusions on the relationship between risk and business value?

To a "pure" frequentist, like Frank Knight and friends:

- The risk judgements of industry use probability in name only; the referent does not display any qualities of the true construct of probability.
- The term is being attached to subjective beliefs attempting to dispel true ignorance – the kind that science has nothing to offer.
- The measurement is only formed as purely subjective uncertainty judgements – a kind that are wholly invalid in pure statistical science and therefore cannot be measured.

As you might imagine, Knight's position from the 1920s did not hold sway, although it is still, in your author's recent experience, being passionately stated and re-stated today. It did not carry the whole argument. Other frequentists were willing to take a more lenient view on the validity of belief data and subjective judgement. In their 1980 paper – On the quantitative definition of risk – Kaplan and Garrick argued the following:

> The major polarization of the argument is between the "objectivist" or "frequentist" school who view probability as something external, the result of repetitive experiments, and the "subjectivists" who view probability as an expression of an internal state – a state of knowledge or state of confidence. In this paper we adopt the point of view that both schools are right; they are just talking about two different ideas. Unfortunately, they both use the same word – which seems to be the source of most of the confusion.

Notice again that even in what will be quite a hard-core paper on the nature of the quantification of risk, semantics is never far away. So Kaplan and Garrick wanted a, once and for all, *semantic* distinction between the two terms we have been discussing so far, between probability and frequency:

What the objectivists are talking about we shall call "frequency." What the subjectivists are talking about we shall call "probability." Thus, "probability" as we shall use it is a numerical measure of a state of knowledge, a degree of belief, a state of confidence. "Frequency" on the other hand refers to the outcome of an experiment of some kind involving repeated trials. Thus frequency is a "hard" measurable number.

The real twist comes however when, out of a wish to try to help us to measure our (unmeasurable) probability, they make the following case:

> Probability, on the other hand, at first glance is a notion of a different kind. Defined, essentially, as a number used to communicate a state of mind, it thus seems "soft" and changeable, subjective – not measureable, at least not in the usual way.

Notice that key phrase – "not measurable" – and perhaps pause a while to worry about it.

COMPARABLE UNCERTAINTY

What happens next is we see the kind of sleight of hand that is not uncommon in communities who are completely familiar with mathematical representation. It is the very same sleight of hand that has taken industry down the path of risk measurement that it has chosen up until now – essentially the trick that people play when they use probability judgements without the requisite agonising over their scientific nature. To give its formal name, this trick is called "The axiom of comparability of uncertainty". Central, if invisible, to how we all use risk in industry, that axiom has the following logic:

Step 1: You can (subjectively) judge the probability of two events; that is admissible.

Step 2: You can (subjectively) judge whether these events are more, less or equally likely to each other; that is also admissible.

Step 3:   We (the experts) can describe for you a "probability scale" (for these sorts of events) by using the rules of frequency estimation as the (mathematical) reference point.

The axiom of comparability of uncertainty says that frequency *can be considered the same as probability* in certain clear ways:

> In this way we liberate ourselves from the restrictions of the relative frequency school of thought (e.g. that only mass repetitive phenomena can be analyzed probabilistically) and create for ourselves a systematic, disciplined theory and language for dealing with rare events, for quantifying risks, and making decisions in the face of the uncertainties . . .

This is not as circular as it first appears, but we are beginning to enter counterintuitive territory – the complexity of a collapsing worldview in fact. Notice how Garrick and Kaplan have had to call their approach a "disciplined theory and language". Once again, there is no escaping the need to address the measurement of risk as, firstly, a semantic problem. By implication, when one does this one is answering a question that specifies which risk dialect one is speaking. The mathematics and statistics we want to rush on and use – to make our risk measurements coherent (and credible) – can only be admissible once we have ascertained the dialect.

The modern discipline of decision science takes this discussion as read. It takes full advantage of this "calibration-led" approach and uses it to create techniques to convert complex, elicited expert judgements of real-world things into representative summary statistics naming these probabilities. The school of subjective Bayesian analysis and also of prescriptive Bayesian analysis take advantage of the same leniency with probability judgements.

It is a key point that these very common shortcuts undergird and facilitate risk assessment techniques. They mean that the people who are experts in their own right in the industries using risk assessment do not have to know anything much about statistics. Of course, very few of us have the services of decision scientists to hand to extract and validate our reasoning models for us when we want to reason about our organisational risks. We tend to do that on our own.

The question of the usability of probability

A clear conclusion, even from just from this evidence, has to be that the first component of our industrial risk measurement is not collapsible onto the abstract probability figure we so easily use. This applies whether that be an assessment of percentages, frequencies, ratios or whatever. Rather, to be a measurement, i.e. scientific, it has to be some kind of valid *and complex* function of knowledge and probability. This is because the efficacy of the use of a concept like probability rests squarely on knowledge. In fact, it rests wholly on our ability to measure the flow of knowledge into well-defined problem spaces.

So what we are saying is that a naïve use of 'P × I' will never be enough on its own.

However in-depth and accurate the 'I' part of this is, drawn as it often can be from real detailed analyses that the company uses for other purposes, the 'P' part will always be fatally flawed – flawed unless it is critically qualified by an assessment of a 'K'– where that relates to knowledge. Which brings us to immediately to another (philosophical) quality control issue for our risk-reasoning fidelity – what can we know?

TAKING A GEO-POLITICAL EXAMPLE

On 12 February 2002 the then United States Secretary of Defence, Donald Rumsfeld, gave arguably his most famous press briefing. It goes by various names, but is remembered as the "known, unknowns" speech. The idea, although it was never originally his, became so attached to him that Rumsfeld would later entitle his 2011 autobiography *Known and Unknown: A Memoir*. In 2016 you can still see him give this legendary briefing, thanks to YouTube™. The exact text of the infamous part, according to the U.S. Department of Defense press archive, is the following:

Reports that say that something hasn't happened are always interesting to me, because as we know, there are known knowns; there are things we know we know. We also know there are known unknowns; that is to say we know there are some things we do not know. But there are also unknown unknowns – the ones we don't know we don't know. And if one looks throughout the history of our country and other free countries, it is the latter category that tend to be the difficult ones.

Rumsfeld wasn't giving a lecture on reasoning, but he was stating a position which was very much about how a large organisation, in this case a government, might reason in complex circumstances. In 88 words he uses derivatives of the word "know" 14 times. He was attempting to summarise a quandary that the U.S. Government (and others) found themselves in vis-à-vis their reasoning on the basis of evidence, or the lack of it. His subject, of course, was a morally ambiguous war in the Middle East, so it was no surprise that he was variously derided and praised for these 88 words.

Philosophically however, Rumsfeld can be criticised for incomplete reasoning himself. After all, he wanted to divide the world of evidence-based reasoning into three data streams: known knowns, known unknowns and unknown unknowns. He was, of course, missing a logical category, that of "unknown knowns". Although this sounds initially ridiculous, it is not so. It is conceivable that "unknown knowns" might be just the right term with which to discuss high-complexity systems: that is to say, the need for reasoning in the space where we have theories about causes and effects, or risks and consequences, we know something about them, but that the theories can only be partial because their targets are too complex to know everything.

For absolute completeness, of course, we should not miss out moral philosophy in the same discussion. Some of Rumsfeld's critics wanted to pointedly say that there were clearly 'disavowed knowns', that is to say morally dubious practices that we pretend are unknown to us when they are known (by us).

As we will see, all five categories (known knowns, known unknowns, unknown unknowns, unknown knowns and disavowed knowns) have an important role to play in assessing the validity of modern industrial measurement and reasoning around risk and resilience.

So here are the terms summarised:

1   Known knowns: situations about which we have exhaustive facts and predictive capability.
2   Known unknowns: situations about which we are clear that we do not have all the facts in answer to key questions, or adequate data upon which to base a sound judgement, but we are aware of all the facts we need.
3   Unknown unknowns: situations where facts are either pertinent, relevant or completely corrective to our reasoning, but we are unaware either of the existence of these facts or of their impact.
4   Unknown knowns: situations where the facts are simply too complex, or too difficult, to extricate and we are cognisant of operating an inferior working theory of the real world.
5   Disavowed knowns: situations where we, or certain parts of an organisation, are in possession of unpopular or inconvenient truths and the larger organisation behaves as if these facts are not known.

What each of these examples demonstrates remains true. Irrespective of whether you accept this design step is necessary, you must accept a very real tension if you want to reason with risk:

The validity of risk reasoning will always be predicated upon the quality of the knowledge – of all types – that is being used.

CONCLUSION FROM THIS CHAPTER

You may have found this chapter unusually philosophical. You might be asking yourself whether this is all very academic. Is it not possible to press ahead with a judgement system that makes a loose use of a helpful construct, like probability, to help people reason without the requisite science? The answer is yes, something that some parts of the requisite science are at pains to point out.

However, the answer is also no. The reason why the requisite science is entirely at home with a justification for this behaviour has also to be noted. The reason is because it can always bring highly complex, expert and involved mathematical methodology to bear on the problem. We are not able to do that.

This chapter has only scratched the surface to ask: when we are not able to do that, are we being sufficiently rational? When we determine that a simple probability figure drawn *ex nihilo* and multiplied by an impact figure is good enough reasoning to measure the risk for our multi-million pound projects and programmes, what ends are we really serving? How responsible are we really being with shareholders' resources? How defensible would such judgements prove to be in a court?

As we dig deeper it becomes clear that when we wish to combine judgements, reduce data and develop systematic priorities, an essential element of any risk-reasoning system, the statistical complexity needed for this behaviour to be valid becomes rapidly overwhelming. Holding our hands out and making the same plea once more – is it not possible to press ahead with a (complexity-intolerant) judgement system that makes loose use of helpful constructs will not avail us.

The house of cards we thus build leads people further and further from accuracy into deeper and deeper errors. These errors either don't matter at all – because they only speak a dialect of reassurance and have no material impact – or they matter a great deal because they are to be translated into material decisions. Either way, this illogical insistence on bad science and irrational thinking destroys value for businesses. In the latter case this might be quite catastrophically.

Probability inference, in particular, for the purposes of risk measurement is a wholly disputed and complex area of science. Even simple examples can show this. Accepting flawed reasoning structures predicated on a misappropriation of this science, because they seem like a good way to simplify complex scenarios, is a folly. The measurement of risk even from these first principles, it is clear, cannot be simple. The choice for our industries is a stark one therefore.

So responsible agents are faced with a choice: indulge in a kind of pseudo-mathematical alchemy that, at best, wastes value and, at worst, stands a chance of destroying it, or face up to the challenge to measure risk properly and add value to your business. We would argue that the latter choice is the only reasonable alternative.

BIBLIOGRAPHY

Holton, G.A., 2004. Defining risk. *Financial Analysts Journal*, 60(6), pp. 19–25.

Summing up
Part 1

THE CLASH OF LANGUAGES

In the world of industrial reasoning around risk, we face a clash of languages on two levels. The first is certainly philosophical. As we observe this discipline in modern organisations, we can detect an addiction to the use of scientific framing. It is easy to see this because our risk activities are not described as journalistic or phenomenological pursuits – the language of wisdom sharing. Rather, they are almost always described as assessment, evaluation or analysis activities – the language of scientific measurement. Of course, it remains possible that we may be using the latter language to add more credibility to behaviours which are really about the former.

The test for whether this is the case has to be an objectification of our risk management disciplines. If we call something an assessment, there should surely be a clear object which is being assessed. If we call something an evaluation, it must surely elaborate on measured values of some kind. If we call something an analysis, the very use of that term connotes that it must be rigorous beyond the fact of mere observation and commentary.

The degree to which modern industry risk methodologies pass even this test is an open question.

What is clear is that risk is certainly a reasoning challenge and, as such, the construct must be housed in some sort of system. If this assertion has to transcend the more dialectic forms of that term, we are on firm ground in expecting that they be evidentially, and not just linguistically, scientific. Thus we must expect to see operational logic, organisational psychology and statistical technique being systematically applied as a key part of the methodology.

The second clash of languages we find in risk reasoning is more pragmatic. It has to do with the integrity of the internal working definitions. It is easy to observe that risk is a term which operates in a continuum of definitions ranging from industrial ethics to hazard-based pedantry. To objectify the constructs in a way that is operationally meaningful, we would suggest that the definition language used has to pass four key tests: that it be semantically coherent, refers to a single abstract, has a validated measurement unit and produces an output which is, above all, framed in a way which is materially relevant to the business in question. In our long experience, few conventional approaches could pass that test.

THE CHALLENGE OF MEASUREMENT

In Part 1 we have explored some of the significant practical problems facing busy practitioners who have to work within extant risk systems. This has already highlighted problems with the consistency of reasoning in these standard methodologies and, most importantly, with the integrity of their measurement designs.

One good consistency of reasoning example is the widespread use of the concept of probability – a central pillar to most industrial risk. In academia this concept is highly complex and highly disputed. Commentators here are also agreed that is very counterintuitive to apply to risk phenomena in real-world settings. Its use there is likely to be inaccurate and inconsistent unless the user is an expert. Furthermore, any valid use of the probability construct in such a real-world setting is always predicated on the quality of the knowledge that informs it.

Here we see once more that significant tension between the narrative and the scientific. The people who assess risks in industry are not expert in probability. Many risk-reasoning systems are not using coherent statistics. Rather, they are happy to designate pure *ex nihilo* judgements as probabilities. This is because we like the authority of the term even if, upon close examination, it does not, in fact, refer to an observable supply chain of causality. This is where we ignore the fact that we are really using the language of probability in a purely narrative sense. We prefer to represent it as a technical judgement of fact when it is only an informed opinion.

The classic reductionism of modern industrial risk to the product of a probability (opinion) multiplied by an impact (judgement) and plotted on a graph to reveal priority (heuristic) fails the dual test of psychological and statistical coherence. Discretised risk events lack enough meaning to be more than casually compared. The commonly used measurement scales, because they are abstract and expedient, contain major statistical non-sequiturs.

The challenge to reason from the outputs of these impoverished designs is non-trivial: the desire is for the interpretation of results to be, nonetheless, demonstrably rational. This presents us with a pressing difficulty. Given their expedient design, abstract metrics and desire to appear scientifically valid, modern risk systems, in the hands of ordinary managers, will simply produce poor reasoning.

BETTER METHODS AND TOOLS

This poor reasoning is not necessary. In the case study we examined it was possible to see that capturing operational logic, organisational psychology and statistical rigour in a coherent methodology was achievable. The consistency of reasoning in a risk assessment can be improved. The size and complexity of the business transformation made it obvious that the industry-standard risk register approach would be all but meaningless. That methodology would produce a large list of independently defined risks without a coherent link to the project decision making or the target business outcomes.

The team in this case needed to embark upon a radical redesign. Their new method would model risk at the meta-level locked deliberately into a volatility tracking system which linked the risk status to the programme critical path. The result was a decision support methodology which was deliberately, and successfully, embedded in the operational oversight at all levels in the programme.

From this case study it is clear that the accepted norms of risk management, measurement and monitoring do not need to have the last word. The determining variables, of appetite for complexity and over-familiarity with accepted norms, do not always determine the design. It is entirely possible to develop systematic processes and tools that benefit from improved reasoning to support decision making under uncertainty. The benefits package of the improved rigour and rationality massively outweighed the effort to get the organisation to adopt them.

Whilst we must try to avoid too histrionic an analysis, or too psychological a narrative, here, what is crystal clear is that organisations who want to use industrial risk must increase their desire for evidence-based practice and their appetite for complexity. To be successful at this we would argue, they have to commit to an intentional journey of systems design.

PART 2
Risk-based resilience

Introduction
to Part 2

Having laid the foundations in part one for a more powerful risk construct – in language, definition, application and measurement terms – this part of the book now turns to address the question of the meaning and the function of the concept of Business Resilience or, as it is more frequently called these days, Organisational Resilience. All resilience forms that we can observe are predicated on a risk construct, however poorly defined this may be. The object of the exercise going forward is to become far more explicit about the dependency that this core concept of resilience has on the concept of risk as we have now described it.

To address this dependence, we must first discuss resilience in a certain isolation. We will begin that conversation by exploring how, just like risk, it only exists in a dense cloud of definition challenges. The role of British or international standards as a possible solution to this, for industry cannot be underplayed. However, upon examination these artefacts, it transpires, have not found themselves immune to having to wrestle with definitions. Resolving even this tension will not be easy. We suggest a definition road map approach.

Seeking a greater reliance on an evidence-based approach for the marriage of risk and resilience as dependent constructs, we examine the potential contribution of theories of human reasoning in the presence of uncertainty. Although a clear set of choices emerge, extant systems apply a highly counterintuitive set of principles. For example, much of the evidence sees the need for a resilience construct to be risk-based by calling for it to be formed out of a naturalistic, human-centred methodology. This is counterintuitive when one examines the current resilience system candidates in industry, which are far from this.

Accepting the marriage of risk and resilience, as dependent constructs, we have to revisit in a more detailed way the question of how risk measurement can inform resilience measurement. The highly flawed nature of the common assumptions, the choice of scaling method and the statistical logic of the conclusion making in current practice should cause us some deep concerns.

The argument that is emerging from the journey of design in this book is that organisations must face an increased appetite for complexity to begin to reason effectively with a risk-based resilience construct. One, perhaps surprising, route to this is a reformation of the measurement method for risk which can still cater for the conventional appetite. We will briefly examine an applied case study that explains how this might help.

CHAPTER 6

What is organisational resilience?

Organisational resilience or, to use its earlier title, business resilience should contain a clue in either title. It should primarily be about helping organisations achieve their goals. Just as we have so far pointed out that risk definition and assessment systems should not be considered in isolation from the strategies, priorities and decision-making controls of the business they support, so too with any business resilience system. Even if resilience, like risk before it, requires us to go beyond the accepted wisdom and innovate a set of dialects and challenge the coherence of the established measurements, this should still be done with the interests of good industrial reasoning in mind.

Resilience as a term is used in a wide variety of fields that include but are not limited to ecology, metallurgy, individual and organisational psychology, health, defence, community, supply chain management, strategic management and safety engineering. *The Oxford English Dictionary* offers us two nuances to the meaning of the term:

1 Toughness: the capacity to recover quickly from difficulties
2 Elasticity: the ability of a substance or object to spring back into shape.

However, if we face up to the reality of how the term is applied in business in 2018 and beyond then, as we had to with risk, we must immediately face the semantic challenge. Does resilience – when it is simply described as some combination of toughness and elasticity – mean enough, in and of itself, to be practically applied to your industrial problems?

Probably not.

The natural reaction, as we saw was the case with risk, has been for people begin to buttress resilience with additional words. Arguably, this is with many more suffixes and prefixes than we have seen with risk, e.g. personal, community, teenager, organisational, health, marital, military, cyber, etc. Our immediate concern in this chapter is to ask what exactly is 'business resilience?' Does that prefix 'business' change the meaning? Can a business be thought of as tough and elastic? Is there a clear observable difference between a non-resilient and a resilient business? We will examine some of the best available answers in a moment. Before that, however, a metaphor.

THE CASE FOR SPACE BETWEEN KEY CONCEPTS

Anyone who is working at present in the field of business resilience, or its close cousin business continuity planning, will know that the difference between the two is a serious point of contention. For some there is no difference, they are merely synonyms. For others there is resistance. The hard-won branding and reputation of business continuity planning, something that took decades to achieve, is seen to be at stake. For still others, business resilience is accepted as a natural evolution of business continuity.

WHICH SHOULD IT BE? WHICH IS THE BETTER TERM? ARE THEY SYNONYMS?

For our journey of design, we believe that there very much does need to be a difference between resilience and continuity. Recognising this is essential to determine the category of reasoning an organisation should deploy. To support that argument, we'd like to offer you a highly useful automotive safety metaphor. Airbags or ABS?

We'd like you think about the car that you transport yourself, and maybe your family in. Stop for a moment and ask yourself a question, but be aware before you answer it that your answer will lead to other questions about your reasoning priorities. The question is this: if you were only allowed to add one safety feature to your family car (in addition to the seatbelts, we'll let you keep those) and the choice was between a comprehensive airbag system or ABS (this stands for anti-lock braking system, a computer-controlled capacity that allows your car's emergency braking to out-perform that of a human operator in terms of stopping distance), which would you choose?

Airbags or ABS?

For those who chose airbags, here are some sub-questions:

- How do you know your airbags are working?
- How do you know your airbags will be effective?
- What does the use of airbags signal for the usability of the car after deployment?

For those who chose ABS, here are the sub-questions:

- How do you know your ABS is working?
- What does ABS achieve when your vehicle is struck by another vehicle?
- If your response to the first question is that you can feel it working, how regularly should you feel it to be considered a safe driver?

BUSINESS CONTINUITY PLANNING IS AN AIRBAG SYSTEM

Airbags are a great metaphor for the classic formulation of business continuity planning. Fundamentally occupying the spare capacity, or redundancy, side of the business efficiency equation, plans provide a classic conservative fallback. As the logic goes, if something is important make sure you have backed it up.

Therein, of course, lies a critical weakness on two fronts. First, there is a very real on-cost for any system that requires unused redundancy as a back-up. In today's world this will be immediately questioned on business efficiency and cost grounds alone. Second, just like your airbags, you simply cannot know in advance whether your continuity will really be up to the job. Not until it has to be fired will it be tested. If it fails in any way, that will be too late.

A key corollary of that is you will never know how effective (including cost effective) your continuity system is because it only returns value in mitigating the loss associated with a, hopefully rare, incident. In fact, that feared incident, to all intents and purposes, might be completely non-existent. The need for business continuity plans is sold on the anxiety associated with its possibility. The core assumption is that real-time planning and decision making would always under-perform when compared to advance plans and contingency.

People may protest that this metaphor falls down. Although you can't test operational airbags in real life, you can test continuity systems. However, the test conditions we have observed rarely amount to more than a much-needed confidence boost on the shelf-life of the written plans – something that many professionals who work in the field will confess with a due sense of realism. The fact remains that the deployment of business continuity still fundamentally adds value to an organisation by mitigating an immediate real-time loss of key people, functions or operability. How much it really does has always to be learned in real time.

That learning, of course, might never happen since when that system fires, it is usually a signal for a greater set of problems to solve. Continuity is, itself, only a partial and time-limited solution to those.

RESILIENCE IS AN ABS SYSTEM

Anti-lock braking is a great metaphor for the added value of reasoning around a resilience construct. This is because, fundamentally, resilience is something that is designed to work in harmony with the business-as-usual system. It is designed to be working alongside it as an optimiser. Its main purpose is still to allow that system to function in what we might call mildly extreme circumstances, in the short term at least. In that sense its overlap with business continuity is quite plain.

The main difference that emerges is that business resilience should operate by creating a superior performance for that business as usual system. This superior performance does not equate to protecting it in the event of a rare failure. It therefore brings the considerable evolutionary advantage of allowing for real-time business learning to take place in parallel with its use. For example, if the resilience provision (which we have yet to specify) is used too frequently under certain conditions, you know your business has a deeper problem. Just like if you are constantly feeling the brake pedal vibrating under your foot, you need to alter your driving style.

Within limits, resilience actually operates therefore in a dual capacity for business intelligence. It acts as a performance indicator and a safety system – a two-in-one arrangement – just like ABS in a car can. This dual capacity rests on the fact that resilience is fundamentally designed to be preventative. So, unlike airbags which, by definition, accept the incident and mitigate the consequences, ABS always militates against the probability that there will be an incident. Thus, within observable parameters, we can suggest that an investment in a resilience capability actually and actively prevents loss and therefore promotes business. Unlike business continuity, however, which is predicated on a business impact assessment, standard resilience approaches rarely offer a clear estimation of a value figure that is being protected.

What this metaphor does is illustrate a key tension that gives us clear space between the definitions in play. Space between something that can damage-limit value loss through the need to manage the (negative) outcomes – business continuity planning – and something that has the potential to add value by contributing increased control to the host system – business resilience.

In definition terms, this offers us a choice of technologies to optimise business operations in the following ways:

The prevailing ethos of business continuity planning is that you do not seek to control the (low) probability of losses happening, rather you invest in impact mitigation.

The prevailing ethos of a business resilience is that you invest in controls which are aimed directly at managing and measuring the opposite. They are aimed at the effectiveness of probability militating systems.

Two further things now go hand-in-hand with this metaphor. Airbags (and therefore business continuity) require that companies accept loss. They are designed to cope with an uncontrollable and damaging incident that managers believe (with however low a probability) will one day happen. As designed, these systems can only return value (beyond the slightly intangible value of reassurance) when that event has happened.

ABS (and therefore business resilience) accepts that a short-term loss of control need not cripple a business. So it makes the business able to cope in and out of parameter operation in that short term. However, if the company were to absorb the benefits of ABS into business-as-usual operation too frequently – in effect give in to the temptation make a safety system a system optimiser – then real trouble would lie ahead.

So even at the metaphorical level both systems (continuity and resilience) require well-defined spaces to work in. Both systems can be demarcated by their different cause-and-effect sequences. Both have differential costs and benefits measurements. In a perfect world you'd like to have both systems, because fundamentally they control different risk streams.

That is precisely why we believe that the definition of resilience should be separate from that of continuity. Both culturally and phenomenologically, they do not address the same risk sources (and beliefs), they do not operate the same control mechanisms and they do not do so with a logically comparable expression of risk appetite.

SOME EXAMPLE DEFINITIONS FROM THE INDUSTRY PERSPECTIVE

Naturally, even if one agrees with this position, there is still the question of the relevance of extant definitions of these concepts away from automotive metaphors, however helpful. We are not the first commentators to discover that the extant definitions of resilience do very little to create any applied clarity to business decision makers or system designers.

The relatively new BSI Guidance on Organizational Resilience standard (Nov 2014) offers us the following:

Resilience is a strategic objective intended to help the organization to survive and prosper. A highly resilient organization is also more adaptive, competitive, agile and robust than less resilient organizations.

Organizational resilience is the ability of an organization to anticipate, prepare for, and respond and adapt to everything from minor everyday events to acute shocks and chronic or incremental changes.

Resilience is a relative, dynamic concept and, as such, an organization can only be more or less resilient. As a result, resilience is a goal, not a fixed activity or state, and is enhanced by integrating and coordinating the various operational disciplines that the organization might already be applying (BS65000:2014, p. 5).

One has to politely suggest that there may be a problem with the clarity, specificity and application of a definition which contains the phrase:

Organizational resilience is the ability of an organization to anticipate, prepare for, and respond and adapt to everything . . .

Likewise, when we look on the wider web for comment then Robert Gaddum (an IBM UK consultant) in his continuitycentral.com article offers the same panacea-like quality to his definition:

The ability of an organisation's business operations to rapidly adapt and respond to internal or external dynamic changes – opportunities, demands, disruptions or threats – and continue operations with limited impact to the business.

Robert Gaddum, IBM UK, www.continuitycentral.
com/feature083.htm, 2004

The phrase . . . internal or external dynamic changes – opportunities, demands, disruptions or threats . . . has more than a hint of everything about it.

For a slightly less inclusive definition, Hubert offers us:

Organisational resilience is the ability of an organisation to provide and maintain an acceptable level of service in the face of faults and challenges to normal operation by preventing, avoiding and resisting damage and recovering quickly.

So what is general resilience according to these definitions?

- Is it the organisation's goal to be adaptable to everything?
- Is it to continue operations in the face of everything?
- Is it to resist any damage and recover quickly?

Or is it all of them in some measure at different times and in different circumstances?

If it is, then we might argue that this fails the semantic test spectacularly. It is hardly helpful to teams who need to design governance, process and tools because it is hardly excluding any eventuality at all from the definition space. One reason these examples of existing industry definitions of resilience really fall short is because they smack, more than just a bit, of always having been written by a committee. Indeed, a key feature of this authored by committee feel to business (or operational) resilience is that they all essentially smack of a reworking of the earlier concept of business continuity planning.

A quick look at ISO 22301, the standard for business continuity planning, ably demonstrates this. It defines business continuity planning in the following two ways. Try reading these definitions twice. First, as they are printed here, second, see if you would notice any difference at all if you substituted the words business resilience for business continuity:

Business Continuity (BC) is defined as the capability of the organization to continue delivery of products or services at acceptable predefined levels following a disruptive incident. (ISO 22301:2012).

Business Continuity Management (BCM) is defined as a holistic management process that identifies potential threats to an organization and the impacts to business operations those threats, if realised, might cause, and which provides a framework for building organizational resilience with the capability of an effective response that safeguards the interests of its key stakeholders, reputation, brand and value-creating activities. (ISO 22301:2012).

How much does this well-defined, long-standing (and legitimate) area of activity actually relate conceptually to something which is distinct from what people are now calling business resilience? Are the two perhaps in a Venn diagram arrangement? Or are they really the same thing described using different sets of words? Notice how the latter definition even co-opts the word resilience into its text.

At this point you might ask: is it a bad thing that Business Resilience is potentially just a makeover of Business Continuity Planning and may not be adding any benefit to the original? Surely that same desire to maintain systemic equilibrium – whatever it is called – is still as essential to businesses risk management processes as it always has been?

Whilst we might agree, we would argue that the addition of this new terminology, if that is all that can be achieved, amounts to little more than rebranding. As such, it really just serves the academic debate and is not helpful for you in terms of building an applied reasoning system to build proportionate risk appetite and controls in your operations.

So we come back to our central point again:

Business resilience ought to be a different concept to business continuity because they are about fundamentally different sources and expressions of risk.

Also, if resilience and business continuity appear, in the current definitions under review, to be terms for roughly the same thing, then that thing is primarily related to impact response and recovery. This requires a systems approach which will fundamentally accept shocks or stresses and then attempts to minimise any disruption caused. Doesn't resilience, by its nature, not convey some kind of prevention activity? Something to be used in advance of any effective response to shocks and stresses?

If we turn, for example, to the field of community resilience we can see this additional concept enshrined in the idea of seeking sustainability.

For example, The London First organisation, in its capacity to address the resilience of the City of London, offers this:

> Community Resilience is defined as 'the coming together of individuals and organisations before, during and after major shocks or stresses to ensure a sustainable business community for the future'. This capability requires both a proactive and a reactive approach, as well as a strong cultural component. Taken together, they enable a business district to survive and thrive for the long term. Community resilience rises above the nature of the shock or stress or the type of business – it is transformative in general.

In that "transformative in general" comment we can see that same spark of reasoning benefit that we discerned in the case study in Chapter 4. Reasoning about risk has the effect of changing, and by that we mean improving, the system that is being reasoned about. Sustainability, proactivity and reactivity in the London First definition are all considered essential and these are, for the most part, built on the agreed core architecture of mainstream continuity. It is quite a pioneering definition.

Our argument is this, therefore: there would be even more benefit if each term (resilience and continuity) were to be defined by a strict exclusion rather than the current obfuscation caused by all these blurred lines. This is the sort of exclusion we might expect to find from a look at some of the more academic definitions of resilience. One might anticipate that these would both conceptualise how these areas and systems come together and how they differentiate.

HELP FROM THE ACADEMIC PERSPECTIVE?

When we do look at the academic perspective, the tension we have noted in the applied arena – between reacting to shocks and stresses or evolving as a consequence of them – rather disappointingly, simply reasserts itself.

Bhamra, Dani and Burnard (2011, p. 5376), looking across uses of the term, endorse a classic formulation of a stabilising response to shock:

> Although the context of the term may change, across all of these fields the concept of resilience is closely related with the capability and ability of an element to return to a stable state after disruption. When the notion of resilience is applied to organisations, this definition does not drastically change. Resilience is therefore related to both the individual and organisational; responses to turbulence and discontinuities.

Ponis and Koronis (2012, p. 923), on the other hand, provide a table of definitions of organisational resilience as well as supply chain resilience and find the opposite idea, that of evolving in response to shock. One definition they rest on is by Sutcliffe & Vogus (2003), who indicate that organisational resilience often has been used to refer to:

a) the ability of an organisation to absorb strain and preserve (or improve) functioning despite the presence of adversity, or to have

b) the ability of an organisation to recover or bounce back from untoward events organisation to absorb strain and preserve (or improve) functioning despite the presence of adversity.

As well as underscoring this point about resilience leading to organisational improvement, Ponis and Koronis also note there is significant overlaps with another concept, that of organisational agility. Sharifi and Zhang (1999) define this as the ability to cope with unexpected challenges, to survive unprecedented threats of business environment, *and to take advantage of changes as opportunities.*

So, the academic literature points to two discrete approaches on organisational resilience. Some are seeing organisational (business) resilience as simply an ability to rebound from unexpected, stressful, adverse situations and to pick up where they left off – not different in any real way to the purpose of business continuity planning. Others, more interestingly, visualise organisational resilience beyond that restoration function. They want it to include the reactive development of new capabilities and an expanded ability to keep pace with and even create new opportunities (Lengnick-Hall et al., 2011; Ponis & Koronis, 2012).

As we continue our journey of design, you will see it is definitely this second approach that interests us. It is our belief that, as an expression of your organisation's risk reasoning, this second definition of resilience is the one which will add value to your business.

WRESTLING WITH APPLIED DEFINITIONS

Even from this brief review, we can conclude that there are no true definitions that we feel we could readily use from industry self-report, international standards or even the academic literature to satisfactorily solve the semantic problem in the case of resilience. Casting a wider net does not resolve the situation; resilience, as a concept, can sustain definitions in quadruple figures these days.

Although the core concept of applied resilience in a business context doesn't have anything approaching the definitional lassitude of risk (from ethics to pedantry), there is still no agreed way to pin down exact definitions for business continuity or business resilience that will receive widespread assent. This is just not going to happen. As we concluded with risk, therefore, the design journey needs to put you in a position to make a stipulative definition – the kind where you are required to take control of what you mean.

Thus, any definition we help you to arrive at must include decisions that are specific to your sector and tailored to apply both to the local and global organisational levels. The same case we are laying out for risk therefore is the one we need to lay out for resilience. How resilience is understood by your organisation will be a combination of how you define it (dialect, semantics and abstraction), by the choices you make about appropriate measurement and by how it addresses the core question of materiality in an evidence-based way.

TRUE BUSINESS RESILIENCE?

Whilst true resilience is very hard to define in any simple statement, as the numerous examples we have shown ably demonstrate, we would argue through our experiences at this point in the journey of design that there are still some core defining characteristics to a usable definition. Let us concentrate on five of those:

1 *Resilience describes a discipline, not a document*
  To establish any control there is clear organisational need for governance, guidance, process, procedures, tools, systems, measurement/metrics and so on, to support resilience activation. The caveat here is that true resilience should not be too speedily reduced to documents and checklists. If resilience becomes a plan, that plan is only a piece of paper (the bête noire of business continuity planning). How a plan interrelates with other operational disciplines and who is responsible for executing the plan (to what competence level) remains a key question.
2 *Resilience should be predicated on competence in resilience*
  Resilience should not remove or undermine the need for business continuity planning in an organisation, because that is a different discipline with different competences. Likewise, emergency and disaster response planning – frequently a separate discipline to business continuity for regulatory reasons – should be managed by appropriate professionals according to how these competencies are defined within the organisational governance. Resilience too requires skilled operators who operate a system which is complementary to, but separate from, these areas.

3 *Resilience embraces the concept of risk-based reasoning*
Resilience adds no new value over historical systems if it is primarily about risk reduction, impact recovery or insurance. Resilience must be viewed and deployed as a strategic enabler. It should align with the main business goals by harnessing upside risks (within ethical parameters) that offer commercial opportunity and advantage to enable the business to prosper. It should do this whilst reacting to risks with purely negative long-term implications. The caveat here is that resilience should not be too speedily reduced to a standard operating procedure in the interests of identifying and solving problems. Rather, it should facilitate risk-based reasoning and decision making.

4 *Resilience should embed itself in the DNA of strategic decision making*
True resilience requires a link to strategic decision making in support of business profit. For this to happen, resilience has to be evident through a direct link to the systems and processes that create high-level decision making. A strategically resilient business is motivated by an appetite for risk and complexity, rather than a reductionist perspective on risk alone. Resilience has to impact the strategic decisions of the network operation. This necessitates some tension in the assessment of priorities, aggregation of data and some appropriate simplification.

5 *Resilience should be linked to metrics that are about profit*
Resilience should enable businesses to profit and prosper under the conditions in which they find themselves operating. Whilst there are real costs in embedding resilience, these should demonstrably pay for themselves in the event of a crisis. In part this is because the organisation finds itself robust and nimble in the face of high challenge and less likely to have to throw (unplanned) money at problems. However, the true profit measure has to be the way that companies can apply resilience to minimise costs and maximise profit. This must be considered a legitimate system property.

If business resilience does offer the prevention of impacts, rather than their mitigation, this certainly infers reduced costs. As a point of credibility, the system should be able to isolate and measure these. Likewise, the capacity to gain competitive advantage in the market at the time of a crisis through resilience is an essential metric. True business resilience at the time of the crisis, compared to competitors operating in the same space, is validated only in part by the manifest ability to maintain operations. This ability should, in turn, only be validated if it creates an increase in measurable profit.

CONCLUSIONS FROM THIS CHAPTER

As you can see, the argument we are building for resilience reasoning is not about an organisation becoming more risk averse. Rather it is about 'doing what you do better' by orientating/aligning/embedding a resilience approach which competitively promotes your business agenda during business as usual and during times of stress or shock.

Stipulating that forward-looking definition and operation for resilience is not without its challenges. Beyond the intellectual and financial investment this requires, there is the need to understand and influence senior management acceptance of the strategic value of this type of approach. There then follows the imperative to train them in its use as a strategic decision input.

The use of the construct of resilience we are promoting does represent a significant cultural shift in this area for most organisations. The benefit from this culture shift is currently quite unclear. This is in no small part due to the host of competing priorities aligned to organisational/business resilience in a cloud of other legacy systems such as business continuity, emergency preparedness and disaster recovery. Even if these competing priorities and definition uncertainties were resolved, not an easy task, there remains the master question of the relationship between organisational resilience and enterprise risk management itself.

What the journey of design we need organisations to take has to arrive at therefore is a definition for risk-based organisational resilience which proves:

Organisational resilience is the optimisation of operations within the appetite for risk.

BIBLIOGRAPHY

Bhamra, R., Dani, S. and Burnard, K., 2011. Resilience: the concept, a literature review and future directions. *International Journal of Production Research*, 49(18), pp. 5375–93.

BS 65000: 2104. Organisational Resilience. ISBN 978 0 580 77949 7

Gaddum, R., 2004 Business resilience – the next step forward for business continuity. IBM UK, www.continuitycentral.com/feature083.htm, 2004 (accessed 16 January 2018).

Pettit, T.J., Fiksel, J. and Croxton, K.L., 2010. Ensuring supply chain resilience: development of a conceptual framework. *Journal of Business Logistics*, 31(1), pp. 1–21.

Ponis, S.T. and Koronis, E., 2012. Supply chain resilience: definition of concept and its formative elements. *Journal of Applied Business Research*, 28(5), p. 921.

Rainer Hübert Organisational Resilience. www.bcm2013.com/papers/StreamC/6 OrganisationalResilienceRainerHubert.pdf

CHAPTER 7

Design for reasoning

This book concerns a new concept that we want to introduce. We have called this the reasoning chain. We argue that it is like those other chains that are so critical to large, complex and dispersed organisations – the supply chain, the value chain and the reputation chain. Management Science, Operations Research and Organisational Psychology, that great Venn diagram of disciplines which research and inform commercial and industrial behaviours, fully recognise these latter three. Actively managing them is deemed critical to business success. This is especially if parts of a business are being conducted in the mercurial contexts of the VUCA environment: an environment which, by definition, does not always play along with the sensibilities of the highly regulated norms of the western hemisphere.

The reasoning chain has *reasoning itself* as the focus – the quality, efficacy, integrity, logic, application and profitability of it within a business. To be a good visual metaphor is to think of the standard three chains as a DNA helix for any business, and we simply wish to add a fourth. To examine this possibility, we have chosen two particular arenas – risk and resilience. The positive effects of each of these, independently and interwoven, are a matter of great current (academic, business and regulatory) interest. They are marked out by the fact that they cause organisations to research, define, measure, monitor and analyse in new ways. They are reasoning disciplines. Thus, their systems need to benefit from a design for reasoning. This chapter will consider briefly the key system standards that would bring this about.

Perhaps the most famous three words ever spoken on this subject are: *cogito ergo sum*. Rene Descartes, a philosopher, mathematician and scientist, coined the phrase in his *Discourse on the Method* around 1637. We translate it as: I think therefore I am. Although it has been argued that Descartes meant us to translate it as: there is thought therefore I am. Since how can a proof that I exist start with the word I? But, I think therefore I am scans better.

Descartes is also credited, although he didn't go on to develop it, with an understanding of the so-called problem of other minds. In short, although I can use my direct experience to know I am thinking, feeling, remembering and so on, I cannot have any direct experience that anyone else is doing so. Thus, I might be the only mind in existence.

As a mathematician, Descartes is further famous for developing a system of geometry which involves plotting shapes in space. The simplest form involves locating a single point in space on the intersection of two linear scales in one plain. If you are feeling sharp you might see where these (Cartesian plots) continue to have a deep effect on risk visualisation to this day.

Since we are in a Latin-speaking mood it might be noted that, if we are interested in reasoning using numbers, another verbal triplet also reaches out from the depths of mathematical history. Euclid, and many other early Greek mathematicians, would round off their proofs with a flourish: *Quod erat demonstrandum*. Translated from Greek this means – the very thing it was required to have shown. In modern maths it is acceptable to reduce this to Q.E.D.

What is reasoning? Well, if you take *cogito ergo sum* and add it to Q.E.D., you have a chance of defining reasoning as it is found today in the empiricist universe of industrial decision making.

Reasoning is the process of thinking in order to demonstrate (and share) the value of what has been proven.

As both risk and resilience are fundamentally rational pursuits they should evidence at least three fundamental things:

1 There is the thought part. How do you understand what data to use? By what, if any, rules you will combine them? How will you explain any patterns?
2 There is the proof part. How do you satisfy yourself that manipulations of your data have been conclusive in a worthwhile outcome that increases your understanding?
3 There is the communication of outcome part. What level of reductionism is necessary in order to have the conversation about the implications of what you now know?

THE STUPID HUMAN?

If that all sounds a little bit too philosophical, then how about this:

How do you know that the reasoning behind your recommendations to senior leaders on risk and resilience is actually good reasoning?

Well, that's where the trouble starts. At the turn of the millennium, if you wanted to make sure your dispersed reasoning system was fit for purpose, you might have invited one of the many Decision Science experts from one of the red-brick business schools to help you. If you had done this, one thing would have been sure to happen. They'd want to spend half of the time making sure that your people felt sufficiently stupid.

This stupidity, although admittedly your consultant wouldn't refer to it as that directly, would have been evidenced when your team had been set up to fail a number of logical tests. The purpose in driving this fundamentally negative message home was to make you aware of the fact that much of the research into human reasoning in vogue around this time had come to the painstakingly researched conclusion that people are at rubbish at reasoning.

Well, people are generally rubbish at reasoning with uncertainty in the pursuit of rational decision making at least – well, under laboratory conditions at any rate. What a raft of experiments had repeatedly shown since the 1970s was that, however well-educated they are, humans are prone to all manner of systematic heuristics and biases in the face of uncertainty. These heuristics and biases, allegedly, made them terrible at risk reasoning which was, after all, a copy-book form of reasoning with uncertainty. By implication they would also be terrible at resilience reasoning since, as we have shown, it has a great deal of overlap with risk.

Here are four of the more famous heuristics and biases that your business school consultants would have been at pains to demonstrate were rife in your organisation:

1 the tendency to select data that supports a pre-existing hypothesis or belief state: confirmation bias or representativeness bias
2 the tendency to favour only small changes to a previous estimate which proves erroneous: anchor and adjustment bias
3 the tendency to overestimate the probability of easily imagined, popularised or sensational risk sources compared to mundane ones: the availability heuristic
4 the tendency, when using conditional events, to assume that knowing the probability 'a given B' the inverse 'B given A' is simply the mirror condition: confusion of the inverse or the base rate fallacy (both failures to apply Bayes' theorem).

Each of these biases (errors in data analysis) and heuristics (short-cuts to avoid exhaustive data collection or analysis) has been exhaustively demonstrated in thousands of laboratory experiments since the 1970s. That was all fairly depressing reading, it has to be said. The thing is, if you'd waited a decade or so and invited a fresh group of decision scientists to come and train your people, you would have heard a completely different story.

A new group of scientists, quite disgruntled with the methodologies of the founders of these heuristics and biases, had begun wading in with compelling arguments to debunk their conclusions. Yes, you could create all of these biases if you asked people very stylised questions about abstract probabilities. However, if you simply provided people with more natural explanations for what you were asking (called the semantic argument), you could actually completely reverse these biases and sometimes remove them entirely. One group of authors (O'Hagan et al., 2006, p. 36) finally broke cover and said what a lot of us had been thinking for a long time:

> All agree that the demonstration of judgement can be flawed does not imply that it always will be flawed. Nevertheless, there has been considerable difference of opinion expressed over just how good or bad judgement under uncertainty is . . .

This new body of research called into particular question the demand characteristics of laboratory experiments using paid students (as proxy representatives of society). This has always been a long-standing debate about the accuracy of social science experiments. However, it also wanted to question the fact that this research was being conducted in a wider academic culture that only rewarded (published) positive findings that tended to support or extend the pre-existing orthodoxy. O'Hagan et al. (2006, p. 46) were brave enough to say something else that needed to be said:

> . . . perhaps errors in judgement . . . occur only because the questions that elicit them are phrased in such a way as to encourage biased reasoning.

These and similar points are going to become central for us as we help you to design the reasoning methods that we recommend you use in your risk and resilience systems. Fundamentally we do still want you to avoid encouraging biases and flawed heuristics in your team where they are likely to occur. More importantly we want to point you in the direction of good applied science for the way you measure and reason about your constructs.

The reason O'Hagan et al. were storming the citadel of the 'stupid human' society was because a whole new set of decision theorists had begun to engage in research looking at 'clever humans'. This they did by examining communities – very much like your own – in what came to be called natural decision-making environments. What we call dispersed systems in this book are very much an example of that. This new work saw the rise of a number of key theories from which you might want to derive some principles:

Support theory – that people make better judgements when supported to unpack the problems facing them more thoroughly.

Cognitive approach – the mainstream literature is flooded with tests of deduction (very often mathematical). However, deductive reasoning might be peripheral to the way that humans reason in real life (see Oaksford and Chater, 2002). Shifting the focus from cognitive shortcomings in the laboratory to the, hugely evident, cognitive proficiency of humans in the complex real world might be a good thing.

Explaining excellence – so much research had been devoted to tackling errors in reasoning. Not enough attention was being paid to the ways in which human beings out-perform computers and solve deductive, inductive and inferential reasoning tasks all the time in their real lives.

Natural decision making theory – highlighted just how effective decisions under conditions of uncertainty were in the real world – for example, in life-saving and critical medical decisions.

Multi-criteria and deliberative approaches – in some larger-scale problems, in particular those that included value elements which were disputable (e.g. communities versus governments), normative probability reasoning was not useful (see Stirling, 1998; Burgess et al., 2007).

One group of theorists didn't want to throw the baby out with the bathwater, so they wanted to take a third-way approach. This was to hold on to the, doubtless valuable, laboratory work on formal decision making under uncertainty where it proved applicable. After all, if your decision making does require you to use (real) probabilities, conditional reasoning, value expectancy and so on – which classical industry risk systems certainly do at the basic level – then some of this research is definitely still valid. These approaches, such as Prescriptive Bayesian Decision Analysis, sought to combine the normative statistics (cognisant of errors, biases and heuristics) with the best elements from these other cognitive, naturalistic and value-led approaches.

So how should you choose to design a reasoning system for risk and resilience today? Who, from these or other theorists, should you listen to? Well, this is a complex question – one that is heavily affected by the way that risk and resilience are currently already manifested in large distributed organisations. For example, if everyone else in your organisation is using a (Cartesian) probability impact plot to represent risk, they will want you to follow suit.

This is where the classical Philosophy lesson at the start of this chapter gives us three handy universal questions:

- How you understand what data to use and by what, if any, rules you will combine them to seek patterns?
- How do you satisfy yourself that you are manipulating your data and drawing conclusions coherently?
- What level of reductionism do you need to communicate outcomes and influence behaviours?

If we examine some modern risk and resilience practices in busy organisations, we can see that coherent answers to these three questions are not self-evident. And yet, without these bare bones, industrial risk reasoning can tend towards nonsense. It will still amass data – multi-page spreadsheets full of symbolic numbers and colours that float around the computers of the risk manager. It will still form conclusions – disembodied ones, such as a list which is restricted to ten medium- to high-key corporate risks. It will be aimed more at low-fi monitoring than at influencing system learning or behaviour at the operational level.

SO CAN WE REASON BETTER?

Some of the theories we have discussed, collectively known as Decision Science, give us evidence that people will be prone to many biases and errors. If that can teach us anything it is this – in building systems, we should be careful to systematically reduce bias in reasoning.

This will be particularly true if the reasoning is distributed and consensual in nature. We know in advance that model-world, hypothetical-time, so-called objective reasoning tasks that capitalise on the normative statistical axioms of value-free scientific expertise are going to impair judgement. Thus, we should be going out of our way design these principles out of our risk and resilience systems. When assessing the utility of existing approaches, we should realise, perhaps ironically for some contexts where there is a low tolerance for complexity, that over-simplification, e.g. by reducing things to one or two simple representative numbers, can exacerbate these biases and heuristic flaws.

Conversely, other parts of Decision Science theory are telling us that human beings can be fantastic at reasoning. This is particularly in real-world, real-time, subjective tasks that capitalise heavily upon prior knowledge, expertise and cultural value systems. If that can teach us anything it is that we should be careful to design these principles into our risk and resilience systems – because it will make them more effective.

In short, risk and resilience systems are more likely to suffer from poor reasoning when their design starts with a hostility towards having a complex, human-centred system of measurement and analysis. The irony is that this is a double-edged sword. It is true that that the less complex (and time consuming) your system, the greater the hope for it being accepted and endorsed in a pressured organisation. This is why so many current risk and resilience systems are predicated on tactical reductionism to a small list of priorities at the cost of elucidating on the strategic causes. This pathology feels doubly ironic because, in most other spheres of business planning, not tackling strategic level drivers would be considered idiotic.

WHAT CONCLUSION DO WE WANT YOU TO DRAW FROM THIS CHAPTER?

A key challenge in your journey of design is to examine the rationale of reasoning itself. Why are you collecting, analysing and generalising from your risk and resilience data? Whom, or what, does the activity serve? Is your reasoning a slave to the *a priori* desire for a shortlist, or simple classification system that can be colour coded? Is this rush for a simple answer to a poorly formed question not treating the integrity of the reasoning method itself as secondary?

Rather than be overwhelmed by postmodern levels of debate and theory, we want you to hold on to some solid design principles. The first is that a rational company should want to forestall any potentially destructive reasoning cycles in the interests of protecting value. The key to that is to create risk and resilience reasoning systems that play to the strengths that formal research theory supports. This would be one that avoids the expedience of any received wisdom that does not do this, even if this wisdom appears to be an industry standard approach among peers or a model that is sold by consultants.

We continue to argue that it is the reasoning itself which delivers the strategic value of any risk and resilience exercise. The organisation that reasons well gains in maturity because its people are channelling their expertise and knowledge into problem solving – not because a spreadsheet has been filled in on time or a plan has been written to a specified standard. We don't expect you to be totally convinced by the cost–benefit of that argument at this stage, but we do expect you to prepare yourself for the strategically compelling case we will bring in the end – a case which leads inexorably to two conclusions:

Effective distributed risk-based resilience reasoning is in a direct relationship with appropriate sophistication.

The purpose of your (measurement and management) system for risk-based resilience remains a question of stabilising business material value.

BIBLIOGRAPHY

Burgess, J., Stirling, A., Clark, J., Davies, G., Eames, M., Staley, K. and Williamson, S., 2007. Deliberative mapping: a novel analytic-deliberative methodology to support contested science-policy decisions: *Public Understanding of Science*, 16(3), pp. 299–322.

Oaksford, M. and Chater, N., 2002. Commonsense reasoning, logic and human rationality. In R. Elio (ed.), *Commonsense Reasoning and Rationality*. Oxford: Oxford University Press.

O'Hagan, A., Buck, C.E., Daneshkhah, A., Eiser, J.R., Garthwhaite, P.H., Jenkinson, D.J., Oakley, J.E. and Rakow, T., 2006. *Uncertain Judgements. Eliciting Experts' Probabilities*. Chester: John Wiley and Son.

Stirling, A., 1998. Risk, at a turning point? *Journal of Risk Research*, 1(27), 97–109.

CHAPTER 8

What and how shall we measure?

In Chapter 2 we introduced an imperative for industry users to define a risk construct, which spoke not to one meaning, but to an interwoven series of appropriate dialects facing different objects and designed to speak to different audiences. In Chapter 3 we strengthened that argument by proposing four key design challenges for emerging risk systems in organisations. These addressed:

1 semantics of the referent;
2 abstraction of objective meaning;
3 measurement of scientifically valid scales;
4 deconstruction of business materiality.

Addressing these first two challenges gets to the heart of the applied meaning of our two central constructs, risk and resilience. We have been arguing that this should not rest with the accepted definitions in current circulation – which can be shown to be, in any case, in such constant debate as to be borderline postmodern. Rather, risk and resilience practitioners themselves must determine what makes a workable version of these concepts to protect and promote operational value creation in a pragmatic way.

As we close out this section of the book, however, we have to recognise that this licence to be pragmatic is also a factor which can substantially weaken the validity of a system. The reason for this is because the third challenge, the design of valid measurement scales, often becomes the key casualty of the very low appetite for complexity this pragmatism can engender. So, the time has come to say something more intentional, and more complex, about where organisations should be going in respect of risk and resilience measurement design.

In Chapter 5 we have already started to address this challenge examining different forms of probability reasoning. This discussion outlined the paradox of simplifying this fiercely disputed academic concept so that judgements can be made in the real world – a real world where this concept is clearly not designed to apply without substantial buttressing of its rationality. In this chapter we will pick up the strands of that debate again and begin to examine the implications of the widespread acceptance of its use to form 50% of the risk measurement argument in any case.

This further discussion on the measurement validity of risk and resilience practices will be in the form of two questions. First, we will consider what it is we should measure. We will examine this by reflecting on the commonly occurring scale choices for risk in particular and unpacking their validity a little more deeply. Second, we will consider the, more pressing, question of how it is we should be measuring in practice. That is to say, what is the baseline statistical reasoning that supports the classical approach? Our conclusions will be frank. First, the scaling choices in the classical approach to risk will be shown not only to be heuristic to the point of breaking, but invalid. Second, we will simply be re-asking, this time with examples, are the managers tasked with measuring and monitoring industry risk registers, applying the baseline statistical reasoning skill to do so?

WHAT SHALL WE MEASURE?

When the dialects are chosen, semantics are clarified and the object that we wish to abstract from the organisation's intellectual capital has been well defined – precisely what is there to measure and how does one arrive at an appropriate measurement of it?

CLASSIC RISK MEASUREMENT

Let's observe that risk is *usually defined* in industry thus: the probability (of a negative event) multiplied by the impact (of that event) on the profits, goals, strategies or social responsibilities of the organisation. This is the ground zero of all industrial risk:

$$R = P \times I$$

Given this attractively simple two-component nature, the results of this formula almost immediately lend themselves to being communicated using derivations of the Boston box, see Figure 8.1.

And that is a problem for industry. A huge problem.

The reason it is a problem basically comes down to a complicity in ignoring several statistical flaws. First, ask yourself how is the measurement of probability and impact, both quite complex concepts, usually managed? Both can be measured by a basic rule of thumb approach. This is made up of three essential questions:

1 Do we think the probability is low, medium or high?
2 Do we think the impact is low, medium or high?
3 When we combine them, which combinations do we consider the top priorities?

If this feels a little too robust, we can observe that it is quite common to see a five-point anchored risk scale as follows: 1 = low; 3 = moderate; 5 = high.

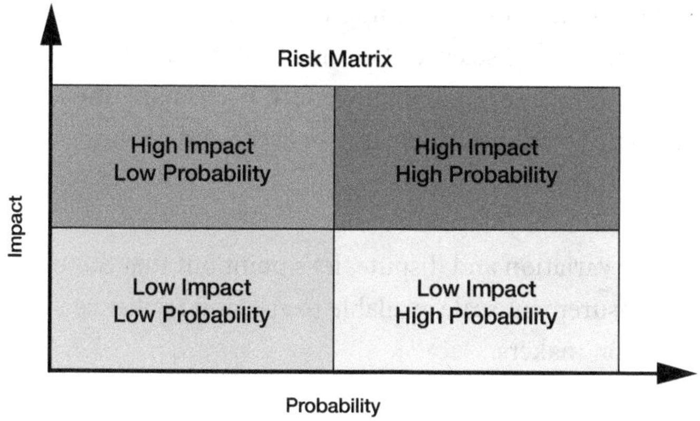

Risk Matrix

FIGURE 8.1 *The classic risk matrix*

If people still feel this is a little vague, a more evidently mathematical scale might be introduced. Impact for example, might be assessed as follows:

1. < 1 million; 2. 1–5 million; 3. 5–10 million; 4. 10–15 million; 5. 15–20 million; 6. > 20 million.

Although this feels mathematically rigorous, and let's face the fact that we might want to feel this to add an allure of authority to our reasoning, there are problems with the statistical logic. To understand that, we need to embark on a brief tangent to discuss the science of scales.

HOW TO DESIGN AN APPROPRIATE SCALE?

Everything that is measured is measured on a scale. Pure scales are easy to spot, seconds and minutes are a pure scale. Sometimes social science creates its own more complex scales, so we will use the term metric to refer to these. Metrics usually combine or qualify pure scales into some sort of utilitarian hybrid. For example, time-efficiency is a metric. Risk too, even in its classic two-part form shown here, is a metric.

Measurement scales are the key unit of any metric of risk, resilience or anything more complex we may want to say about predicting their commercial effects. The choice of the scale upon which to measure something is always a question of science. The answer chosen has a dramatic effect on everything else – a dramatic effect, particularly the validity of what you come to believe when you are at the end of your measurement.

Notwithstanding a little variation and dispute, let's point out that there are really four kinds of measurement scale available to risk and resilience practitioners and decision makers:

1 nominal,
2 interval,
3 ordinal,
4 ratio.

Time is almost a perfect clearing house concept to summarise the different ways in which these scales can be used to relate meaning because, with a teeny bit of tinkering, time can be measured using any of the scale types. Observe:

Nominal

Nominal scales, sometimes referred to as categorical, always refer to a quality not a quantity. For example, the questionnaire that asks you whether you are: A. male, B. female, C. mind your own business. A, B, C or 1, 2, 3 or anything else can be used to 'nominate' the quality in question.

Time is measured using a nominal scale when we talk about it as *ante meridiem* or *post meridiem*. These categories describe when a time is found, but offer absolutely no more accuracy than that. It splits all of the time of day into two nominal categories and tells you which one it is in. That's it.

Ordinal

An ordinal scale refers to direction as well as providing nominal data. If I say that George, Jane and Jenny competed in the javelin contest and

Jenny and Jane came first and second, then you have nominal data (who) and ordinal data (winner, runner-up, third place). Notice it doesn't tell you anything about how close the competition was, though.

Time can be measured on an ordinal scale when we split AM and PM into ordered regions, e.g. night-time, dawn, noon, afternoon and evening. Notice that ordinal data only adds one level of detail, order – it doesn't say anything about important things like how long the period is. In fact, these are generally of unequal and variable lengths, but they remain meaningful to us.

Interval

An interval scale adds an all-important missing piece to ordinal data. That is, as the name suggests, the idea of a regular interval. Scores on a test are usually interval scales when the difference between any two points on the scale, e.g. 1&2 versus 7&8 are of the same order of magnitude.

Time can be measured on an interval scale when we use the twelve-hour clock: 1 and 2 pm are the same distance apart as 1 and 2 am; the intervals are regular even if the nominal level is referring to two completely different things.

Ratio

A ratio level scale is really the master type of scale. It possesses all the qualities of nominal, ordinal and interval scales and it adds to these an absolute reference point, that of a zero. A ruler starts at zero and increments in millimetres up to infinity. However far away you get, you can always relate it to a regulated distance from that absolute.

Time, when we use the 24hr clock, is being measured (very nearly) as a ratio scale. It has a zero hour and it goes up to 24. The interval between 7 and 9 is the same as that between 3 and 5, and their absolute distance from zero is also calculable.

Properties and statistics	Nominal / Categorical	Ordinal	Interval	Ratio
Shows values in an order		YES	YES	YES
Allows counts / frequency distribution	YES	YES	YES	YES
Calculate Mode Value	YES	YES	YES	YES
Calculate Median Value		YES	YES	YES
Calculate Arithmetic Mean			YES	YES
Quantified difference between values			YES	YES
Allows addition or subtraction of values			YES	YES
Allows multiplication and division of values				YES
Has a real zero				YES

FIGURE 8.2 *Statistical properties of scales*

So there they are:

- nominal/categorical data: tells you what describes something;
- ordinal data: tells you what comes before and after what;
- interval data: tells you what comes before and after using a relative fixed interval;
- ratio data: tells you all of the above in an absolute interval based on a true zero.

Now that you are familiar with the kinds of scales one can use, consider the following table of statistical properties shown by each (Figure 8.2).

HOW SCIENTIFIC ARE OUR RISK SCALES?

With this tutorially safely logged, and with some important gaps shown by the table above in our peripheral vision at all times, let's take a look at the common scales that are used in the classic risk assessment.

High, medium, low

In that first example, the ubiquitous high, medium and low (H.M.L.), it is an easy spot to see that probability and impact are being measured at the nominal level of scaling. You have simply placed each of your defined events risk into two categories: a high, medium or low category for probability and a high, medium or low for impact. People familiar with this scale will know that trying to apply the risk formula at this point, i.e. multiplying them together, produces this rather mumbled "high–high" or "medium–high" sort of result. The fact is that, referring to our table above, we can see that any aggregation attempted at this level of scaling is a statistical *non sequitur*. You cannot perform this transformation on categorical data. Yet somehow, in the interests of a simplified argument, this is what we go on to do.

Emboldened by breaking one rule of Statistics we go on to break another of Mathematics. We now take these nominal categories and arrange them onto the axes of a Cartesian plot as if they were actually ratio measurements. This is a transformation that is wholly inappropriate for nominal data. The Boston box plot, if it is referencing a high, medium, low scale, is wholly illegitimate. Any insights it brings are (mathematically) fallacious.

Five-point scale

Those who are using five-point scales, or greater, may feel that argument wouldn't apply to them, but that is not the case. A well-designed five-point system seems designed to work as an interval-level scale. From the table above and we know that these have superior mathematical abilities. Were this true, it would make aggregation of five-point scales legitimate.

How true is it though? If 1 = low, 3 = moderate and 5 = high, what is the difference between 4 and 5? Is it exactly the same difference between 1 and 2? There the answer has to be no, because these differences are linguistic rather than numerical. There is no absolute unit of measurement here. So, far from being on the border of interval scaling status, this seemingly more accurate scale is only a borderline ordinal level scale.

The problem with ordinal level scaling is that you still cannot legitimately aggregate it and you certainly cannot multiply two different ordinal scales together to generate a metric. Neither can you claim that this scale is appropriate for representation on a Cartesian graph, even if you do go to the trouble of drawing gridlines to designate the boundaries.

Banded scales

This is where those who go to the trouble of creating more complex scales might feel a little superior. A scale from 1 to 20 million would appear to be a true ratio scale. That means it can be aggregated and it can be entered in multiplications and viewed on Cartesian graphics. So this is the minimum kind of scale that risk measurement should use. There is a lot riding on that assertion. The banded impact scale we are discussing is likely to be the most sophisticated level of measurement that we will see in many modern risk systems.

There is, however, once again a problem. In the interests of helping people make more grounded and logical summary judgements, the banded scale is still a hostage to inaccuracy. Leaving aside the fact that people are still being asked for judgements, not measurements, in such a scale, consider the following two possibilities.

A score of 2 (because the impact is judged to be of the order of 2 million) compared to a score of 4 (because the impact is judged to be of the order of 12 million).

A score of 3 (because the impact is judged to be of the order of 10 million) compared to a score of 5 (because the impact is judged to be of the order of 15 million).

Now if we do the maths:

4–2 is a scale difference of 2 but it relates to a value difference of 10 million.

5–3 is a scale difference of 2 but it relates to a value difference of 5 million.

This scale has the pretentions of the continuous measurement we would find in a ratio scale. We might feel it is allowing us to add subtract multiply, aggregate and plot meaningfully, but it is not. It is still only an interval level scale. So plotting is dangerous and using it to multiply values is off the menu.

Taking what we have learned so far, it is easy to see that the final step in most risk measurement systems has a significant inherited flaw. We often group similar risks into larger, simpler objects on the basis of their relative combined magnitude. Often the desire is to compress them into a risk shortlist because this is simpler for managers to understand and communicate with. However, because of these scaling problems, that transformation is actually statistically indefensible.

HOW STATISTICAL ARE OUR SCALES?

Leaving aside questions of complexity and pleas for heuristic-level reasoning still having awareness-raising value, whether the scales we use to measure, plot and create metrics from our probability and impact variables are meaningful is not a question of preference or expedience. It is a question of statistical validity. What this simple breakdown shows – given we know from experience that the appetite for complexity usually settles around five-point scaling using high and low categories in most applied risk systems – is that this classic form of risk measurement is woefully invalid.

The choice to continue using it, therefore, will be a question of accepted practice and that much-valued expedience. The invalidity of these choices of scaling method, as anything beyond a fundamentally *narrative device* dressed in the authority of pseudo-numbers, is incontrovertible. And if you are trying to convince your board and your shareholders that you have actually been measuring something using a valid process, that is a problem. A huge one.

HOW SHALL WE MEASURE?

So, the scales we use to measure risk aren't good enough; whilst this is problematic, it is not fatal – we can simply use better scales. Our journey of design, at this stage, cannot involve launching into a sophisticated argument about measurement theory. We recognise that many of the managers who take on the responsibility for risk and resilience may not have been professionally trained to answer the questions we have raised thus far. However, we must take a further professional step and also recognise that they are not likely to be experts in Statistics. This means, even if the problem of scaled measurement were addressed, others remain.

In some senses the remainder of this chapter has to function as a short master class to help discern principles of design for risk and resilience measurement. These are principles which we hope you will see do level a profound further challenge on the validity of much of the current practice of measurement in risk and resilience systems. Reasoning statistically is professionally unavoidable, given the claim that risk and resilience systems in industry are there to protect and promote value. We already know from the extant research discussed that people struggle with this in general, but what about specifically?

BEING MEAN

Let's start simply. Please take the following problems on the same face value that you once gave them when you were asked similar things in high school examinations.

> *Question 1*: Suppose I tell you that on my 10-mile journey to work I travelled at 60 miles per hour. I came home by the same route, but traffic was bad, so I only travelled at 40 miles per hour. If I then ask you what my average speed for the total journey was, what would you say?
>
> *Question 2*: Suppose I asked you, in the toss of a fair coin, what the probability of seeing a head or a tail would be; what would you say?
>
> *Question 3*: Suppose I asked you, in four tosses of the same fair coin, which of two sequences I was most likely to see: heads–heads–heads or heads–tails–heads. What would you say?
>
> *Question 4*: Suppose you are invited to examine three ordinary playing cards, one of which is a queen. I shuffle these, look at them, but don't let you see them, and then place them face down on in front of you. I ask you to place your finger on the card you think is the queen. Once you have made your choice and before your card is revealed, what is your probability that the card you have indeed chosen is the queen?

I then offer to help you by turning over one of the remaining cards that I know not to be the queen. Following this I ask you two further questions.

One, what do you think your probability that the card you have chosen is the queen (the same question again). Two, would you like to change your choice to the other unseen card? What would you say?

In Chapter 5 we took you on a short statistical journey to exemplify the challenge of making reasonable judgements with a simple probability exercise using coloured sweets. The purpose of that was to underscore some rationality standards which might make a risk assessment exercise more consistent. In this part of the journey this is no longer the aim. Rather, we are taking a deeper look at one of the single most problematic set of heuristics for any resilience and risk measurement system one could care to design. Here we are using the term heuristics in the general sense, i.e. reasoning in the absence of a complete algorithm. This is rather than the specific sense of the 'heuristics and biases' literature we quoted from earlier. The heuristics we are referring to therefore are those of the over-confidence that educated professionals hold in their own mathematical abilities.

Time and again, in a typical sample of educated managers from a range of industries where I have used these examples in risk manager workshops, the following are the usual answers given:

Question 1: Average speed is 50 mph.
Question 2: Probability is 50%
Question 3: Heads–heads–heads and heads–tails– heads are equally likely.
Question 4: There is a one-in-three chance that I have chosen the queen before you turn over the other card. This changes to a one-in-two chance when you do. I don't need to change my choice because each remaining card has an equal probability of being the queen.

And that, dear readers, is a problem, a huge one, because of the following:

Question 1: Average speed is 48 mph.
Question 2: Probability is 100%

WHAT AND HOW SHALL WE MEASURE?

Question 3: Heads–tails–heads is more likely than heads–heads–heads by a ratio of 3:2

Question 4: There is a one-in-three chance that you have chosen the queen before I turn over the other card. Once the additional card has been turned over, the probability that the un-chosen card is the queen is two-thirds in this example; you should always change your card.

The question we have to ask then is how?

Not how can these counterintuitive answers be right. They are right. Rather, how is it that people feel so resistant to them being right, and so tricked when the proofs are revealed? People feel especially tricked in the case of this last problem. More importantly, if we assume it is not a lack of mathematical ability that is causing the general difficulty people have in solving these types of puzzle, what is causing it? Finally, if people are generally rather poor (generally heuristic at this kind of reasoning), doesn't that raise a suspicion? A suspicion that the statistical validity of metrics they might have created in their own risk systems could be equally faulty or even more so?

WRESTLING WITH A BIT OF A MATHS LESSON YOU DON'T WANT

You may have noticed that the questions have been arranged as a logical progression. They begin with a calculation using two figures and a statistical function. They graduate to single estimates of probability followed by chained probability estimates and rounding off with the necessity to understand the behaviour of conditional probability.

You might detect in that progression some of the characteristics of classical risk measurement. For example, we could ask whether risk really as simple as the product of Probability and Impact? If the risk system involves the views of more than one person or team, how do we best aggregate the judgements of different judges of the same risks? If the risk system makes measurements at different times, how should probability estimates be updated in the light of any new information relating to the probabilities over time? These are all quite critical statistical questions for any logical measurement system.

We have already cited the evidence that people are more error prone when problems of this kind are related in the abstract forms we have used. So you might rightly ask whether it isn't it a bit disingenuous that we have gone ahead and done this to you? The reason for that is simple, however – it is not an attempt to trick you or make you feel foolish where a more semantic approach would lead to accuracy – it is a reflection. We are reflecting how most risk systems are, in fact, predicated on this level of representation. These sorts of computations are unquestioned at the outset. So we must start there, because it is imperative that they be questioned.

Risk managers and risk team members around their table, once they have listed important risks, are generally tasked to provide probability and impact judgements for them. Such teams are encouraged to aggregate their different judgements as a way to resolve any disagreement. You are encouraged to multiply the (probability and impact) terms together to reduce the risk index to a single risk score. You may then go on to aggregate collections of these single compounds to reduce the final number of risks in the system to an absolute priority set, sometimes, although not always, a top ten. All of it is based on the sort of statistics we are now discussing. All of this is risk management 101. The challenge is to move to risk management 102.

WHY IS THE AVERAGE SPEED 48 AND NOT 50 MPH?

Let's start at the beginning. Why do most people answer 50 mph when the right answer is 48 mph? What stops them from getting it right? Well, there are two related explanations, one of which is to do with

Statistics and the other a matter for Psychology. Let's begin with Statistics. What people generally do, when faced with this question, is calculate the average. This they do in perhaps the only way they remember as shown here:

$$\frac{60 + 40}{2} = 50$$

What they may be unaware that they are doing is calculating not *the* average but *an* average – in this case the average they are using is the Arithmetic mean. The problem? That is the wrong statistic for this question. What people should do is just a touch more complex, and there is usually a bit of forehead slapping when you remind them what that is.

Speed cannot be a raw number because speed is a rate number. It is not reporting a simple amount, rather it is reporting a value which itself represents a distance over time. You cannot calculate the average rate of speed unless you take the time travelled into account. The formula Speed = Distance/Time is normally able to be recalled if people are asked to.

So, if I am travelling at only 40 mph in the afternoon, it will just simply take me longer to cover that same distance I covered at 60 in the morning. My average speed for the day has to take the differential time spent at each speed into account. To calculate this using the Arithmetic mean you would have needed to calculate a weighted Arithmetic mean where time would be the weighting factor.

Why do most people get this wrong? Well, that choice of the wrong statistic is not simply attributable to faulty logic. It is equally attributable to what Psychologists call cognitive heuristics. Cognitive heuristics explain why those high school education algorithms leap so powerfully to the front of the mind when someone is asked to calculate an average. When you are asked "what is the average", particularly when it is a problem that simply contains two numbers, your brain takes a fast-track to those synapses which register a general meaning for average in your consciousness. So you add the two numbers and divide by two.

We might also note, for those of us who confess to maths anxiety, there is a certain immediate gratification in selecting this solution because it means we do know the answer. Psychology also tells us that people stick to the answer they have worked out when they feel it is a cognitively compelling solution. In the average person's mind there is generally not a more compelling heuristic vying for attention – one that might cause them to ask the right question: which average is the appropriate one to use given all the facts?

If there was, the answer would be that the fastest way to solve the average speed for the day problem is not even to use the weighted Arithmetic average. It actually is to use the harmonic mean:

$$Harmonic\ mean\ =\ \frac{2}{\frac{1}{40} + \frac{1}{60}} = \frac{2}{.025 + .016667} = 48$$

What even this simple explanation shows us should be a sobering thought. Few of us, your authors included, remember enough maths to reason from first principles, that is without using cognitive framing devices or short-cut rules in our heads – especially for what appear to be quite simple problems. On top of that few of us, if we are honest, have ever heard of a harmonic mean.

The diagram on the facing page (*Mathematical Means* by Dzenanz – Own work. Licensed under Public Domain via Commons), or something like it, is commonly used to illustrate the properties of different pure mean scores.

The average length of line **a** and line **b** can actually be represented by four means: A, G, H and Q. A is the arithmetic mean (notice how it tries to smooth out differences). G is the geometric mean (notice it is always shorter for uneven lines). H is the harmonic mean (notice how it is affected by the big difference between **a** and **b**). Q is the root mean square or quadratic mean – a little rich for our blood.

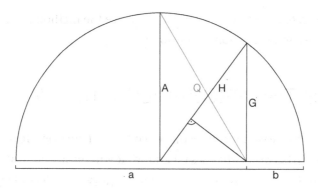

FIGURE 8.3 *Common mean measurements*

Look at Figure 8.3 again and slide the tick mark so that it is exactly half way between **a** and **b** (i.e. **a** and **b** are actually the same length); can you visualise what happens to all of these means? Therein lies our problem when it comes to the measurement of risk and resilience variables. A is the only mean that many people think Excel can calculate, or, worse still, that exists. It is of crucial importance to notice that there is no such thing as an average (or a mean) – there is only the right statistical measurement to inform us of the properties of a system.

We shouldn't feel bad, or maths anxious, that we get such a simple problem wrong. In their online article for the *Economist at Large* (http://economistatlarge.com/finance/applied-finance/differences-arithmetic-geometric-harmonic-means), the authors explain why different means are needed for different kinds of everyday problems. They do this because they too have noted the following:

Many people (including journalists) routinely use the wrong type of average – leading to incorrect results and often poor decisions . . .

. . . choosing the correct mean is essential to correctly estimating the central tendency of a population or calculating investment returns. Although the concept of an average may seem simple, it is imperative for a user to carefully consider which mean to use – and to communicate to reader or intended audience the method of deriving the average and the rationale for doing so.

WHY IS THE PROBABILITY 100%?

This time the reason is purely one of cognitive heuristics. It is the difference between what is said and what you think you hear. Any derivation of the "in the toss of a fair coin" language is highly likely to fire another powerful cognitive heuristic. This one is around solving probability questions. That heuristic simply says that "the toss of a fair coin" is usually used to signify a fifty–fifty probability. You simply don't attend to the word "or" in the sentence. Heads or tails (notwithstanding vanishing probabilities of coins landing on their sides or falling through black holes) accounts for 100% of the possible outcomes. Fifty–fifty is only the right answer when asked about the probability of a single outcome such as a head.

WHY IS HEADS–TAILS–HEADS MORE LIKELY?

The simplest way to explain this answer is to use a tree diagram of the outcomes (Figure 8.4).

So why do people get this wrong? Well, the answer is not as simple as solely the faulty use of a cognitive heuristic in this case, although we can observe one. Consider the following "rule" that people might apply to this problem. The probability of a single outcome in a coin toss is 50%, the probability of any two in succession is half that at 25%, and the probability of any three in succession should be half that again at 12.5%. By this logic, HHH and HTH should be calculated to have the same probability.

Why this is wrong is because the problem in question is about when a sequence will turn up in an actual run of four tosses, not any hypothetical

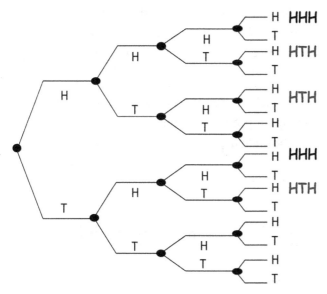

FIGURE 8.4 *Coin-tossing decision tree*

run of three. People are focusing on the wrong statistic once more. In an actual run of four, as Figure 8.4 shows, you do see a slightly higher probability of the HTH outcome. The reason you see this is all at once fascinating and depressing. It is fascinating because chains of outcomes in coin tossing are actually fiercely statistically complex. For a mind-bending discussion of this topic, see R.S. Nickerson's paper which points out many interestingly counter-intuitive facts such as:

- THTH will beat HTHH in a race about 64 times out of 100.
- The short sequence HHH will win a race against the longer THHH only one-eighth of the time.
- HHHHHHH takes on average 254 tosses to occur whereas HTHHTTT takes only 128.

This is slightly depressing because, as Nickerson himself concludes:

I suspect that the occurrence of sequences of heads and tails in a series of coin tosses is not a topic to which most people give a lot of thought. For writers of textbooks on probability theory, however, coin-tossing is the prototypical example of a random process. The phenomena discussed in this article are illustrative of counterintuitive relationships that can hold among probabilistic variables . . .

. . . Such surprises are compelling evidence of the wisdom of caution in drawing conclusions about probabilistic relationships even if they appear, at first blush, to be obvious.

Nickerson, 2007, pp. 527–8

WHICH BRINGS US TO THE QUEEN

The first three Statistics challenges are, you will agree, fairly simple problems and we can remedy poor judgement relatively easily, just as easily as we can remedy poor scale design. Finding the queen is far more psychologically sobering. It is actually, unbelievably to most of us, also a simple problem of conditional probability which can also be worked out easily. The reason it is more unsettling is two-fold.

First, educated people almost always get the probabilities wrong – they cannot reason easily with conditional probability.

Second, and more importantly, people have a tendency to become irrationally angry when they get the answer wrong and usually spend a period of time directly challenging the answer, itself, as wrong.

So let's just recap the typical flow of events in this most famous of challenges.

In the knowledge of which card is where, I lay down one queen and two other cards and ask you to choose a card indicating your belief about your probability of having selected the queen. This you do, indicating a (correct) probability of one third.

I agree to help you by revealing to you that one of the other cards is not the queen. I ask you whether you would like to change choices and I also ask you to state again your belief about your probability that you have chosen the queen.

Typically, people don't see the need to change cards and they re-evaluate their probability to fifty–fifty.

This answer is completely incorrect. The correct answer is that the remaining card has a two-thirds probability of being the queen whilst your choice retains a one-third probability.

The reason the answer is incorrect is because it fails to take the conditional probability structure of the problem into account. Most people reject initial attempts to inform them that their estimate is incorrect, sometimes passionately. The debate over this type of counterintuitive conditional probability has actually been raging since the nineteenth century. It continues to rage across the Internet as new waves of naïve participants are subjected to this particular statistical torture.

JUST TRY IT?

There is an easy way to satisfy unequivocally in your own mind exactly what the solution should be. That is actually to enact this game over and over with a friend. Settle on a consistent strategy, be this always switching cards or always staying with your original choice. A tally mark system will reveal in about twenty minutes or so that you win twice as many times with a switching strategy as you do with a sticking one. That is what will happen. No fuss, no maths, just a fact.

THE "COMPLICATED" EXPLANATION

If you do want the fuss and the maths behind that fact, well, the main culprit is Reverend Thomas Bayes. His theorem was simply an elegant way to formalise some rules of conditional probability. In its simple resolved form, Bayes theorem reads as follows:

$$P(A|B) \; = \; \frac{P(B|A) \; P(A)}{P(B)}$$

In words that goes something like this: the probability of A being true, given B has happened, is equivalent to the probability of B being true, given A has happened, multiplied by that same probability of A being true and all divided the probability of B.

To understand the 'find the queen' problem is to understand that it has a conditional probability structure. This is always very counterintuitive. The key is to understand that your target probability, the one you are actually being asked to calculate in this problem, is this: what is the (conditional) probability that you have chosen the queen *in light of the fact* that you have been shown that a second card is not the queen?

Using the notation above, this target probability, that you have chosen the queen (A) given that I have chosen to show you card number two (B), can be written as P(A/B). These two probabilities must be considered jointly – it helps a great deal to keep this front of mind. That target value can be calculated using the theorem, remembering that this describes the progression of *conditional probabilities* as follows:

1 The first term to calculate is a new probability P(B/A) – that I showed you card two, even though you have the queen.
   Supposing that you do have the queen (something I would know but you would not), I now have only two cards from which to choose. I will choose to reveal to you that one of them is not the queen (something that I would know). With two (non-queens) to choose from, this is simply fifty–fifty. But this is not the end of the theorem, or of the game. We still have to resolve the P(A) expression in that numerator. What is the probability that you have the queen? This is easy to do because we already know the answer. The probability that

you did, in fact, choose the queen from the three cards on offer is one in three.

2 We now have all the terms in the equation to calculate the probability that we care about, namely the expression on the left P(A/B). Your probability of having the queen, given that I have shown you card two.

3 This probability is equal to one-half (the probability I showed the card) times one-third (the probability you did choose the queen at the outset) divided by one-half (the probability I would show you the card that I did).

4 The answer is one third.

Do not be confused, however. This new value describes the conditional probability. Although it is easily confused with your original probability, when all three cards were unknown, it is not that same value. Everything hinges on that fact. One-third describes your probability of holding the queen in the second stage of the problem, i.e. when one of the other two cards has been turned over *already*. It is crucial to realise this is a new probability, and few people do. Realising it gives you the key to unlock the answer.

5 The probability that the queen is anywhere else, other than under your finger, must be two-thirds. Since there is only one card that can refer to now, your probability that this card is the queen is two-thirds.

So, if you switch to card three, you will double your chances of finding the queen. If you are still confused, play it over and over for real. Those facts, the real facts, will out.

The core thing people struggle with is that the mistake always feels more logical than the answer. If you have been trained in the rules of conditional probability, you will not make the mistake. Few people facing this problem are in that category. For them, from a cognitive workload perspective, it is too tempting to think your way out of the problem by answering the question you are never being asked: in a choice between two cards, what is your probability that one of them is the target?

The real choice is between two cards that carry an event history which impacts their (conditional) probability structure. There is a supply-chain of uncertainty. The idea that, instead of accepting this, your card should be allowed to *increase* its probability to fifty per cent cannot logically happen. Bayes' theorem does not allow you to update your probability *when no new information about* your card has ever been provided to you.

That last point is the only sleight of hand that actually ever happens and the reason, just as an aside, why it is crucial to speak in the above explanation exclusively of "your probability". The conditional probability structure of this problem only comes about because of a total imbalance of information. People always fail to consider, when they try to calculate their way out of this, that the final twist is that there is no twist: I always know where the queen is. "We" never had a probability of choosing the queen, only you did.

You don't know where the queen is, and that lack of knowledge can be summarised as a one-third probability. This is true both at the outset and, by the rules of Bayes' theorem, after I have revealed another non-queen card to you. I, on the other hand, have always had a one hundred per cent chance of finding the queen. I have perfect knowledge. I am revealing *only some of it to you.*

If it doesn't tire you out too much to think about this problem a little more deeply, consider another scenario, one where this perfect knowledge is not there. Consider the case where we are playing this game but neither of us knows where the queen is. Imagine that I turn over card two *not knowing* whether it is a queen, but it turns out not to be the queen. Now what is the probability that you have the queen?

Answer? Fifty per cent.

If that makes you want to rip your hair out, then our work here is done. It's time to recall what we told you in Chapter 5: The accuracy of any probability judgement always interacts with the available knowledge that informs it.

SUMMING UP WHAT AND HOW TO MEASURE

What this chapter has called into question is whether the form of measurement and deduction used in most mainstream risk register approaches is valid. The answer is that it is questionable at best. We have been able to show easily that most mainstream approaches to standard measurement in this field are a weaker measurement than we'd really expect from a professional system. They err on the side of having scales which are designed to be expedient to use rather than showing a valid grasp of scale rules. This weakness is then compounded by a quasi-statistical, and illegitimate, use of the outputs.

We can also show that testing basic statistical judgement skills, such as calculation of an appropriate average, proves these skills may be absent or poorly formed even among professionals. Furthermore, those deeper skills which pertain to conditional probability, essential to the user who claims to track probability and impact of multiple risk events over time, quickly collapse on rudimentary testing. This area proves much more complex than may at first have been believed by the designers of current systems.

Modern risk and resilience systems rely on averaging, and their rationality is heavily centred on conditional probability. Whilst people self-report their confidence to assess these, their technical ability to do so accurately under controlled testing shows this confidence to be misplaced. Cardinal statistical rules, it is easy to show, are often deeply counterintuitive, perhaps upsettingly so, for the untrained person.

We might therefore be left to face a stark conclusion, that probability judgements in particular are so intractably complex, so unwieldy a concept to measure, giving so questionable a return in meaning, that the wisest choice might be to abandon them in our model. If we won't accept that because we find (a less accurate and less complex) probability too useful or too accepted a construct, then what the designers and users of risk systems must accept is a stark choice.

They must come to the sobering conclusion that we are using inaccurately formed numbers and illegitimately manipulated calculations to buttress the legitimacy of what is actually a very weak methodology. As such use is scientifically invalid, even when the users are naïve to that invalidity, would it not be better for all if risk and resilience were to revert to being narratively described rather than numerically measured constructs?

If this disruption proves too hard, then the task must be to transform the current crop of risk assessment approaches into good science. We could do this by undoing the damage that our desire for computational and communications expedience does to the integrity of the measurements. We could accept the need to undo the damage which occurs when we are demonstrably intolerant of using Statistics and Mathematics within their own rule base simply because our appetite for complexity is too low.

CONCLUSIONS FROM THIS CHAPTER

Risk-based resilience systems present us with psychological and statistical design problems to solve if we are to hope for an efficacious and valid business tool to be the result of our efforts. Measurement rigour and expert judgement are the critical source of validity to any risk and resilience system.

Risk and resilience systems designers must face the empirically demonstrated realities about how people measure and reason in these contexts. This requires us to reject the design and use of the classic-form risk measurements of today, mindful that we are connecting the results of these exercises with the value-creation of our businesses.

Academic evidence tells us that even educated people reason with uncertainty very poorly when the questions are in the abstract. Most modern risk and resilience systems have a measurement prospectus which is fundamentally abstract. A key flaw in this approach is attempting to ask people to reason narratively, which is perfectly legitimate, with the aim of then treating the results as if they were numerical values, which is absolutely not.

If we wish to continue to place psychological stock in communicating our risk "measurement" in numbers and calculations to prove we have been reasonable, then the disastrous short-cuts that have become the norm can no longer be maintained.

We cannot assume that the busy people tasked with designing and operating risk and resilience measurement systems will immediately become experts in measurement theory and statistics. It is imperative therefore that they defer to experts in measurement theory and statistics to support and validate the design of their systems. These experts should be tasked with crafting a measurement system that has been deliberately designed to satisfy three system edicts:

1 *It always uses an appropriate measurement scale to create reasoning data.*
2 *It always applies the appropriate statistics and Mathematics to produce effective data and complexity reduction.*
3 *The probability construct informing the risk construct is always applied with rigorous accuracy – a practice which requires statistical expertise to execute.*

BIBLIOGRAPHY

Holton, G.A., 2004. Defining risk. *Financial Analysts Journal*, 60(6), pp. 19–25.

Matuszak, A., 2010. Differences between Arithmetic, Geometric, and Harmonic Means. http://economistatlarge.com/finance/applied-finance/differences-arithmetic-geometric-harmonic-means (accessed 16 January 2018).

Nickerson, R.S., 2007. Penney ante: Counterintuitive probabilities in coin tossing. *The UMAP Journal*, 28(4), pp. 503–32.

CHAPTER 9

Reforming conventional risk measurement – a case study

By this stage in our journey of design, you may be feeling that what has been achieved so far is tantamount to a certain iconoclasm. We've said that risk and resilience constructs are much too disputed and much too poorly defined to be effective. We've said that the basis of much risk and resilience reasoning is unfounded, being far too reductionist to be useful. We've said that classical risk measurement systems are much too unscientific to be effective.

The lynchpin of these and other arguments, quietly bearing the strain the whole time, has been what we are calling appetite for complexity. What we have been saying up to this point is that this appetite has been responsible for so much compromise that the architecture of modern risk and resilience systems is, itself, almost wholly compromised. Certainly for when it comes to adding value to an organisation beyond seeking reassurance that risk is, somehow, "being assessed".

INTRODUCING IMPROVED APPETITE

In this second case study, we would like to recognise a highly reasonable question that may be forming in the minds of some of our readers. That question is this: *What can you do to improve risk reasoning when you already know the appetite for complexity in your organisation is low and is not likely to change?*

This is a non-trivial question, as many risk and resilience managers will find themselves in this place. The first and clearest argument has to be that the appetite for complexity should be increased, given the compelling case we have made.

However, that is hardly going to help if an organisation is wedded to a more simplistic worldview based upon an institutional use of accepted norms. They will see, so our Risk Managers can tell us, no compelling reason to put more time and resource behind the existing effort. Thus, they will keep requiring the current outputs even if these are driven by appetite for credulity not accuracy, efficacy, or business impact for that matter.

The key to evolving that model under these sorts of constraints, and even possibly hostility, has to be to accept these. This is where everything we have said so far may seem to come to a temporary halt. What needs to be introduced here is not, we agree, iconoclasm. What is needed is something to stimulate a modest increase in the appetite for complexity in order to pave the way for further reform. This is the 'evolution not revolution' argument, which many beleaguered risk practitioners reading this book might prefer to see.

So, do we have any insights to bring to bear? The answer is perhaps. The reason it is perhaps is because a small-scale outbreak of iconoclasm is still going to have to occur. It is just that rather than focus, as we have been doing so far, on the whole rationale and system design, it can be targeted at just one part of it – the mechanism for measuring risk. Here we can see whether it might be possible to retro-fit some improvements – for example, to add the influence of knowledge on the assessment.

So, let's suppose the following are a given in your organisation:

- There is a very low tolerance for complexity of risk reasoning.
- The leaders are wedded to the usual idea of 'bivariate risk', e.g. one usually expressed as probability multiplied by effect.
- The main mechanism for prioritisation decisions and the desired output of it is probability and effect plotted against each other.

If this is your organisation's risk culture, then we know most of its reference grammar for speaking about risk, i.e. the answers to our key questions of dialect, semantic, abstraction and measurement, although maybe not materiality. So how would you create that subtle step change in the appetite for complexity without overtly criticising the impoverished reference grammar itself? The answer is to reverse engineer (some of) the rationality behind it.

AN EXAMINATION OF BETTER REASONING

The following methodology has been abstracted from a larger body of work in risk systems thinking that I researched with the National Air Traffic Services (NATS) in the UK in 2000. That much larger body of work was with a view to helping the management culture react to the many new, and non-technological, risk sources that quickly beset NATS as a result of burgeoning air travel over the UK brought on by the cheap flight revolution.

Space doesn't permit any discussion of the comprehensive risk system that this research created; just one tiny piece of it is of interest to us here. It concerns a thought experiment that NATS management undertook to examine the way they thought about, non-technical and non-safety, programme risk management.

Before you read about this work, please firmly note that The NATS of today is not at all the organisation it was in 2000. For one thing, back then it was wholly state owned. No assumptions about the current risk practices of NATS should be made in any way. Eighteen years is an eternity in such a high-performing, safety-critical industry.

As we are dealing with a case from 18 years ago, at the time of writing, it is also important to note that a great deal of the academic thinking fuelling the thoughts in this book was not really available at that time. Risk was in its relative infancy. John Adams' breakthrough work on social geography has only been in circulation for less than five years. The dominant engineering metaphors of Jim Reason's, highly influential, work on human error in engineered systems had only really come to the fore two years before that.

SETTING THE SCENE

This chapter introduces the idea of changing how you measure risk by introducing better tools to do so. This is the smallest step change we could suggest and still be talking about improved reasoning. It is the least disruptive change we could imagine that would not simply be window-dressing the faulty logic, semantics and statistics we have been describing so far.

Suppose then that your risk management system is one which discretises project risks (as single events) and wishes to articulate a risk level for each? This is done by way of assessing the probability of the event and then multiplying it by the (perceived) impact.

If probability and impact are non-negotiable outcomes for your measurement system, then how do you reverse engineer greater rationality into these measures? One way to do so, and you will need some support from your organisation to increase the measurement complexity, that is unavoidable, is to accept these sorts of metrics as central, but to work more laterally towards them. This you do by strengthening the verifiability to their evaluation.

The approach you would need to sell in is threefold:

1 Increase the logic of the reasoned uncertainty, to make it more transparent.
2 Add bandwidth measurements to allow modelling (with uncertainty) rather than fixed hard values.
3 Formalise this new measurement process into software.

INTRODUCING A REASONING TOOL FOR RISK

Consider the following input – output dashboard for use by a risk manager. It is a piece of software which allows the direct manipulation of any value in the nine "dials" shown. This includes directly typing in a value or even choosing a pre-scored low, medium or high.

Before you protest that a nine-factor risk model is already way too complex for your organisation, consider this: not everyone in the

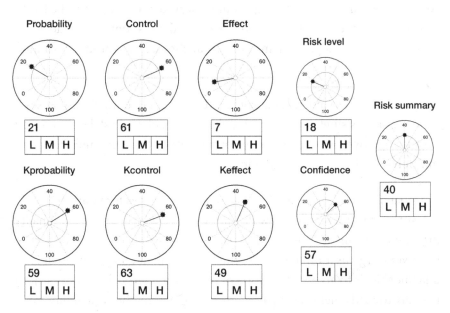

FIGURE 9.1 *HuRisk input dashboard*

organisation needs to see this complexity, nor does anyone need to use it. Should you wish, any risk could be assessed by providing one score. That is actually a decrease in complexity from the accepted norm.

However, there are other, more detailed, scoring permutations that you might like to take advantage of when you have the time. That's because this is a fully propagating scorecard. Reading right to left, it is made up of that one master summary and two sub-scores each supported by a set of three further detailed scores:

- changes in the master risk summary propagate backwards to all other dials;
- changes in the risk level and confidence dials propagate backwards to the three dials supporting them, and also forwards to the master risk summary;
- changes in the detailed scores propagate forward to the single summary and then to the master risk summary.

RISK REASONING SCENARIOS

Ignore for the moment that this particular scorecard is not actually set up to relate probability and impact as the two-factor summary for risk, NATS did not view risk in these terms. Just be aware that it could be set up to do this. It is the way that this propagating design mediates the appetite for (scoring) complexity, rendered in a single software housing, that is important. So, notice that the design will facilitate any of the following risk-scoring scenarios:

1 Pseudo-deterministic scenario: I wish to identify an overall risk score (here called Risk Summary) and I need this to be made up of two components (here construed as Risk Level and Confidence Level).

The user (risk manager) can follow the steps of an existing (low-complexity) risk assessment with ease. She or he can identify a risk event.

She or he can proceed to score that risk event by providing only two scores. These can even be just a preference for high, medium or low. The system will take these two scores and combine them to form a risk summary score. The summary scores will automatically plot in a Boston Box.

With one descriptor, two scores and one plot, the risk event in question has now been assessed according to all of the existing reference grammar. Crucially, there is no need for an increase in the appetite for complexity. In fact, it has actually made the scoring process easier to administer and audit. It brings a complexity reduction in process. This is risk 101. Job done.

So where is our reverse engineering argument? Well, this comes in two forms. First, when you offer the organisation a software tool for risk which is this dynamic and easy to use, irrespective of their actual tolerance for complexity, you will see a Trojan horse effect. They will quite like the scientific appearance, the real-time computation and the instant visualisation. (They may also like to hear that individual risks could be assessed by multiple scorers offline.)

Second, people are bound to ask about the remaining six dials in the system, and this is especially because their scores react to any changes made further up the line, so they are obviously part of the assessment. Furthermore, their titles are intriguing – why are these factors set out in this particular array? This is the second part of the Trojan horse effect. You simply say that it would be possible to score the most important risks in more detail using these factors.

2   Heuristic reasoning scenario: suppose, because the power is evidently here at my fingertips to do this, that I wish to score my important risk in this greater level of detail, what should I do? The top three gauges are fairly obvious. Two of them don't require you to do anything very different to your normal assessment. You judge the raw probability of the event occurring. You judge the impact it would have. These scales are serendipitous because they are the same ones you always use.

The third scale is not hard to understand. It is just a matter of nuance. Given that you have assessed the probability and impact, can you judge your organisation's levels of control over either? Clearly, you can. Now your Risk Score is being derived from three scores. It has, almost imperceptibly, become multi-attribute.

The lower three gauges present more of an initial challenge, but this is eased when you point out they represent exactly the same question being asked three times. That question is: to what degree is the assessment you have made on the gauge above based on expertise and facts compared to being a raw judgement? Using these (knowledge) qualifying scores, you are allowed to represent that thought in a transparent way.

3   Fully heuristic reasoning scenario: industry is full of clever people. Those people, with an assessment like this in front of them, will ask clever questions – for example, changes over time. Once I have an assessment, can I revise any one of my factors because of some future learning or actions? The answer is yes. If I only have time to revise a higher-order score (e.g. risk level), is the nuanced pattern from an earlier, more involved, assessment now erased? The answer is no, it is preserved. As I measure the same risks over different times, could I make reference to their previous scores so as to observe any trends? The answer is yes.

WINNING THE COMPLEXITY ARGUMENT

When the really clever people ask the next question, you have won the complexity increase argument: just how are the risk level and the confidence level actually being combined?

The reason you have won the argument is, to be fair, because of something we haven't mentioned yet, but when we do mention it you will see that you have moved from a classic (static) risk assessment technique to a true (if heuristic) dynamic risk modelling environment. It still has the same recognisable reference grammar, it still speaks the same risk language, but it speaks it with greater sophistication (or, in our terms, with a greater appetite for complexity).

SYSTEM ADVANTAGES

Before we get to a discussion of that sophistication, let's just recap how far a system like this can bring you along the journey to better reasoning:

1 As score propagation keeps all scores on display, you have a nuanced understanding of the attributes of this risk and a "classic" understanding of it too.
2 Risk priority is still reducible to a summary score. However, the user can shuttle seamlessly back and forth between the high-level summary and the rationale for it.
3 Control has been introduced as a mediator for severity – after all, control is inversely proportional to risk. If you can control either the probability of an event occurring or the damage it causes when it does occur, you have the power over business outcomes.
4 The (deterministic) impact of knowledge has also been introduced away from being confabulated in probability. This deepens the assessment by qualifying the accuracy all of the – probability, impact and control – judgements.
5 Risk is an evaluation, rather than a mere judgement, because of the modest increase in the logic caused by the number and the meaning of the attributes and scales.
6 Time can automatically be introduced and trends assessed.
7 Multiple scorers can assess the same risks and seamlessly compare outcomes in and over time.
8 The (main) user still gets a single risk priority summary. The user still has the facility to plot a risk matrix which adheres to the standard rules of the Boston box.
9 Since these facilities are automated and highly transparent, the time spent generating this analysis is far less than the manual time required to administer the average risk register spreadsheet and manually generate its associated power-points.

Has the complexity increased? Yes. Has the utility of scoring matrix increased? Hugely. The team using this scoring system will reason better about actions.

RISK TOLERANCE JUDGEMENT

One hugely important reason why this is so, is the thing we haven't yet mentioned. There is one more point of reference that is not obvious from this dashboard, because it is hidden as a set-up variable. As an entry question to this dashboard, the user is asked one further and very simple question, which is this: what is your tolerance for risk? That is assessed on the same 1–100-point scale:

- 1 indicates you are highly risk seeking.
- 50 indicates risk neutral, i.e. you are neither risk seeking nor risk averse.
- 100 indicates you are highly risk averse.

The power of this metric is found in two key facts which are critical to the subversive increase in rationality this system offers.

First, it is this score which drives the algorithm which combines the risk score and the confidence score to give the final risk priority. As the system is bidirectional, it also propagates more simplified scores backwards through the system. Risk appetite sits between confidence and risk firstly as a moderator:

- In the risk-averse condition, it causes any uncertainty over the knowledge on display – i.e. the confession that the judgement could be wrong – to increase the final risk score by a linear factor.
- In the risk-accepting condition, a lack of knowledge does not amplify the final risk, it is allowed to simply stay in play.

The second fact this metric introduces should never be underestimated in terms of its analytical power. It sets the user free to use scenario-based reasoning, to attempt predictive risk judgement. This works because the scoring is multi-attribute and the propagation is statistically logical. Thus, it is now possible to create a range of risk outcomes based on hypothetically different tolerances. In statistics this is known as sensitivity analysis.

What happens is that now, across your entire risk portfolio, you can examine the impact on relative priority by setting different risk appetites. Clearly the result of that will be once again that the poorly understood concept of probability will now be supplanted by the impact of user knowledge.

In high-knowledge conditions the risk scores will be insensitive to appetite – because they are accurate already.

In the low-knowledge condition the risk scores will by highly sensitive to appetite – because they should already be considered more volatile when you are reasoning from impoverished knowledge.

MODELLING INSTEAD OF SCORING

We need perhaps three final words on modelling potential: first, for a modest increase in analytical burden, which is as we have said tantamount to adding three more assessments in reality (tolerance, control, knowledge), there is a huge hike in the rationality available to the risk manager to do their job. This comes with no loss in the summary capability of this scoring system to satisfy the desire for simple one- or two-point outcomes and plots. Second, you can simulate in real time and over time because it is in software now. Third, you can actively compare different scorers and talk about shared uncertainty.

All of this is possible, and much of it is highly desirable. The baseline complexity, for those who want to keep it low, has not really changed. Sublimated into the better reasoning architecture is the power to be better informed and more logical prior to that communication. The modelling capability (multi-attribute, multi-scorer, sensitivity analysis, over time) is a huge hike in reasoning power. It conveys risk not just as guesses about probability and impact but as volatility and knowledge rolled in.

For the risk manager who solely wished to identify risk events, to score them using a two-point reference system and to plot and prioritise them relative to each other, there is no disadvantage from using this dashboard. That exact level of effort (in fact less than this since we allow high, medium and low inputs and the outputs are automated) is all that is needed to get a classic risk register from this system design. No change.

Let's state something one more time, however. This two-point risk reasoning approach is bad reasoning. It is destructive of value.

For the risk manager who wished to support the appetite for complexity that the two-point reasoning system permits, but also to quietly subvert it behind the scenes by increasing the scientific rigour of the evaluation and the analysis of the self-same set of risks, there are huge advantages in using this tool. Everything changes – measurement, logic, statistics, modelling – and with them reasoning power and problem solving. They all change from measurement to modelling, and that is a huge gain in the likely business value of this approach.

SUMMING UP

We said at the outset of this chapter that this would be a simple case study into a reasoning tool for risk assessment. You may feel the need to disagree. For those who are feeling duped by all this talk of propagation, sensitivity and multi-attribute reasoning, and see that as a huge ask in terms of complexity, let's state a few things one more time.

- To operate this system, you only need two scores. That is the same number of scores that people have been using all along.

- The basic outcome of this system is the same prioritisation mechanism people have been using all along.
- The basic visualisation of this system is the same plot people have been using all along.

What this system does is actually add value to that same approach because it can do those same things much more efficiently – many manual aspects of the tasks are now automatic. In short this system, or something like it, can always be working within the existing reference grammar of classic risk assessment without increasing the organisation's appetite for complexity one bit.

It can do that.

It can, and should, also do much more than that.

Reverse engineered into this system, which supports the organisation to do what it wants to do, is another system which can help take the organisation leaps forward to what it should be doing. For a relatively small gain in scoring complexity, the power of multi-attribute scaling now improves reasoning. The algorithms which run the analytical side are "psychometric". This is in the sense in which they convey psychological properties into the assessment – for example, quantifying uncertainty, tolerance and diligence in a transparent way and using behaviourally anchored scaling rather than abstract statistics.

Also, being reversed engineered into the existing (impoverished) reference grammar for risk assessment, there is the potential for a new reference grammar based upon it. This can be fed in through small-scale increases in complexity, particularly those around scoring sophistication. It can be fed in a little or a lot depending on appetite. This is what makes the thinking behind this reasoning tool unconventional. This is what makes it genuinely heuristic. Reasoning can be improved on a needs basis. This can be done at different levels of sophistication and different times quite seamlessly.

CONCLUSIONS FROM THIS CHAPTER

W e started this chapter with a key question that many risk assessment teams do face:

What can you do to improve risk reasoning when you already know the appetite for complexity in your organisation is low and it is not likely to change?

One answer is to offer flexible increase in measurement sophistication on a needs basis. This paves its own way because it improves the way that the conventional and valued forms of risk reasoning are functioning. The more powerful analysis capability to create more flexible forms of reasoning is designed to win people over with its efficacy. It is better for problem solving, decision making and action planning. It leads people into better reasoning without abandoning the methods they are comfortable with.

This offer can come at a small price. The only thing that the organisation does have to change, and this only as much as they feel necessary, is their appetite for complexity (of scoring and insight generation). This change can be stimulated and supported:

- as a response to the data from a simpler assessment that warrants a deeper analysis;
- in a behind-the-scenes approach as only the risk assessment panel need do anything different;
- by intelligent people realising the power of better reasoning is not so very far away from what they were trying to achieve in the first place.

This should generate the necessary appetite for complexity and, if necessary, the upstream reporting could remain unchanged – although it will be better quality.

So we end this chapter with a simple answer to its opening question. Using a more rational approach to risk measurement allows the risk management team to argue the clear value in changing the appetite for complexity by making the business value of changing it clear. This value becomes apparent by the rationality of a system such as HuRisk initially in a Trojan horse role. This is because when people can be put in a position to see that far more value adding reasoning is just around the corner, they tend to turn the corner.

Introducing a HuRisk-style approach to rational risk measurement is, we offer, a clever and effective disruptor that helps risk management teams in low-complexity organisations to move the game on.

BIBLIOGRAPHY

Adams, J., 1995. *Risk*. London: University College London Press.

Reason, J., 1990. *Human Error*. Cambridge: Cambridge University Press.

Summing up
Part 2

I n this part of the book we turned our attention to the meaning of a
construct for organisational resilience predicated on risk and therefore
laying bare their co-dependency. We began to unpack the definitional
debate around organisational resilience and its implications for reasoning
design. This inevitably led us back to a renewed consideration of the
rationality of what and how should we measure to make an applied
reasoning system from the joint constructs.

THE CONTINUED CLASH OF LANGUAGES

R esilience, just like risk, can be seen to be surrounded by a dense cloud
of possible definitions. Although British and international standards
have played an important role in attempting to bring clarity, they have not
proved immune to having to wrestle with multiple and conflicting options.
In the available language for resilience, we can detect that same addiction
to the use of scientific framing that we saw with risk. This is rather than
the, better suited, language of wisdom sharing.

If a reasoning system joining risk and resilience constructs together is to be evidentially, as well as linguistically, scientific, we can expect the marriage between the two disciplines to be an uneasy one. If each construct were more adequately defined, it would clash with and act as a disruptor to its own currently accepted semantic.

THE DEEPER CHALLENGE OF RISK-BASED RESILIENCE

To objectify a joint construct in a way that is operationally meaningful, we would suggest that the resilience definition used has to pass those same four key tests that objectify risk. These are that it be semantically coherent, refers to a single abstract, has a validated measurement unit and produces an output which is, above all, framed in a way which is materially relevant to the business in question.

The challenges we met in defining the quality of reasoning for the risk construct will, of course, be amplified in any construct that includes it: the need to measure with statistical coherence; addressing the inexpert application and the counterintuitive nature of probability; and predicating confidence on the quality of the knowledge.

The academic literature from key schools (heuristics and biases, and natural decision making) that comments on this judgement under uncertainty presents us with significant challenges. These also deserve to be far more disruptive in our context. So when users are not statistically expert there are two important conclusions we should not ignore. The first is that very poor reasoning is more likely from an abstract judgement system. The second is that better reasoning will result from a narrative and semantic one.

Given their expedient design, abstract metrics and desire for scientific face-validity, the current crop of risk-based resilience constructs, in the hands of ordinary managers, will simply produce poor reasoning. This is an inescapable fact. The persistent desire for undeserved rationality continues to present us with the same pressing difficulty, which is rationality itself.

BETTER METHODS AND TOOLS

P oor reasoning is not necessary, even if the environmental and cultural conditions do not support a wholly revisionist agenda. We have demonstrated how the integrity of the risk measurement approach can be specifically improved within a low tolerance for complexity. Here the target behaviour was to frame an increase in the sophistication of the scoring methodology in an attractive package of support for the base methodology. The software application that deliberately facilitated the base method in such a way as to offer a step change in reasoning with little additional effort acted as the Trojan horse to achieve this.

This risk software tool made the existing preferred approach easier to execute, visualise and report, so it could not be rationally rejected on appetite for complexity grounds alone. Always visible within the system was an enhanced set of metrics for more rational risk reasoning. This was an increase in power and functionality which would become very attractive, in the first instance, for high-priority risks. The Trojan horse effect comes about where an easily accessible, and evidentially more powerful, rationality would be a more natural course.

THE HOUSE OF CARDS

A s we progress it becomes increasingly clear that the accepted norms of risk and resilience management, measurement and monitoring do not need to have the last word. The determining variables, of appetite for complexity and over-familiarity with accepted norms, do not always determine the design. It is entirely possible to develop systematic processes and tools that embody the research evidence on improved reasoning and decision making under uncertainty. The benefits package of the improved science should massively outweigh the effort to get the organisation to adopt them when they are sincere about reasoning well.

The type of systems that are in vogue for hard-pressed organisations to measure and manage their risk and resilience outcomes seem to rest upon a house of cards argument. Yet so often the discipline remains unrepentant. There is too little time, there are too few resources, board room leaders don't want paralysis by analysis, and we need to keep things simple. What we have is better than nothing. So the mantra goes.

In no other discipline does this kind of hokery really apply with such, ignore the pun, resilience. You shouldn't take the authority of mathematical housings and statistical reasoning and then wholly dismantle the integrity of their rule base. It is not all right if you do this whilst suggesting that this is largely fine due to the need to do something on a tight timeframe, or with a level of appetite for complexity that is not commensurate at all with the evidence, sophistication and power of the desired outcome.

This attitude creates a profound credibility gap and it is at its most significant not because of sour grapes by more technical professionals taking umbrage at their tools being mangled by cack-handed application. It is at its most significant because it is poor-quality reasoning. Poor-quality reasoning that leads to, at best, spurious and, at worst, dangerously misleading outcomes.

STARTING A REFORMATION

If both risk and resilience are decidedly occluded constructs, to say the least; if neither accepted practices, industry bodies nor the academy can provide us with a validated road map to better reasoning; if ordinary multi-disciplinary experts lack the training to design viable measurement and clearly struggle to reason well within the existing abstract frameworks, it is perhaps time for a reformation. The reformation could advance something like this.

When organisations use words like assessment, evaluation and analysis attached to construct like risk and resilience – which have become legislatively, regulatively and operationally quite important artefacts in our society – the use of these concepts should shoulder the burden of their full scientific rigour. They must be used because they relate to a supply chain of ideas leading to the genuine synthesis of insight formed from deconstruction and construction, not simplification.

When these weighty scientific terms are used instead to add gravitas to a process that is reducible to the manipulation of meaning-impoverished three- or five-point heuristic judgement scales, we should pause for reflection. When these processes, so named, are being inconsistently applied to support an appetite for complexity that will not exceed the production of a short list supported by a three-colour priority scheme, we have a duty to question the integrity of what has gone on. We must accept that gentrifying the language around demonstrably scientifically inadmissible behaviours and dressing their outcomes in a layer of mathematical hyperbole amounts to a conspiracy of disingenuity.

To suggest, as is most commonly the case, that this absence of genuine rigour is acceptable nonetheless because a) there is no time for a more rigorous process; b) senior leadership have requested prefabricated and simplified outputs; or c) this is what everybody else does (and every consultant supports) must be viewed as borderline ridiculous.

In no other industrial reasoning would such a slipshod approach to rigour or accuracy result in anything other than a visit to the courts, wholesale malfunction, disaster or all three. In fact, in a final twist of irony for this debate, it is the routine presence of such disastrously *laissez faire* behaviour that gives industry its supply chain of seminal test-cases for future risk training courses. To name but a choice few across key sectors in the last forty years:

- aerospace: Challenger shuttle and Concorde disasters,
- oil industry: Piper Alpha; Exon Valdez; Brent Spar; Deep Water Horizon,

- automotive: Firestone Tyres and Ford; Mercedes A-class; VAG emissions scandal,
- nuclear: Three Mile Island; Chernobyl and Fukoshima,
- consumer goods: Persil Power; Melamine in baby milk; Nestlé mother's milk scandal,
- industrial: the collapse of Enron and Arthur Andersen,
- banking: Bearings; Northern Rock; and a small matter of a global banking collapse.

What joins so many of these events together in the consciousness is the spectre of that most famous of sayings: "this must never happen again". Yet, history is not our friend in that assertion. Every one of the organisations concerned, in what is less than forty years, has had the capacity to learn from the investigations of the preceding events. Every one of them has benefited from the ongoing and wide-ranging debate around the scientific, social and global framing of risk management. Every one of them has been regulated in relation to its risk diligence. Every one of them has had a risk management system (and in the case of Arthur Andersen actually sold capability development in risk). In fact, one in particular, the Shell Group, designed "the" risk management system that still shapes the expectation of the industry standard today, from government, to the BBC, to NATO, to WHO and at the desk next to yours in the office.

Whilst we must try to avoid too histrionic an analysis fuelling a kind of punk Psychology narrative here, one thing is crystal clear. If you want to use risk-based resilience in a large, complex, distributed organisation, you can't just take this stuff down off the shelves. Evidentially, you still have to take a journey and three words simultaneously encapsulate and evaluate where that journey needs to lead:

Appetite for complexity.

PART 3
Deeper into systems

Introduction
to Part 3

RISK AND RESILIENCE AS
DISTRIBUTED SYSTEMS

The third part of this book now has to move away from considering risk management and organisational resilience design at the construct and measuring/modelling interface. Instead it is now important to ask, how should these constructs and measurements be designed so that they apply to large, complex and distributed organisations as reasoning systems? Reasoning systems which will not be in isolation, but which will have to interact with a range of other legacy and complimentary systems which may share objectives with them.

A WORD ON SYSTEMS

When we speak of systems, we want to carefully balance three possible definitions: the first mechanistic – this refers to the intellectual capital mechanisms used by an organisation to promulgate the expectations of the risk-or-resilience approach. Most typically these manifest themselves as standards, governance, processes and procedures, training and compliance-checking methods.

The second systemic: this definition is the degree to which the risk or resilience approach has, itself, been designed to function as a system, as opposed to a series of stand-alone concepts, judgements or even as a linked series of descriptive narratives. When we say that risk is systemic we mean that it will be a multi-component, multi-attribute, multi-stakeholder device encased in a suitably complex process for measurement, deployment and quality assurance.

The third is digital: this definition, which is of accelerating importance as the digital age expands its reach, refers to whether any part of the risk-or-resilience approach has been computerised. Here, we are referring to purpose-built, dedicated software devices rather than the off-the-shelf use of generic office tools such as Microsoft Excel, although we do defer to the undoubted power of Excel in the hands of skilled user-programmers.

A natural corollary of these uses of the term system will, of course, be the temptation to want to view them as simply the component parts of a unified risk and resilience system for an organisation. Semantically this is entirely fine, as system is an enormously flexible idea. We would, however, add the caveat that such a broad definition would have to be defensible, in respect of intentionality and integration, rather than just conveniently descriptive. The term has to do more than point to a loose collection of concepts, processes and tools as "our resilience system". This is not a firm enough use to warrant being called a system.

It is not our intention to use the concept of system in technically specialist ways, such as those found in the various applications of the term Systems Theory. Rather we wish the concept to operate as a parsimonious description which refers to, but also collects together under an agreed housing: recognisable artefacts (such as a policy); familiar behaviours (such as a measurement activity); and observable outcomes (such as decisions or actions).

A WORD ON DISTRIBUTED

W hen we use the term distributed, we also have three meanings in mind. These correlate roughly with organisational size and diversity as follows:

In a medium-sized organisation, distributed has to refer to a multi-site operation to make any sense although, at a push, employee numbers and organisational complexity on a single site (such as an airport) may make a case for the need for distributed reasoning.

For much larger organisations there are two linked dimensions to the use of the idea of a distributed system. The first is geographical size, where multinational or global operation naturally implies multicultural operation.

Also for much larger organisations the second dimension, a key determinant of risk and resilience efficacy, refers to whether the organisation operates in any VUCA (Volatile, Uncertain, Complex, Ambiguous) environments.

In any of these three uses it should be clear that our notion of distributed reasoning should always connote two key ideas. First, distributed would refer to reasoning by individuals and groups who are separated in space. Second, reasoning that takes place in two distinct time frames. The first can be thought of as over time – the collection of data, population of algorithms and production of results that is not possible within a very short timeframe. The second refers to the same behaviours above but at different times – conclusion-making can therefore interact with changing patterns thrown up by measurement trends or a chain of effects from actions in response to an earlier system output.

A WORD ON DESIGN

In this part of the book we wish to push into more and more practical and applied territory. To do this we will begin with a critique of the 'silver bullet' argument in this space, how industry standards might be applied to risk-and-resilience systems (Chapter 10). We will examine, where we can find it, compelling research evidence that supports the efficacy of using these sorts of guidance to aid thinking and shape the design of an organisation's reasoning system.

Following on from those conclusions we will review the outcomes of a hierarchical content analysis addressing eight of the most prominent and available international standards linked to risk, continuity, resilience and governance. This is with a view to understanding any common factors and controlling themes. The result will be a prototype tool based on a general deconstruction of these types of instruments into a principles-led approach. This is proposed as a potentially fruitful method for responding to the very large behavioural burden that any use of multiple standards would amass upon an organisation's management.

In search of further design principles, we will revisit more fully the strengths and weaknesses of a Business Continuity Management system (Chapter 11). By this we will be able to explore which organisational structures explain the intentions behind an existing systems approach. This analysis will take the form of speculative success and failure factors for existing business continuity systems as a route to stylised principles and systems standards for a future resilience-and-risk reasoning system. This will include examining the, sometimes absent, interactions with: financial rationale; existing business process; appetite for reassurance; differentiation from other similar systems; and the maturity of the risk measurements.

Building on this thinking we will begin tackling the placement of a resilience system in a large, complex and distributed organisation

(Chapter 12). We will need to clear away some of the definitional confusion around where, in an organisation's pre-existing structures, such systems need to sit. This quickly becomes a journey of definition by exclusion – we examine those areas where businesses should resist the temptation to roll pre-existing approaches together under a new heading of resilience. We examine the logic and operational coherence of such a move. Depending on the appetite for complexity of the organisation concerned, we examine the pros and cons of seven scenarios for the placement of a resilience system. To aid this process we propose a staged template based around organisational decision making.

Concluding this part of the journey of design, we discuss an infrastructural approach to resilience systems design for large, complex, distributed organisations. This seeks from first principles to reject most of the pre-existing compromises of meaning and application brought on by the need to meet the constraints so far discussed. In their place we present a seven-stage design process which examines a completely new and operationally coherent methodology for resilience systems design and integration – for example, including a systematic analysis of the required behaviours and decision thresholds of all risk reasoning systems in play. We note, once again, that the key determinant of this systems integrated design and likely success is a requisite appetite for complexity to design the system that is needed rather than the system that is wanted.

CHAPTER 10

Taking a standard approach – a hybrid case study

In Chapter 6 we began to define organisational resilience, noting as we did that this construct went by a range of names and definitions. In that first discussion we touched, very briefly, on one key resource that sets out to provide a definitive position – this is, of course, the Standard. The International Standards Organisation (ISO) and The British Standards Institution (BSI) have both, in recent times, published formal standards on Organisational Resilience (ISO 22316 in 2017 and BS 65000 in 2014). When these weighty propositions already exist, you might be forgiven for wondering why we are still asking about the core definition of resilience in this book. You might further ask why we consider the inherent and/or necessary complexity of a resilience reasoning system, as we have argued it so far, to be such an open issue. Surely, with an ISO and BSI to refer to, everything that organisations might need to know would be two small purchases away?

It is not at all surprising that organisations who wish to be more continuous, resilient or risk resistant do often resort to the advice of standards organisations. These can be expected to show them both the light (of guidance) and the way (of accreditation). It is tempting to think that a potentially fast route to delivering resilience is for an organisation to set up a team who can be simply be tasked with implementation of the Standard. This means they do not need to wrestle with contextualising and designing a complex reasoning system in the ways we are laying out here. They can simply smooth a path for the organisation to comply with a pre-existing, and validated, Standard. If you already are a busy and complex organisation, this is indeed a very attractive proposition.

From our own point of view too, this proposition ought to be pushing an open door. Not only should the dialect, semantic, abstraction and measurement challenges we have been discussing come somewhat ready-solved, but the materiality case itself should also be compellingly made, albeit at a higher level. This might be at an industry-wide, regulatory or even international level. The further possibility of a community of users sharing wide-ranging data sets to mine for prototypes and lessons all seems very alluring. So there is only one question that the huge set of advantages from aligning with agreed Standards opens up, and it is a simple one: Does it work?

Does alignment with BS 65000, or something similar, go on to produce higher levels of organisational resilience? The answer to that question, however, is not simple.

In part this is because British and international Standards are not developed by magic but by sweat. They are developed in a collective process using invited expert groups. The experts are selected from representatives of organisations who have either a relevant track record, or a recognised expertise, or a pressing professional interest in the subject matter. They are bought together to form a technical committee. Such a committee might typically comprise of representatives of industry bodies, research and testing organisations, local and central government, consumers and Standards end users. Development of any Standard is an intellectual process. This is, of course, guided by specific principles and it is very involved, usually taking between one and four years, depending on the complexity and the range of stakeholders involved.

The approach – collective development by representations of organisations having expertise and interest in the subject matter – does sound very authoritative. However, in the real world, we need to pause briefly and ask: is that the same thing as a process of facilitated by experts with a validated track record of efficacy in the subject matter? Is that the same as experts who have unequivocal evidence of the actual business benefits delivered to real organisations from their ministrations? What we will find is that the answer, to that deeper question, will come with some considerable hesitation. We should, of course, recognise immediately that this could be a moot point. After all, one of the key reasons Standards may be written is very much to address the absence of such a thing. However, scientifically and pragmatically this should introduce a small note of hesitation around the authoritative status of the output.

If it is indeed in this latter spirit that the technical committee have been brought together, in order to become, and remain, an available body of professional opinion, this is not the same as the collation of appreciable and evidential facts. That is a small, but very important, distinction.

BSI will bring such groups together and facilitate the development and review of their Standards at a mostly international level. They do this with a set of specific and rigorous principles. These are set out as a terms of reference to guide development. The process of development, remembering that this can run to years, is detailed in Figure 10.1. As a further quality assurance mechanism, following adoption, Standards can be reviewed at any time and, while the responsibility lies with the technical committee, public consultation is always a feature of this process.

So it is fair to say that Standard creation, especially in new areas, is an art not a science. This is because the intellectual capital forms around a coalition of the interested and the willing, not the validated. This goes some way to explain that, whilst Standards are regularly reviewed, there is little evidence of thorough testing and evaluation of their implementation. This is particularly true in our area under discussion here, and this raises a challenge. Is the business benefit from the good practice they are calling for

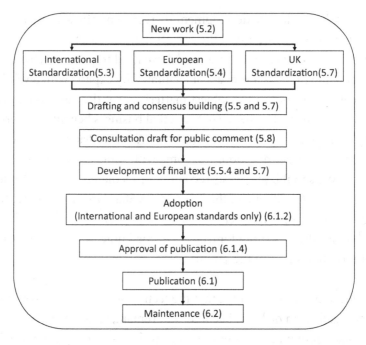

FIGURE 10.1 *The BSI Guide to Standardization. Section 1: BS 0 A standard for standards – Principles of standardization.*

WWW.BSIGROUP.COM/DOCUMENTS/30342351.PDF

an assumption therefore and not a proven fact? The benefit an organisation will see is clearly believed to be an emergent property of the rigour of the development process. A process which, not to belittle it but to underscore a fact of it, is really an application of collective wisdom.

So, it remains important, in our busy, largely complexity-intolerant environments, to call the validity and the efficacy of that collected wisdom if not into question, then at least into court. This is where we would like to turn our attention in this chapter.

A HYBRID CASE STUDY

We need to first say a word on the chapter title. The reason this chapter is entitled a hybrid case study is twofold. First, it is because we have brought together two related pieces of work that happened at different times to inform it. The first of these is a critical evaluation (Hierarchical Content Analysis) of eight risk and resilience Standards. These eight were chosen because they all apply in differing ways to our large complex distributed systems context. They will be listed in a moment. The second piece of work is an academic literature review. Using the Content Analysis as a launching point, this is seeking to uncover any formal evidence which supports the efficacy of Standards in risk and resilience. After all, organisations should not be tasked with the sorts of efforts such Standards require without being able to bank upon their likely effectiveness.

The second reason this is a hybrid case study is because, although the literature review was conducted after the Content Analysis, the argument flows more easily for you if we consider them in reverse order. Just on a point of science, we need to highlight that the argument is therefore somewhat hybrid in this form, but the points are easier to make.

THE ACADEMIC REVIEW OF STANDARDS' EFFICACY

Two things that are going to make the use of Standards attractive to organisations surround questions of ease of use and evidence for success of implementation. Such questions address how much confidence organisations should have to use a Standard out of the box. For example:

1 Has anyone else reviewed the efficacy of Standards in an appropriate context that might inform our choices for large, complex distributed systems?
2 Is there any research evidence which would prove or support their effectiveness in such a context?
3 Is there any coherent view in the academic literature about how the best way to apply of this kind of artefact to a business?

When one examines extant and formal academic literature, it is possible quite early on to see that these simple enough questions do not have ready answers. Some overall conclusions are:

- There is no review of collected standards in the risk and resilience area.
- Individual standards are frequently introduced, described and discussed as a way to talk about *potential* benefits.
- There are some, but very few, examples of comparisons, but only in very limited and specific contexts.
- No critical reviews exist and, more importantly, no comparative reviews exist, to challenge the received wisdom that an organisation must apply these standards discretely, i.e. they cannot be combined in some way.

To say that again in a nutshell, we note that there is no published evidence to demonstrate the usefulness or, more importantly, the effectiveness of these sorts of Standards. Where they are being referenced in published material this is very often in the early part of such texts that concerns itself with discussing definitions. This is an understandable, if self-fulfilling and rather circular, reference to the credibility of Standards. What it does not do is critique their authority or effectiveness because it is not describing evidence of application and use.

Searches in Google Scholar on the eight individual Standards from our Content Analysis exercise reveals very little. Similarly, for comparison, we note that evidence does appear for any specific Standards in other fields leaving us to conclude the search is appropriate. There is simply a lack of literature related to our subject: a lack of evidence.

When searching using the mainstream Google, rather than Google Scholar, almost all the relevant hits refer to the British Standards Institute itself, or articles which are promoting the use of Standards. These articles, unsurprisingly, do not offer any discussion of their validity. Also, this search technique points out what we have noted before, that there are many consultancies offering support to implement particular Standards (e.g. Frazer Nash, Steelhenge, Regester Larkin, Price Waterhouse Coopers, Deloitte).

In terms of any active practical discussion as to how Standards should be applied to business, there is direction, of course, in some of the Standards themselves. There are also pointers to related articles, but these have been expressly written to support them. The existence of particular Standards is being acknowledged through referencing in some examples. However, this is usually in the context of organisational resilience more broadly and, again, not in that essential evidential way we require. This material is not referencing proof of effectiveness.

To form a belief in that effectiveness therefore we have to take the, scientifically dubious, step of falling back onto general opinion. Overall, there seems to be an assumption that the rigorous and lengthy development and approval process is what gives Standards their authority. Across the board there seems to be a lack of post-implementation evaluation, either at a local organisational level or at a national/international level.

Academically speaking this is a tumbleweed moment. What it equates to is that there is no strong evidence emerging of case studies reported in the academic literature which support the utility and efficacy, or even try to examine the processes, of these Standards working. Not as yet.

IS THERE ANY RESEARCH EVIDENCE SUPPORTING THE POSITIVE USE OF STANDARDS?

We might want to broaden our search for validation outside the academic spheres of influence and ask, has any other community reviewed the efficacy of these, or similar, Standards in a context that would be appropriate to us? The closest thing we can find to a considered review of Standards is the RESOLUTE project. In 2017 you could find this at www.resolute-eu.org/. This is focused on the retrieval of evidence, assessment and synthesis of knowledge on resilience, aiming to support RESOLUTE research methodology and produce a suitable conceptual framework. However, the resilience in question concerns Urban Transport. Whilst this project reviews some relevant standards (e.g. see pp. 67–71), it is pertinent to note that it particularly critiques them rather than supports them.

Authors Raz and Hillson, in 2005, did compare nine Standards for Risk Management. This looked at their terms, scope, steps and emphasis. This analysis was used to draw conclusions about future Standards. Whilst drawing comparisons of the content, and identifying potential shortfalls, they still did not directly measure effectiveness. Added to this is the fact that the paper is rather dated given how much activity the risk and resilience area has seen in the last decade.

We have been able to find no evidence related to the specific Standards in our case study, and that may be a feature of the fact that we have found very little evidence related to Standards in general. Searches on Google Scholar on performance, evaluation, evidence, testing, effectiveness and impact all return nothing that is usable. The conclusion we draw from this is that there is a lack of evaluation of Standards in general and the examples from our set in particular.

One might argue that some of these are actually quite new so and have left little chance for that critical reviewing to have happened in business performance terms. However, the paucity of any real evidence of assessment of the efficacy of any such Standards, not just our particular eight, leaves us to believe that this is not a rich vein of academic or applied concern. Our search has been fruitless. Against the following Standards no reviews can be identified at the time of going to press:

- BS11200
- BS65000
- BS31100

- BS13500
- NFPA1600
- ISO22301

Whilst these standards are referred to in publications (e.g. Pollock, 2016), there is little in the way of evaluative material. Searching for comparative evidence for other Standards, the studies we found are still relatively limited. There are articles looking at the impact of specific Standards, particularly ISO9001 and ISO14001 (e.g. ISO9001 on the performance of service companies; financial impact of ISO14001). We find some commentary around using standards by a specific population, but not around directly testing the impact of them (e.g. Bakar et al., 2015). One of the few studies that does some research of implementation was by Link and Naveh (2006). They studied 40 organisations who reported how they implemented ISO 14001 (environmental management standard) requirements. They reported how the Standard impacts on their environmental and business performance. This, however, was not supported by analysis of financial data.

HOW SHOULD STANDARDS BE USED?

In this consideration we still have two questions to ask. First, is there any coherent opinion in the academic literature about how these artefacts should be viewed? Second, is there any evidence of good practices being caused directly by applying Standards.

STANDARD APPLICATION

Looking at material published post 2016 on Google Scholar (up to date and giving time for newer Standards to have embedded) provides virtually nothing. There is only either descriptive data, or examples of the standard owners, or consultants, trying to sell the standard itself or its application (e.g. see Kerr (2016), White Paper on Organisational Resilience espousing the BSI model).

EVIDENCE OF VALID GOOD PRACTICE BEING CAUSED BY STANDARDS?

On the question of evidence of valid good practices caused by Standards, the short answer to this is no, not really. Even for the, arguably more authoritative, International Standards Organisation, evidence of attributable validated good practice remains slim and apocryphal.

It is worth remembering that this institution is a non-government bridge between public and private sectors. The degree to which it is an authoritative Standard setter is self-proclaimed. All of its Standards are voluntary and consensus based. Historical evidence shows that the ISO believes this has led to competition and innovation, but there is no evidence to back up this belief.

In conclusion, this comprehensive and up-to-date review has not able to find any compelling evidence of the validity and impact of international Standards or British Standards in a business context. Furthermore, this remains accompanied by precious little in the way of any general view of standards at all from a critical perspective. The conclusion this research leads us to is as follows: *In the collective wisdom of standards, there is a constant, and un-tested, assumption of good practice as a result of the development process and the application of collective wisdom.*

CASE STUDY PART 2 – FINDING FACTORS TO SHAPE PERFORMANCE

One day in 2015 a large, complex and distributed organisation – a major, and very fine, British high street partnership – asked two breakthrough questions to develop their approach to Business Resilience:

First, could or should resilience really become some sort of superordinate discipline for the partnership? That is to say should all the other, older and very similar, disciplines just be rolled up into a single set of core practices for the whole organisation? Could they collectively be re-badged and re-launched as, simply, resilience?

Second, could one define the content of this resilience concept by examining and combining the merits of all the current Standards for these approaches? That is to say, if the organisation satisfied all of the conditions laid down by the current body of Standards, would that organisation not be, inherently, resilient?

To address these very insightful questions, they issued us with a challenge which was simply this: is there no tool or methodology that we might use to work out – in a single assessment – the degree to which we comply with any and all relevant Standards?

A CONTENT ANALYTICAL APPROACH

Pre-informed as we are now by our literature review, we can see that the answer would be no. As an applied examination into the efficacy mechanisms of Standards therefore, the Content Analysis we are about to discuss is highly notable. It is a one-off. No-one has ever examined any standards in this way before. Although it pertains to relevant examples in risk and resilience, this analysis still addresses the, somewhat larger, proposition of the use of any Standards. Such a methodology might of course also prove quite subversive of expensive, demanding and often lengthy, Standards.

Purpose of the case study

The purpose of this case study was to look for a small set of underlying operational capabilities that predicted wide-scale Standard compliance. We decided the best approach would be a naïve critical realism. So we examined a cross-section of seven of the most common Standards in use internationally taking each one entirely on face value. Finding that Supply Chain risk, as a specific discipline, had no Standard at this time, and knowing it was an essential component of our sponsor's organisational life, we also included a Business Continuity Institute report on the causes of Supply Chain disruption (for simplicity we will include this under the term Standard in the remainder of this chapter, but we recognise it is not). The list of eight was:

1 Business Continuity Management (ISO 22301)
2 Organisational Resilience (BS 6500)
3 Risk Management (BS 31100)
4 Crisis Management (BS 11200)
5 Emergency Management (ISO 22320)
6 Disaster Management (NFPA 1600)
7 Supply Chain Management (BCI 2015)
8 Effective Governance (BS 13500)

HIERARCHICAL CONTENT ANALYSIS

This analysis technique is inclusive and painstaking being as it is, simply, a systematic deconstruction of the meaning of the phrases in a text. Content Analysis is a highly involved and iterative process, but an isolated example might help illustrate how it progresses:

Every behaviour statement in the eight Standards was isolated into a long list. As an example, BS65000 (Organisational Resilience) contains the following three behaviours:

a) Understand the trade-off between cost and resilience.
b) Ensure plans are regularly and appropriately exercised.
c) Integrate all operational disciplines into resilience systems.

As this is a hierarchical analysis, these three resilience behaviours can be mapped to their different core competencies:

- Cost assessment/management.
- Training design/testing.
- Operational Integration.

Once all the behaviours have been discretised and classified in this way, the competencies can be meaningfully clustered. For example, the behaviours above relate to two clusters:

- Measurement (cost assessment and training design [the behaviour was "ensure"]).
- Placement (i.e. understand how the behaviour fits into the rest of the organisation).

This gives you a flavour of how the analysis progresses to build up a hierarchical model of what the content of the Standards actually requires. Given its dependence on language, this is a soft approach, but it is no less technically valid for that. Standards, being a highly structured form of writing in the first place, lend themselves to this type of hierarchical deconstruction very well. We found that a three-level model best suited the data.

LEVEL 1: CORE ELEMENTS

Core elements are the highest level of description. These might be termed strategic requirements, in that they relate to the common generic content of all eight Standards. They can be thought of as answering the question:

How do I describe the high level classes of action these combined Standards require?

We could not find a Standard that did not have all of the following five core elements:

1 Placement: the degree to which where a capability should be situated in an organisation is specified.
2 Policy: guidance on the exact nature of the policy architecture needed.
3 Purpose: stipulation of an exact purpose for the capability.

4 Process: instructions given on the type, organisation and outcome of necessary processes.

5 Measurement: the specific measurement activity, metrics and scales recommended to quality-assure the capability deployment.

LEVEL 2: KEY COMPONENTS

At the next level of detail down we are asking a different but related question of the data:

What are the high-level components (what we term key components) which determine, explain or justify the meaning of these five core

TABLE 10.1 Key components

Core elements	Examples of key components
Placement	Three key components explain all this material: • reflection in the strategy of the company • demonstration of operational viability • demonstration of intra-/interoperability
Policy	Six key components explain all this material; examples include: • demarcation of clear roles and responsibilities • appreciation of the scope/complexity and values of the company • senior team involvement in process and outcome
Purpose	Eight key components explain all of this material; examples include: • strategic value (appetite for complexity) • support structure (fit for purpose) • organisational impact assessment
Process	Thirty-one key components explain all of this material; examples include: • written plans and tools (procedures) • adaptive capacity (information management) • capability/competence focus required
Measurement	Eleven key components explain all of this material; examples include: • systematic risk appetite • legal and regulatory compliance • monitoring of systems maturity

elements? These might be termed the operating requirements for the Standard, in that they describe the sorts of support processes needed. An examination even just of the relative numbers of these key components is already informative (Table 10.1).

Examining the number of (operationalised) key components it takes to explain any (strategic) core element is informative. On one level it can act a proxy for the strength of their mandate in the Standard. For example, there is a very clear top line implication from this data analysis:

If you are to deliver the behaviours outlined in all eight of these Standards in your organisation, you will need highly detailed processes (made up of 31 different components) and very involved measurement systems (made up of 11).

It should be noted that a lower number of explanatory components (e.g. for Placement and Policy, 3 & 6 respectively) doesn't equate to less importance. The requirements might be described in fewer broader statements but still be (as is the case here) nonetheless complex.

LEVEL 3: OPERATIONAL BEHAVIOURS

As we have said, this Content Analysis is iterative. Although we can use core elements and their components to hierarchically summarise the (strategic and operational) landscape of the Standards' combined requirements, the behavioural element remains the most interesting. For the managers on the ground these behaviours will remain the core currency of Standard compliance, since they will describe what people must do. Here, the facts are sobering:

To meaningfully apply all eight of these Standards to your organisation requires a staggering 165 separate operational behaviours. Table 10.2 shows a breakdown of the whole hierarchy.

TABLE 10.2 Operational behaviours

165 operational behaviours	59 key components	5 core elements
29 behaviours, e.g. *competitiveness*: Risk Management creates and protects value	Operational viability (1 of 3 key factors)	Appropriate placement
11 Behaviours, e.g. *governance attributes*: all governance materials are in a single, unified, transparent whole	Scope, complexity and value (1 of 6 key factors)	Compelling policy
23 behaviours, e.g. *documentation scope*: documentation reflects size, scope and complexity of the organisation	Balanced risk and opportunity (1 of 8 key factors)	Detailed purpose
71 behaviours, e.g. *supplier resilience*: seeking reliable and validated evidence of key supplier resilience	Intra-/interoperability (1 of 31 key factors)	Effective processes
31 behaviours, e.g. *evaluation rigour*: the system is developed in a continuous, purposeful and rigorous way	Validation on cost (1 of 11 key factors)	Valid measurements

Looking at the demand characteristics of just the behaviour examples above: try to imagine the introduction of a single new approach in your business that requires 165 of such behaviours. Easy? We thought not. The conclusion of this Content Analysis draws us up very short. The burden of meeting all relevant Standards in the risk and resilience area cannot be easily reduced to a handful of pertinent meta-behaviours across the piece. The total burden of the literal requirements of all eight Standards cannot, therefore, be easily met.

This fact actually shines a new light on any current attempt to apply a single Standard within a business. For example, think about a team accountable for Operational Resilience. They may be driving to the best of their ability to make the organisation compliant, or even certified, against a relevant Standard such as BS6500. This will require them to create large operational behaviour changes in at least 28 areas. This will involve gathering much resultant data from, and delegating many consequent tasks to, lots of other people in the wider organisation. That workload grows proportionately with the rigour with which they pursue the exact requirements of their Standard.

Now consider in the next office, or maybe in another seven offices, other teams are doing the very same with supply chain risk, emergency planning and so on. Imagine how this workload grows so as to satisfy operational changes in 165 areas over 59 key components of your business. Imagine also, those teams in the organisation upon whom all these different behavioural requirements are likely to fall. Chances are these will be a small number of critical groups made up of the same people.

It would seem that we have hit a dead end. This detailed analysis shows how impossible the task of meeting all the relevant Standards would be.

OPERATIONALISING STANDARDS –
A PERFORMANCE-LED APPROACH

Or perhaps not.

The target of a Hierarchical Content Analysis is a parsimonious model that still respects all of the relevant content. When applied to Standards we can see that this is a strength – the analysis was comprehensive – and a weakness – the content would be operationally overwhelming. This, however, is not the end of the argument.

This first analysis highlights the challenges of literally operationalising standards as written. What we can see is that this might be possible for one Standard, but becomes prohibitively value reducing for each additional one. We say this is value reducing because of a key point of context. Nearly all of the behaviours laid out in these Standards are indirect activities, i.e. few, if any, are found in a direct line to profit. A problem that only deepens when you accept that these 165 "compliance" or "quality assurance" behaviours are wired like a complex matrix into another, pre-existing, set of external and internal governance that companies may already be struggling to manage. Without a direct case for business value, it becomes hard to see why any organisation would tolerate all the administration never mind the pressure of culture change.

Most importantly, it is just a substantial failure of joined up thinking in organisations to treat these Standards as isolated best practices for different teams when all of them predicate success on total organisational roll-out. When their requirements are collected into a total overall burden, it is hard to hide from that implication. When it is not broken up to become the individual prerogative of one or other department (such as Supply Chain), the pan-business, multi-disciplinary workload of all of them could be operationally overwhelming.

A HUMAN FACTORS APPROACH

Performance-Shaping Factors were invented in Air Traffic Controller studies sometime in the early 2000s (Richard Scaiffe, NATS, personal communication) – a technique emerging from Hierarchical Task Analysis (HTA) they pertained to model the cloud of conditions which mediated the, otherwise quite prescriptive, performance required by core tasks revealed by the HTA. A simple, everyday example can suffice to establish the principle.

Each person who drives a car has a complex baseline set of core competencies for the many tasks involved. From a personal perspective each of us can think of friends and rate their relative driving skills.

When it snows, our baseline ability to drive becomes somewhat challenged, as it does when we are tired, or about to miss an important interview, etc. The core ability to drive hasn't actually changed, what has changed is that there are temporary Performance-Shaping Factors in the internal and external environment which affect it.

The modelling of Performance-Shaping Factors offers us a key route out of the impasse of a completely overwhelming set of behavioural requirements for literal Standards compliance. What we can do is revisit our existing Hierarchical Content Analysis and look for these instead. We can extract not all of the specific behaviours required to meet a set of Standards, but a set of factors which mediates combined performance across them.

ARRIVING AT PERFORMANCE-SHAPING FACTORS

Our desire here is a smaller set of outcomes than either 165 or 59. We cannot simply revert to our five common elements because these are clearly too high level and, also, these are a vertical cut through the data. The factors which shape overall performance have to ideally be a horizontal cut across all five of these elements simultaneously. So the research question is clear: could this same detailed literal operationalised data be described by a smaller set of horizontal business-level behaviours? Could these sensibly exemplify unique sets of the underlying operational behaviours across all the existing model's components?

If we could do this, the resulting set of business level behaviours would only be valid if they passed two further tests. First they would be valid business actions that could be referenced back to the original Standards. Second, they would have to demonstrate a high natural correlation to the operational behaviours already identified. This could be achieved if the master behaviours encapsulated a unique set of demand characteristics that were common to the operational behaviours in question.

Such an exercise would be describing a set of Performance-Shaping Factors for the entire pool of behaviours in this data set. These would also be able to act, therefore, as a measurement benchmark to predict competence. The key question is: would the number of factors needed to create a parsimonious solution to explain all of the data be any less overwhelming than the 165 behaviours already identified across 59 components?

The answer to that question, to cut quite a long and involved story very short, is yes. We re-analysed the content data and found that a horizontal matrix of seven Performance-Shaping Factors satisfied the above criteria. It summarised all 165 operational behaviours across, rather than within, nearly all of the 59 key components. There were still some minor gaps, but very few.

To put that another way, meeting the behavioural requirements of all eight of the Standards above can be explained by a methodology which measures only seven predictive Performance-Shaping Factors. These factors summarise (almost) everything the Standards are expecting to find, or to stimulate, at the business level, in every organisation. Table 10.3 summarises this model.

MEASUREMENT AND METRICS DESIGN

In Human Factors, a comprehensive Content Analysis is always needed for psychometric questionnaire design. As we had one to draw on in this case, it was a relatively easily mater to explore what type of (performance) metrics this exercise would be able to support. We focused on two performance areas, document validation and general performance prediction.

We chose documents validation as a key metric because two from the five core elements in our model focus on the creation of organisational documents. These are the Policy and Process requirements. Either the documents that organisations already have, or those that they specifically produce in response to a Standard, could now be behaviourally benchmarked. We developed two metrics – policy coherence and procedural coherence.

TABLE 10.3 Performance-shaping factors

Performance-shaping factor	Indicated by	Predicts behaviours
Strategic adequacy	Senior involvement in governance setting; explicit strategic value; situational awareness of leadership; explicit appetite for risk	9 Placement 5 Policy 4 Purpose 6 Process 9 Measurement
Operational capability	Matches scope complexity and values; has clear support structures; is fit for purpose at ethical, organisational and human levels; has evaluable capability	7 Placement 2 Policy 3 Purpose 22 Process 12 Measurement
Multi-disciplinary role clarity	Principles of operation defined; clear multidisciplinary collaboration; strong communication	0 Placement 2 Policy 2 Purpose 16 Process 0 Measurement
Organisational impact validation	Has managed reputation; performs impact assessment; valid documentary and systems presence	0 Placement 0 Policy 3 Purpose 19 Process 7 Measurement
Feasible intra-/interoperability	Explicit operability across extant systems; operability with key partner organisations; regularly monitored operability	13 Placement 1 Policy 6 Purpose 3 Process 3 Measurement
Risk cognisant	A balanced risk and opportunity is a live feature; situational awareness in play; tolerance for complexity explicit	0 Placement 0 Policy 5 Purpose 5 Process 0 Measurement
Stakeholders	A qualifier for well-rounded approach stakeholder involvement in and stakeholder management through the design was seen as important	0 Placement 1 Policy 0 Purpose 1 Process 0 Measurement

In terms of measuring Standards-induced general effectiveness, we note that businesses would struggle with an audit covering 59 components. However, a health barometer method to assess effectiveness across seven factors felt like it might be more readily accepted. Such a model ought to be able to act as a high-level predictor of the operational effectiveness of all of these Standards, and indeed any similar ones. To this end we also created a prototype deployment effectiveness questionnaire.

Document analysis

A document analysis system, based on the seven Performance-Shaping Factors in our model, resulted in twelve indicator scales, six in each of the two areas as shown in Table 10.4.

An example of one of ten anchored scales from the deployment effectiveness questionnaire is shown in Table 10.5.

TABLE 10.4 Twelve indicator scales

Policy coherence indicators	Process coherence indicators
Strong governance	Leadership strategic awareness
Senior authority/support/involvement	Fit, competent and adaptive
Scope, complexity and value	Multidisciplinary roles, responsibilities and communications
Roles and responsibilities	Planned, tested, resourced and costed
Intra-/interoperability	Situational intra-/interoperability
Demerit points	Reputational intelligence

Fit, competent and adaptive	Adaptive and fit for purpose: The RCR process shows clear signs of commitment to adaptation and learning built in 1. Clear steps to convert and exploit operational information into actionable plans, especially to address critical dependencies and single points of failure 2. Commitment to an adaptive capacity through internal and external lesson learning and error sharing as part of mandated formal training 3. Risk management is detailed, structured and timely and identifies tools (e.g. techniques, templates, software, documents) that help people manage risk within the organisation's framework

FIGURE 10.2 *Process coherence question set*

TABLE 10.5 One of ten anchored scales

Effectiveness scale	High-performance behaviour description	Modest-performance behaviour description	Low-performance behaviour description
3. Understanding of the scope of risks, incidents and crises	We have deep horizon scanning to anticipate, identify, monitor and evaluate the trends in critical strategic, financial, operational and reputational areas	We have horizon scanning to anticipate, identify, monitor and evaluate the trends for a broad catalogue of different risks	We have horizon scanning to anticipate, identify, monitor and evaluate the trends only for certain kinds of risks

As a final exercise in this case study, we used these prototypes to assess the resilience policy, procedures and effectiveness index using Unilever as the guinea pig organisation. Time does not permit us to relate that data in any detail, but these metrics tested very favourably indeed.

THE BENEFITS OF A SYSTEMATIC ANALYSIS

It is fascinating that, rather than seeing Standards as a set of discrete (and demanding) requirements on a business written vey much as a *fait accompli*, they can yield so much more. At this detailed level of content analysis we have shown that the operational burden of literally meeting just eight Standards is just simply too huge. This is a key finding.

However, precisely because those eight Standards are so similar at the deep-form level, they do lend themselves to the extraction of their intentional performance content. Or to put that more simply, you can extract a small number of highly valid and very specific Performance-Shaping Factors common to them all. Furthermore, you can go on to define a set of benchmarking metrics based on these which organisations can use to test effectiveness and perform gap analyses.

CONCLUSIONS FROM THIS CHAPTER

We accept that Standards can never provide the silver bullet argument, however conscientious the people and process which produce these. Repeatedly calibrating entire operational systems around a general advisory schema is not effective. You still have to bear the intellectual burden of designing a system fit for the organisational context. We have suggested that this system might do better to enshrine the performance characteristics and competences that many Standards are advocating, rather than seeing the Standards themselves as its script. This is for a range of reasons.

Industry Standards attempt to be comprehensive. Thus, used in their current form, they potentially bring a cost to user organisations from their complexity – a performance factor which makes them, individually and collectively, more likely to fail than to succeed.

The goals behind using industry Standards can be thought of as those of improved operability, value creation or both. Pursuing these goals in a large business would benefit from an analysis of the combined burden of all of the relevant standards to be used upon the whole organisation – a number that might be quite large for a complex organisation.

The combined impact on an organisation of following many Standards may be occluded at present by a division of labour between key disciplines and departments leading on different areas in isolation – a challenge which deepens when the work called for by each taps into overlapping resources, intelligence and data for what are ostensibly unconnected reasons.

Just the organisational resilience and risk management areas are, as we have already pointed out, highly complex and diverse. This explains why there are many national and international Standards aimed at helping organisations tackle aspects of these and related areas more coherently. We also note that there is a paucity of formal evidence to support their effectiveness. The goal of improved operability, or value creation, from the use of such Standards has to be predicated on accepting their wisdom on ethnographic data alone.

To access this wisdom through the discretised application of numerous different approaches seems ineffective. This would be doubly the case if there was a way that it could be more generally distilled across subjects. Due to their typically involved approach to definitions and actions, and their meticulously authored nature, Standards do lend themselves very well to hierarchical content analysis. Due to their proliferation, searching for common factors across a number of thematically related examples is advisable for any large, complex organisation.

When we conducted this exercise it revealed that a core business competency model can predict valid transfer. This in turn means that assessment tools can also be created to help organisations assess gaps, benchmark performance and track progress. Once again, on the assumption is that the wisdom found in these standards is worthwhile.

Taken together, these actions create a systems approach to meeting resilience (and other) standards that meaningfully embraces, but simplifies, their many requirements. It does this in a sensible, logical and cross-business manner. This would appear to be an enormously fertile ground for future strategy and further research.

BIBLIOGRAPHY

Bakar, Z. A., Yaacob, N. A. and Udin, Z. M., 2015. The effect of business continuity management factors on organizational performance: A conceptual framework. *International Journal of Economics and Financial Issues, 5*(1S).

Kerr, H., 2016. Organizational resilience. *Quality, 55*(7), 40.

Link, S. and Naveh, E., 2006. Standardization and discretion: does the environmental standard ISO 14001 lead to performance benefits? *IEEE Transactions on Engineering Management, 53*(4), 508–19.

Murphy, C. N. and Yates, J., 2009. *The International Organization for Standardization (ISO): Global governance through voluntary consensus.* London: Routledge.

Pollock, K., 2016. Resilient organisation or mock bureaucracy: Is your organisation "crisis-prepared". www.epcresilience.com/EPC/media/ MediaLibrary/Knowledge%20Hub%20Documents/J%20Thinkpieces/ Occ16-Paper-Resilient-or-Mock.pdf

Raz, T. and Hillson, D., 2005. A comparative review of risk management standards. *Risk Management, 7*(4), 53–66.

CHAPTER 11

A systems evolution approach – experiences of BCM

L owering the academic guard of the last chapter a little at this point – in favour of an increasing emphasis on pragmatism – we need to be allowed to speak a little more ethnographically. That is to say, we are now going to describe the nature of the (organisational) world from an observational point of view. The descriptions we wish to discuss in this chapter will doubtless be plotting on a curve for our readers.

There is still much that is practical yet to say about a systems design for risk and resilience reasoning that applies an appropriate synthesis of operational logic, organisational Psychology and statistical rigour. However, at this juncture it would be fatal to consider this to be possible, even aided and abetted by the design templates we have discussed thus far, *ex nihilo*. Large complex, distributed organisations just aren't like that.

If we think that risk management and operational resilience can be introduced from a clean slate, we ignore a crucial state of affairs that will apply in many businesses, which is this. There will already be legacy systems in place. In all likelihood one of them will be an expression of Business Continuity Planning – the kind of system which, as discussed in Chapter 6, always plays a critical role in shaping the cultural expectation around resilience.

With this in mind, it is now necessary to make a detailed examination of Business Continuity Management (BCM). Reflecting on practical challenges experienced over many years of observing many organisations, we have constructed a two-part taxonomy. The first part examines nine performance attributes that lead to the likely failure of a BCM system. These are covered in two sections – those concerning organisational culture and those concerning the relationship between BCM and business as usual. The second examines eight performance attributes that lead to the likely success of a BCM system. These will also be in two groups covering more effective Human Factors and what we will call organisational synchronicity.

Our conclusion will be that, however it is done, poorly or excellently, BCM systems are prohibitively difficult to design, execute and embed. At the risk of appearing dogmatic, we feel that the chief enemy of effective practice is a tendency towards seeking reassurance from a system that has a low appetite for complexity. Conversely, effective practice would be predicated on behavioural evidence of business effectiveness coupled to the most appropriate appetite for complexity. However, counterintuitively in this case perhaps, we may need to prepare ourselves for the possibility that the business case (costs vs benefits) for that more effective system do not to stack up.

BCM systems should only be considered effective if the business case does stack up, that is to say the linkages between their goals and outcome measures align in a materially coherent way with those of the operation concerned. However, a sobering fact of that conclusion is that the system would also, by necessity therefore, have to subject itself to being critically judged on its merits as a business engine.

THE CHALLENGES OF BUSINESS CONTINUITY MANAGEMENT

To begin to examine the cultural expectation of BCM on resilience, let us set the stage with three propositions. When it comes to the status of pre-existing Business Continuity Planning (or Management) in many large, complex, distributed organisations today, we find variations around the following states of affairs:

1 Business Continuity Management does not, on the whole, have a reputation for creating sustainable, effective and enduring processes. Rather its practitioners complain of an uphill struggle, a frequently unwilling organisation, lamentably low levels of resource, a minefield of compromise and a regrettably short shelf-life for its end product, "the plan".

2 Business Continuity Management systems do fail in predictable ways that the discipline recognises and regrets. This is all the more frustrating because this need not happen. Business Continuity Management excellence tends to be a boom-and-bust trade. The boom, unfortunately, is often signalled by the presence of a recent failure of audit, or the fact that a major continuity crisis is filling the windscreen of the company C-suite.

3 Business Continuity Management systems can, and do, succeed using more than the tenacity of the hard-pressed managers at the helm. This is when the organisation has a mature appetite for an embedded system integrated with their operational aims. This may be more probable when a Business Continuity Plan has recently been instrumental in actually protecting people, assets or profits from a major shock.

Taking these three propositions forward, we would like simply to open up a conversation about failure and success. This will form an important stratum of observational data for the approach to operational resilience for an organisation with pre-existing systems – an approach, we conclude, that will have to be a process of evolution not revolution.

WHY DO BUSINESS CONTINUITY MANAGEMENT SYSTEMS SOMETIMES FAIL?

The multiple operational reasons why a Business Continuity Management system can have a very hard time penetrating an organisation and developing effective traction are a perennial topic. The simplest general reason is easy to articulate – no one cares enough. This can be broadly summarised into two key problem sets, shown in Figure 11.1. One is that business continuity, because it is predicated on a risk management core ethos, often only speaks one dialect of risk, that of (re)assurance. The other is omnipresent – the question of demonstrable business value.

Business Continuity Management systems can be designed (and one might argue that all the early ones were) primarily to "trade" in risk reassurance. They embed themselves best into cultures that value governance and compliance mechanisms to exercise control. Since that is a policy debate

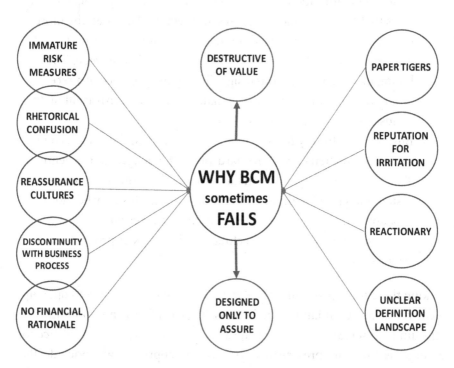

FIGURE 11.1 *BCM failure tree*

(or even a regulatory one), systems almost always find themselves positioned as an indirect within a business. Much like safety and other assurance exercises historically were, these will tend to embody a checklist-dominated exercise around the soft end of the organisation's licence to operate. To put that another way, Business Continuity Management is simply not seen as a *direct* business process, i.e. one which is affecting profit and loss. This is despite the fact that it attracts a great deal of attention very quickly if it is seen as to blame for a loss.

Languishing in this indirect space, the system may even come to be perceived by some more hard line commentators as destructive of value. This is because, much like safety and risk, it suffers from a particular kind of evidence path, one we might call "the myth of the non-event". Value is added to the business because something, not routinely meaningfully quantifiable, did not happen. So the system is slightly doomed to be seen as an overhead, an inconvenience, a cost. By dint of time use and process burden, it may even be accused of slowing a business down.

Financially tight, time-poor organisations will always struggle to accept the myth of the non-event as a value-adding argument. This is the source of a major complaint from continuity managers, and safety/risk managers, sometimes the same manager of course. It's an argument which might be better won if business case creation was a critical part of its justification. A decision we have to recognise could just as easily downgrade the importance – on business value terms – as upgrade it. Not a popular subject.

UNPACKING FOUR ORGANISATIONAL CULTURE REASONS WHY BCM CAN FAIL

This problem of business (decision making) penetration and the associated lack of traction experienced by some continuity managers is a *de facto* reason why continuity systems are hard to design and execute. They constantly teeter on the edge of potentially wasting their own effort and resource, let alone that of the business. Four Performance-Shaping Factors are noteworthy in this debate: unclear definitions, reactionary approach, causing irritation and the reputation of their output.

1 Unclear definition landscape

Good Business Continuity Management should not be the opaque work of a specialist group. This group should not feel that it is tasked with the ownership of a system of opaque risk and business impact assessment. These impacts should not be managed by the inconvenience (and cost) of isolating back-up, redundancy or contingency. These strategies should not, themselves, need to be kept in the consciousness of the operational players through detailed, but extra-ordinary, training exercises to rehearse real-time preparedness.

If that sounds a little backwards, consider this: allowing BCM to create its own definition citadel – something that might be a search for validity and recognition – potentially further alienates it from a business value argument. When there is never a clear definition of the exact business risk–cost–benefit case for this effort, it will be seen as an end in itself.

The harder path is to define a large percentage of the BCM impact in the exact currencies of the normal business value and strategic decision-making processes.

2 Reactionary approach

The motivation to have a system must be examined. One can observe in many businesses that this is reactionary. A pervasive story of a major loss somewhere in the recent history of the company (the list at the end of Part 1 of this book offers a range of candidates) may be the catalyst. This causes two mindset reactions in the host company and across its sector. The "this must never happen again" mindset and the "we must learn the lessons" mindset (even though it almost always will, and we never really can, see Lauder, 2003). In any large, high-paced, cost-sensitive, competitive business these are two of the worst kinds of mindset for making structurally effective decisions about continuity system performance. These are reactionary, a nervous instinct from a vulnerable leadership that got something wrong.

The harder path is to defend a BCM approach that is not to be seen as an airbag system for a hard-pressed business. Rather, to promote it to the value-creation decision-making arena, where its outputs can be precautionary, yes, but also empowered to be proactive not reactive. This is much like our argument for the difference between continuity and resilience.

3 Reputation for irritation

This is a sensitive political point to make. Many organisations find the business continuity management team's expectations of them, particularly the data hunger and the basic paranoia of the poor end of that systems thinking, annoying. It can be an unwelcome task, particularly if it is a perennial one about auditing documents and phone-number lists and seeking sign-off signatures for wording changes. It is never anyone's true priority and so, after fleets of e-mail reminders, it is often (eventually) done under some kind of sufferance. The managers running the system are sometimes laconic about this. At other times they are mildly incensed that no one sees the (un-validated) importance of their work.

The harder path is to create a BCM culture that is owned and prioritised from top to bottom in a business by dint of the business value it can be demonstrated to add.

4 The creation of paper tigers

Part of the psychology of the above dynamic is to do with paper tigers. This is an old Chinese expression referring to persons, things or institutions that are initially imposing but do not stand up to challenge. In our use of the term, the tiger is quite literally made of paper too. It is the unqualified acceptance that the system is a success if it creates a Business Continuity Plan. This might be without stopping to verify that it enshrines an accurate definition of the goals of the business: without an evidence-based model of the drivers of Business Resilience; without it needing to actually function as a real plan, i.e. designed for shelf-life and to be executed and efficacious in real time; when the document itself, rather than professional competences, is the output. When this exhausts almost all the resource of a traditional team, and a great deal of the goodwill of the operating business, getting a plan across the line each year becomes its own arch quality assurance device.

The harder path is to identify business critical benefits that make up the target efficacy and generate those as a living plan – as the competencies of a business value-creation engine.

These four features: unclear definitions, reactive approaches, systems that irritate busy people, and paper tiger outcomes are all a real possibility for any hard-pressed BCM team facing the resistance of a business. Real care must be taken not to allow the host business to set them as the arena for compromise. They are a recipe for failure.

THE CHALLENGE OF RULES FOR BUSINESS

Any social scientists, like ourselves, working in industry are, at some point, taken under a friendly arm and given an explanation of the rules of business. The basic rule is the harshest: "it's about profit, you idiot". A key adage is "look at what you make". Few organisations make business continuity management, or public affairs, or safety. These social science-, management science-facing ideas are actually our ideas, the management scientists, the operations researchers, the business schools and universities, psychologists and sociologists.

To a business person, the working concepts of an effective business continuity system can remain quite obscure. They are tough to abstract meaningfully and therefore very hard to measure in those familiar terms of profit, turnover, volume or share-price. When activities are not direct to the value chain, or supply chain, it is often hard to see why they merit a seat at the strategic table. This is except of course briefly, and by special invitation, when things have gone badly wrong.

Rather than cry about this, systems designers need to actively look at how their philosophy is perhaps contravening the accepted rules for business. Of the many possible sources of disconnect between BCM and business, we have highlighted five:

1 NO FINANCIAL RATIONALE

Businesses work, in the main, by making profits. Very few business continuity plans highlight, or incur, costs beyond the overhead for the staff to develop the processes and plans. That and the cost, if there is any, of the training exercises – a levy which is often, quite injudiciously, handed straight to an external consultant. The management system is not offered to the business decision makers with a cost–benefit options appraisal, or even necessarily a bill, attached. The costs stay invisible.

2 DISCONTINUITY WITH BUSINESS PROCESSES

The relationship between BCM and the rest of the business has not been made clear. Some might like to see business continuity, much like some see safety, as absorbed into the 'business as usual' behaviours of the organisation. That is to say, its aims should be completely aligned with what the business does. Others think that the system should always be wholly audit performance driven and external to the direct stuff of business.

It's rare for Business Continuity Management systems to actively manage this 'same but different' challenge. If the system is too independent, and unlike any of the business processes it is purportedly serving, it will be completely alien. People who wish to reject the additional burden can make easy recourse to its lack of business relevance and a status of corporate assurance, with a faint tincture of "unnecessary". To combat this, a certain utility/transferability of logic (financial or operational or otherwise) must be part of the outcome.

3 REASSURANCE CULTURES

Organisations which desire reassurance and compliance are not making a mistake. However, as organisational size and complexity increase, the difficulty of the senior team in having direct line of sight to the operation increases exponentially. Governance structures become more complex, just as time (for boards) comes into shorter supply. "Positive reassurance" becomes the (time-saving) norm and the leadership begin to govern by indicators – a proactive set of narrative devices giving, not knowledge, but confidence.

This potentially cripples the necessary senior engagement that effective systems need to survive. As the positive assurance mechanism sets strict standards of brevity – BCM's diversity and complexity is a disadvantage. The culture (excepting detailed audits) stops paying enough attention. A culture of reassurance does grievous harm to BCM operability and authority.

4 RHETORICAL CONFUSION

BCM systems classically orbit two fears. One, that the businesses encounter unavoidable short term shocks unprepared. Two, that they are suffering from long-term deleterious stresses but ignore them. Not being able to recover quickly from a shock and being degraded by a stress are what keeps the BCM manager awake at night. Where the rhetorical confusion can quickly arise is at the interfaces with other insomniac managers.

There is often a blurred interface with the corporate risk register. To what degree should Business Continuity Management encompass the key "corporate risks" of the business? The answer is unclear. The corporate risk register and the continuity risks are at quite different levels and overseen by different teams. The second blurred interface is with emergency and disaster response planning. The two-way obfuscation between emergency and continuity is normally hidden under a convenient diagram. The third source of confusion is the interface with normal operating, where business continuity simply struggles to join up.

5 IMMATURE RISK MEASURES

The classic forms of risk found in most business continuity systems are simply too immature. This is for all the reasons of construct validity already discussed at length in this book. Risk event reasoning without interconnectivity, sensitivity to time or operational context, and any model of volatility, will not be effective beyond reassurance. BCMs almost always recommend a "robust" red, amber, green style of risk effected by a democratic (and usually very speedy) process. This immature measurement significantly degrades the clarity and efficacy of any long-term positive business impact.

These five features: lack of finance data, discontinuity with business aims, a drive for reassurance, blurred interface with similar systems, and immature risk measurement are standard pitfalls that a BCM team can only avoid by setting themselves a much harder set of goals. Real care must be taken not to allow the team itself to seek to make compromises here. This is a recipe for a titular system.

HOW CAN BUSINESS CONTINUITY MANAGEMENT SYSTEMS SOMETIMES SUCCEED?

The picture we have painted is that BCM systems can fail because generally they are: prevented from being clear; expected to work as a reaction; and billed as a distraction from the real work. Their outputs can be lacking in financial rationale, continuity with business process, leaning towards reassurance over substance, hard to separate from the priority of other similar systems and forced to use and report low-utility, highly summary indicators.

For a system to succeed, the obvious thing to say is that these failure points need to be overturned. Whilst this is true, it is also not completely true. The one-to-one relationship between failure performance-shaping factors and success ones is a little bit of a suspect argument. In considering success factors, we may want to imagine that the successful system, rather than being a hostage to fighting against organisational inflexibility, is a force organisational development.

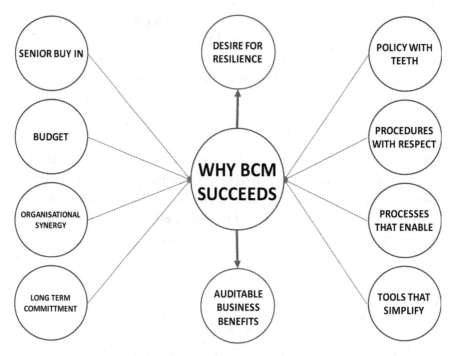

FIGURE 11.2 *BCM success tree*

With one eye on this possibility, our success performance-shaping factors fit into two key schools of thought. These are more effective Human Factors and what we might call organisational synchronicity. Together they represent the pursuit of auditable business benefits as the way to validate a continuity management effort.

MORE EFFECTIVE HUMAN FACTORS

Effective Human Factors do not come easily to busy, large, complex and distributed organisations. The responsibility for negative performance factors discussed so far cuts both ways. The organisation might do better to meet the continuity manager half way. Likewise, the success factors discussed below should not to be considered as unilateral.

1 Policy with teeth

If you are a large company and you have policies, whatever these are for, the thing that matters is that the policy has teeth. By teeth we mean that the policies are: cleanly written; free from contradiction or bias; underwritten by consequences for infringement; and supported by example in the senior leadership. They should also be enabled by a set of standard operating procures, augmented by clear operating processes in a supportive culture which assesses them regularly through effective audits.

All of that is easy to say, and indeed companies do say it all, but it is far less easy to do – a problem always magnified across geographical and cultural borders. Policy is a hard instrument to use effectively in large distributed systems. When it comes to continuity or resilience we need to ask two questions. First, is there any policy at all? Second, is it a real policy, or a form of words which satisfies as reassurance and little else?

2 Procedures with respect

Where good policy should mandate expectation, good procedures should qualify execution. Too hasty a set of "musts" created in isolation for a policy, too sharp a set of teeth in fact, is an easy error to make. These quickly prove to be baby teeth if they can't translate into the application of a cognitive behavioural approach. Procedures must form the enabling instructions of policy.

These have to be written (or modified) to make the implications of any business continuity policy actionable. They justify the impact on time and resource, and they describe the actual cognitions and behaviours of the operational agents in a real operating culture. This should include an understanding of the real human cost of operating in certain cultures so as not to request what everyone knows to be a cultural impossibility.

Procedures with respect should not compromise the ethos of continuity, just make it more practical. As these interface with serious threats (human, epidemiological, episodic or otherwise) or pressing ethical questions, they have to serve the organisation within the constraints set by its policy, its values and the realities of its operating environment. Lacklustre operating procedures are barely better than guidelines and will be treated as such.

3 Processes that enable

Policy sets framework. Procedure delivers practical detail. The purpose of process is to make following procedures effective. Processes are pithy – they bridge the mandatory aspects of policy/procedure with the practicability required for real-time operation. A good process embodies the Human Factors that enable competence. It is pragmatic enough to describe the problems which are to be solved in reality. Processes are an art form and they have to be a constant transparent work in progress. Designed like this, they operate as a feedback loop of problem solving and lesson learning that may lead to a future change in policy.

4 Tools that simplify

When organisations are large, complex, diverse and dispersed, the agreed governance we have described so far creates systemic pressure – for example, keeping data in good enough shape to make a process work efficiently. The most efficient form of data that a continuity system can use is the kind that it can reuse: that is to say, data that is already collected for another business specific reason. A well-constructed tool that that takes time and effort out of the process of using data is powerful. It will be a Trojan Horse function for the BCM. That is to say, tools that simplify make following the rules the easiest and most effective thing to do.

These four features: authoritative policy; well-crafted procedures; enabling evolving processes; and simplifying tools form a key part of the landscape of a successful BCM system design. There is no question that they are detailed and involved and require regular maintenance and support. There is also no question that with proper attention to these, BCM will be able to support and interact with a business to deliver value and benefits to it.

ORGANISATIONAL SYNCHRONICITY PERFORMANCE-SHAPING FACTORS

Organisational synchronicity is a way of saying that continuity, when the system is in place and operating, should be appropriately harmonised with the goals, targets and valued outcomes of the organisation. It should map to the operating environment and culture of the organisation (assuming these are in a good state of health). We have highlighted four factors here. There are others. These support the successful deployment of a continuity system when it is well designed in the ways we have outlined above.

1 Senior buy-in

An overused term and, at times an oxymoron, senior buy-in remains key. The leaders of the organisation set the operational tone of the culture. Senior buy-in for BCM amounts to many things: agreed funding, agreed importance and appropriate lobby. The thing that translates most effectively is overt modelling of agreed behaviours. Continuity can easily be compromised by a word and deed mismatch.

2 Budget

This is the simplest thing to say and the hardest thing to achieve. Budget is needed: for the BCM function to exist; for its tools to be well designed and iterated; and for research into effectiveness, metrics and course correction. Usually only the first is provided. Often, as these things go for everyone, it is provided and then cut. Budget has to play a deliberate and overt part in the appetite for complexity of the BCM system. An ideal financial rationale for a business continuity management system should be as follows:

- Directly identify which profit, turnover and volume is being protected by the approach and which is not.
- Set the business delivery level that can be expected during a continuity incident and another level for crisis – express this as an appetite for business loss.
- Develop countermeasures which are linked to operational drivers and have an explicit cost and effort to maintain.

- Return a costs–risks–benefit business case for the overall management system.

Rarely, if ever, does the business part of a Business Continuity Management system come in such a serious form. This is part of the reason it is easy to ignore.

3 Organisational synergy

The continuity team should become experts in the organisation cross-functionally. How else can they reflect the real organisation in their systems? If they have this valid expertise, the system can be a source of critique to propel as well as protect the business. Although BCM should be separate in some ways from business as usual approaches, if it provides a critique of the business as a creative synergy it can become a business optimiser that can be measured alongside value chain profit and supply chain efficiency.

4 Long-term commitment

If the desire for continuity has been reactive, perhaps to some serious loss judged preventable, perhaps to some failure of audit, perhaps to some change in policy or regulation, that has to be fine. If it is more sensibly planned, but still suffers from the negative performance factors we have highlighted above, that has to be fine too. If it is a knee-jerk reaction from a senior leader transplanted from another organisation, or sector, who wants "what we used to do at X", that too has to be fine.

Whatever the mandate, we would argue that the most compelling positive performance-shaping factor after organisational synergy is this. To see continuity as a capability development exercise embedded into the culture – where measuring outcomes and training people is its absolute epicentre. This capability needs to be allowed to mature through being actively monitored and optimised over a long game. The leadership must recognise that continuity is here to stay and should be therefore not be judged year on year, by isolated indicators, but in the long-term health of the organisation by integrated measures.

With these four features: senior buy-in to the processes; budgeting as a normal part of business; a developed sense of synergy with the goals of the organisation; and a long-term commitment to judging efficacy at the infrastructural level of a business driver, we can measure synchronicity. The business continuity management system will be synchronised to the priorities and to the capabilities of the organisation it serves.

CONCLUSIONS FROM THIS CHAPTER

The experiences of an organisation with Business Continuity Management can affect their design of a resilience system markedly. BCM is very difficult to do well and key tensions are evident:

First, there is the trans-material nature of its outcomes. BCM has credibility when it adequately reflects the operational priorities and business metrics of an organisation. However, to be effective behaviour change mechanism, it has to also define the parallel reference grammar, objectives and trade-off mechanisms of a separate construct namely continuity.

Second, it is often placed organisationally in an indirect position and may be allowed to focus on a success criteria set that is about things not happening. However, defining its objects of reference within the positive currencies of the business is a key success driver.

Third, it is frequently perceived as a reassurance-based exercise. However, it fares better with a planned organisational synergy where it is allowed to embody and influence actual strategic decisions. These need to be formed in a precautionary and predictive language rather than the default protection language preferred.

Fourth, operatives who deliver it are under pressure and can sometimes allow its own administrative burden and outcomes to become the key success criteria. The real need is to design an integrated cognitive and behavioural schema. That is to say, the outcome should be operational competency to think and act differently.

TOWARDS SUCCESS

BCM success can be thought of as driven by better human factors: clear and enforced policies, accurate behavioural procedures, processes enabling people to execute tasks, tools to create efficiency. It is also driven by stronger organisational alignment: knowledgeable senior end users; effective resourcing; links to core organisational aims; a commitment to the long term. It should display the rules of business: greater financial rationale; tighter alignment with business process; functional not just reassurance outcomes; clarity and maturity of risk and impact measures.

Where BCM pre-exists in an organisation, the design of a resilience system will need to be a process aimed at evolution not revolution. This should continue to recognise the clear space between the concept of continuity and the concept of resilience outlined in Chapter 6. However, organisational experience of BCM will be too powerful to ignore. Where factors to frustrate its success have built up, those are likely to beset resilience too. Conversely, the factors above which promote its success are, in fact, the factors which would ensure its evolution into a business engine.

Our main conclusion is that if you can evolve BCM thus far, then you place it, conceptually, not very far at all from being an ideal template for a resilience system.

CHAPTER 12

Resilience and other legacy systems

This chapter will continue with our pragmatic theme as we create the building blocks for the creation of risk management and operational resilience systems in a modern, large, distributed organisation operating in a VUCA environment. This will be in order to help us to continue to consider all of the practical implications of a central question in this discipline:

Where does an evolved resilience risk reasoning system belong when one takes into consideration all of the other legacy risk systems in a large organisation?

By using the term legacy systems, we are referring to any number of a range of possible risk reasoning systems that are already present in an organisation. One obvious example, as the last chapter examined in detail, is Business Continuity Management. However, there are several others: Issues and Incident Management, Crisis Response, Emergency Planning, Disaster Recovery (both in the geopolitical sense and in the Information Technology use of the term); and Pandemic Preparedness.

Particularly for the large multinational organisation, one would expect to see a risk management landscape made up from something resembling this list. So how does a resilience construct, like the one we have been discussing, fit into that schema? This is a question that is all the more poignant when one considers that these current systems may already be in historically quite uncomfortable jurisdiction relationships with each other.

We need to continue to practically examine this question for two main reasons. First, to avoid criticism of too academic an approach; to avoid being accused of considering resilience systems planning in splendid isolation from a true operational context; of proposing a clinical best case scenario, even though this is something which is practically quite unrealistic. Second, to keep using this title "system", at this stage in our argument, we simply need to begin to talk in less general terms. We need to begin to define real lines of demarcation that can help you, the reader, make sense of your business context and make real choices about the design and placement of a system specific to your context and not a general system in any (and therefore no actual) context. We must help you specify a system which deliberately informs strategic business decisions.

This chapter will be in two sections. The first, shorter, section will explore a case study that reflects on the positioning of a resilience system which was designed to wholly replace a legacy Business Continuity Planning system. This will discuss some of the actual trade-off mechanisms in a mature organisation that also happens to be one of the world's largest and most diverse companies operating in over 200 countries. The second, more detailed, section will describe a model of eight infrastructural decisions that large, complex, distributed organisations should address order to integrate resilience.

Our conclusion will be that without a requisite total systems approach, and the appropriate appetite for complexity and culture change this brings, the effectiveness of resilience will always be heavily compromised. Resilience, conceptually and practically, demands that the recipient organisation evolves its structures to support a formal reasoning chain.

REVISITING A METAPHOR FOR THIS STATE SPACE

L et us, just for a moment, revisit that helpful metaphor we introduced in Chapter 6 – that forced choice between an anti-lock braking system (ABS) and an occupant airbag system. In that example, if you chose ABS your reasoning might go something like this:

ABS is better than airbags because it is a preventative system. It is designed to stop the car from being in a crash in the first place. ABS responds to unseen threats, such as ice, and keeps the car under acceptable control. ABS is an assistance system, optimising the control envelope of the vehicle allowing it a broader sphere of safe operation.

If you chose airbags, your reasoning might go something like this:

Crashes are the single biggest threat to driver and passenger safety. They will happen. Airbags substantially mitigate the effects of all serious crashes. Serious crashes are close to inevitable and not safeguarding people from their effects is intolerable.

One side says it is better to avoid crashes. The other side says it is better to be able to mitigate their effects. If we were to pause this discussion and ask two related questions, an interesting new design constraint might be admitted to this discussion:

To team airbag let's ask, what is the relationship between your airbag, your seatbelt, your crumple zones and your collision bars?
To team ABS let's ask, what is the relationship between your ABS and your tyres, your brake pads and your sensor array?

To both we are really asking: what is the state space *within which* you are expecting your preferred system to excel? What we are driving at is that it is simply no good (even metaphorically) thinking about resilience and risk reasoning system options in isolation from the state space in which they are designed to operate. That is being too academic.

In the real context, two state spaces offer themselves for consideration. One is business as usual and the other is the company's coping strategy for (inevitable) business interruption. Business Continuity, arguably the airbag approach currently supporting most normal operations, fundamentally addresses the latter. It is a business interruption system. The value-add calculation expects business interruptions to be lessened by anticipation or mitigation. An observation that should quickly come up however is that it is not, of course, the only business interruption system – it is one of several. What about Emergency Planning, what about Crisis Management and so on? These are as much a part of the operating context as the business interruptions themselves.

ADDRESSING THE LEGACY SYSTEMS – A CASE STUDY FROM UNILEVER

Let's turn for help to a real example from a real global company. They made some choices that might surprise you. Following a global review of (the repeated Audit failure of) Business Continuity Planning, Unilever decided to design a forward-looking Resilience and Continuity system to replace it. This was the first decision point. Where does resilience interact with BCP? It doesn't, it replaces it. In replacing it, we still inherit the question above. An examination of the (complex) management structure (in policies and procedures) proved that this new system had to trade in a crowded marketplace.

Here is a second decision. Resilience and Continuity must address one of five classes of business interruption. Four other systems of command and control were also in play. The remit of the Resilience and Continuity for this company was therefore to sweep up into its capability all the functions of the existing BCP approach. However, that must exclude the following: Disasters and Disaster Recovery; Pandemic Preparedness; Emergency Planning; and Crisis Prevention and Response.

If this seems surprising, you might want to ask: what was the logic? The logic was simple and, as will become clear, answers several of the questions raised by our model thus far. This is in terms of fit with (pre-existing) strategy, governance, standard operating, tools, outcomes and Audit. Let's look briefly at the logic of each of the exclusions:

DISASTER RECOVERY

If the company has assets and people in a disaster-prone area (i.e. where such things are common) it is the responsibility of that business, under the Safety and Insurance governance of the company, to put highly specific local disaster recovery planning into place.

Resilience will occur inside that specific context therefore. Once the business has responded to the disaster, resilience is the wish to preserve and quickly return to normal (or enhanced) post-disaster recovery operations.

PANDEMIC PREPAREDNESS

Preparation for pandemics was specifically mandated by the company executive at a particular point in global history, that of the major avian flu outbreak in the early 2000s. Some might argue, with the benefit of hindsight, that the real pandemic, like the Millennium bug, was a pandemic of unnecessary worry. That aside, Pandemic Preparedness was considered the responsibility of the corporate business under the Occupational Health governance of the company. Every division of the business was required to have a plan (written, approved) and a prepared response (stock piles of vaccine, critical employee lists, etc.).

Resilience will occur inside that specific context therefore. Once the business has activated the pandemic plan, resilience embodies the desire to offset the medium-term impacts on continued normal operations.

EMERGENCY RESPONSE

Protecting employees, populations, assets and the environment from emergencies is mandated under the company's Safety and Insurance governance for all businesses – on the basis of risk. Every business therefore has to have a written, proportionate and appropriate site-emergency plan. This, where necessary due to the need for coordinated response, will be shared with other local agencies, e.g. fire, medics, police and so on – agencies with whom the local company will hold joint training exercises.

Resilience will occur inside two specific contexts therefore. First, to plan to support the return to normal (or enhanced) operation during the emergency cool-down. Second, to have interacted (perhaps through prioritisation of business value chain assets) with the "loss-prevention appetite" of the emergency risk assessment.

CRISIS PREVENTION AND RESPONSE

Understanding the likelihood, severity and consequence of a business crisis is the responsibility of every manager in the company. It is mandated by the Crisis Prevention and Response policy and procedures. A single formal process of declaring and responding to a crisis is mandatory.

Resilience will occur, as was the case for Emergency Planning (unsurprising since emergencies may become crises) in two contexts. The crisis may, itself, be a failure of planned resilience, i.e. a loss of control in standard (resilience) operating. Also, crisis response automatically calls for an enhanced short-term form of resilience planning to take place.

Why did things need to be made quite so complicated? The answer is that they already were that complicated to start with. They often are in large, complex businesses. Business Continuity Planning, as was, existed in this company as part of a history of the development of many risk control devices. The decisions taken around its remit were, by and large, a wholly informal and *ad hoc* response to evolving responsibility and industry practice. They were also a response to a blinkered use of standards (such as BS 25999–2).

Most large-scale distributed companies operating in a VUCA context are likely to find themselves in similar historical definitional complexity. Resilience thinking can come along, as was the case here, when many other risk control systems are mature and fully embedded.

IT IS POSSIBLE TO DEFINE A RESILIENCE RISK REASONING SYSTEM BY EXCLUSION?

Notice how each exclusion is logical on the basis of one of our key infrastructure factors: that of governance. All four areas of exclusion had already been written into the corporate governance. They had owners and responsible named individuals. They had Audit and reporting. If resilience were to come along and take the reins so to speak – because disasters, pandemics, emergencies and crises might rightfully fall under the purview of the definition of resilience – what would happen? Would Safety, Security, Insurance, Occupational Health and Corporate Secretaries' be required to hand over their jurisdictions? Would Resilience supersede all this pre-existing governance? Would it become, in fact, a meta-construct?

The conclusion, in this case, was to decide no, these other systems would not be superseded; resilience and continuity would need to be complementary. The fitness for purpose argument suggested that a new (proportionate and appropriate) governance and system would be required to meet the (profit and loss) challenges of needing to be resilient in the globalised VUCA environment – that need that was not being met by the legacy BCP approach. This replacement system was to be designed to address this as well as to strengthen all the other legacy systems, not supplant them.

For completeness, reflecting something like our Strategic Adequacy construct from Chapter 11, six other operational, exclusions to the remit of Resilience were in the formal procedure:

1 Sales and Operability Optimisation
2 Supply Chain Complexity Reduction

3 International Sourcing Strategy
4 Proactive Stock Keeping Unit Harmonisation
5 Manufacturing Core Technology Convergence
6 Manufacturing Interdependency

Those readers who work in manufacturing will recognise these, or similar things, from their global playbooks. These are all strategic business optimisers that, in one form or another, businesses use to leverage scope and scale. These too were excluded from a resilience argument simply because they were not deemed to be business interruption systems.

TABLE 12.1 Excerpt from the Resilience Handbook

Area	Owner	Focus	Governance Source
DISASTER (e.g. typhoon, bush fire)	Business leadership	Response to known disaster types of reasonable probability/experience	Health and Safety, insurance loss prevention
PANDEMIC (e.g. SARS)	Business leadership	Response to an anticipated or feared breakout of an epidemiological nature. A special case of Disaster Planning	Health and Safety
EMERGENCY (e.g. ammonia release)	Facility/ Asset director	Foreseeable and realistic threats to personnel or assets	Health and Safety, insurance loss prevention/security Procedures
CRISIS (e.g. loss of control of product incident)	Business Unit Crisis Coordinator and Procedure leads	Organisational readiness for the possibility of a crisis within the risk profile of the business concerned	Crisis Prevention and Response Framework Standard (and 6 Standard Operating Procedures)
RESILIENCE & CONTINUITY	Resilience Lead as identified level, e.g. Category Brand	Identification of company-critical business risks and opportunities, an appropriate and proportionate response including transparent cost of control and business risk appetite sign off	A cross-border sourcing solution for a brand-critical SKU

Here we see another of our key points from Chapter 11: resilience has to be business rational but it can, and should, be differentiated from becoming business as usual.

In this case study this huge global company took a very clear position on definition and, when you examine the result, you may or may not fully agree with it. This was to position resilience within the existing logic of its legacy systems. This excerpt (Table 12.1) from their Resilience Handbook summarises the rational very neatly.

In summary then, Resilience and Continuity Approaches do not encompass any classes of business interruption that are already covered by pre-existing alternative governance requirements. Rather they are designed as a business risk tool to help (the company): win in the market during a crisis, minimise business interruption from network disrupting incidents and drive growth through fitness to respond to risk and opportunity.

THE CASE FOR INFRASTRUCTURAL THINKING

Whilst this definition by exclusion above might be thought of as highly restricting, it may of course see greater organisational acceptance since it is not disruptive. It will highlight only a unique value add for any new concepts resilience thinking can bring to an existing system set – notwithstanding the conflict of jurisdiction that these other systems often mask. A key criticism we might level at Unilever's choices is that using the policy and procedure *status quo* was the wrong starting point. The existing operating framework was not being called into question.

A resilience risk reasoning system ought to be viewed through an operating framework lens. The effectiveness of large complex dispersed organisations is always founded on the fitness of their operating framework. Any new, or evolving, capability is in a relationship with four states of that framework.

From much risk and crisis management literature these are in a largely agreed continuum:

1 Normal operation: the execution (and iterative design) of the core operating model.
2 Incident management: the formal state of "problem resolution" for and identified significant error or threat.
3 Emergency/crisis management: the formalised suspension of some of the normal operating procedures to respond to a significant threatening event.
4 Disaster response/recovery: the overwhelming of parts of the entire operation by a, usually externally mediated, catastrophic event.

This taxonomy actually offers us seven placement/integration options for a resilience system jockeying for position with legacy systems:

1 Resilience describing the recovery process from extreme shocks to the business.
2 Resilience defined as the recovery process from any crisis, emergency or disaster that hits the company – a definition very close to BCP and BCM.
3 Resilience defined as supporting the management and recovery process from either incident, emergency or crisis response.
4 Resilience as a business tool set to enhance normal performance and also help strengthen the response – through speed, flexibility, agility etc. – to normal incidents.
5 Resilience as a tool set to evolve the business as usual model to make it resilient by design (directly and significantly preventing incidents, emergencies, or crises).
6 Option 5 as a prevention mode with a secondary response mode designed for the duress of emergency, crisis, or disaster.
7 Total resilience, all of the above prevention, response and operating enhancements integrated meaningfully across all operations and significant events lifecycle.

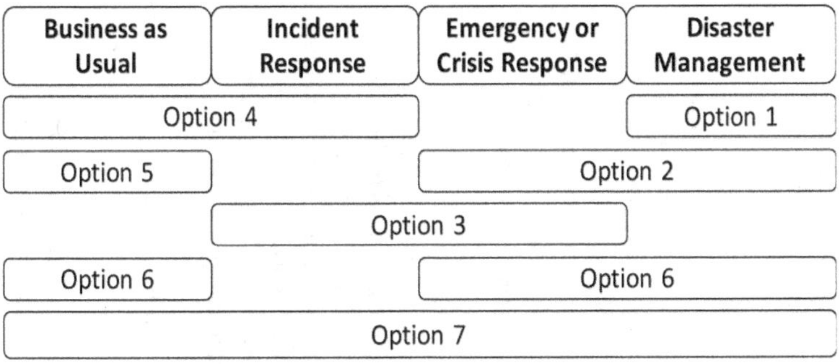

Business as Usual	Incident Response	Emergency or Crisis Response	Disaster Management
Option 4			Option 1
Option 5		Option 2	
	Option 3		
Option 6		Option 6	
Option 7			

FIGURE 12.1 *System positioning options*

The difference between these options might seem overly fined tuned but, in fact, they are real design choices that are critical for a focused system. By either design or default, your system will have to occupy one of these positions. They are critical because, even at this high level, they delineate the expected cognitions and behaviours of the human operators and the mode of operation for key decision makers – be this normative or extraordinary. Some of the ramifications of each resilience option are shown in Table 12.2.

Choosing the option is often a pragmatic operating choice. An operational response to some formal identification of vulnerabilities, such as the outcome of an enterprise risk assessment, has been required. The sacrifice of this approach is obvious – there is no clarity; clarity not just of what we mean by resilience, but of what we mean by all these other things and how they relate to, or evolve in the face of, a resilience construct.

This table shows us that the solution to resilience system positioning will not be found in operational semantics. The definitional architecture is simply too blurred. The compromises are too great. The function of resilience risk reasoning ends up falling uncomfortably between two stools, differentiation and embedding.

Differentiation – make it a separate system: like the FMCG example at the head of this chapter, you can be very clear about actively excluding

TABLE 12.2 Resilience options

Option	Main triggering condition	Mode of response	Main advantage	Main disadvantage
1	A disaster	Disaster recovery plan execution	Is reserved for only the most severe incidents when the company is in deep shock	For most companies disasters are rare and the overhead needed to maintain a live system will be questioned
2	Initiating emergency/ crisis plan or a disaster	Suspension of normal operating to react to/ manage serious event. Disaster recovery plan execution	Resilience thinking makes most sense when companies can see live disruption and feel the benefits from plans, decisions and contingencies	Disasters are rare; crises and emergencies less so. Fundamentally reactive. Crisis management mode may see itself as authoritative until BAU is restored.
3	Incident or escalation	Deployment of Standard Operating Procedures or preformed contingency/ emergency plans	Restricted to but empowered in out of normal operating conditions, can set the standards for behavioural control	Blurred boundaries with incident, emergency and crisis governance still leads to reactive approach
4	Normal business process	Strengthening the business through anticipating and preparing for predictable incidents	Occupies most of the normal range of business activity and so can be integrated into normative processes	Does not make the business resilient or continuous in the case of VUCA operating or affecting decision making in extreme conditions
5	None	Strengthening the business to maintain a view on operability and contingency as part of normal working	Integrated and accepted as a part of normal business	Not delineated as a distinct capability to enable extraordinary empowerment, prediction or mitigation
6	5 & 2 combined	Seen as normal process, extended to ramp up in critical circumstances	Incident management is a distinct operational discipline	Shared with 1, 2, 3, 6 & 7
7	"Readiness & Response"	A total system informing a proportion of all business modes	A constant set of perceptions and behaviours irrespective of the mode of operation	Hard to keep differentiated from normal operation and protect from compromises

resilience from existing operational areas. It is not the same as an emergency response, a disaster recovery, an incident management procedure and so on. It is something different. This still leaves it to be defined by negation and to be challenged to go on and create its own unique selling point.

Embedding – a component of all systems: alternatively, as the seven options above illustrate, you can incline to a sort of operational syncretism. This is where resilience seeks to be either a component, a contingency of or an available option set, to be used vaguely by all other modes of risk and threat response that support business interruption. The aim is to do this without causing any changes to the overall infrastructure.

Differentiation and embedding, in different ways, are both design by compromise with a *status quo*. When it comes to reasoning design for efficacy, this is really not the way to go.

CONCLUSIONS FROM THIS CHAPTER

This chapter has focused on designing resilience as a system in a triple context. One, that of being taken seriously in a business – not a hollow shell of documents and ideas. Two, that of being defined with a strict relationship to all other similar or affected systems that are already in a mature organisation. Three, that of being able to deliver a demonstrable business value.

We noted, in the Unilever case study, that a resilience system can operate as an upgrade for a historical Business Continuity Planning approach. To do this, it was designed from the perspective of how it tessellated with, but did not disrupt, the many other risk-based business interruption systems, such as Crisis Management, that were already in play. We considered this design by exclusion approach to be extremely limited. It did not seek any kind of synergistic outcome where the many approaches might be rationalised as to their aims, costs, benefits, operational burden and outcomes to the overall business.

We noted that this example really belongs in a larger class of design considerations. This is where all such systems interact with four system states for parts of, or the whole of, a business such as business-as-usual or incident response modes. For resilience design to speak effectively within this four-part model we found that two positions were tenable: differentiation of a unique additional contribution; and embedding of all the risk systems in a cross disciplinary hierarchical arrangement.

Although tenable and observable, these are both in reality design by compromise. Neither were predicated on system effectiveness and both should be rejected.

CHAPTER 13

Taking an infrastructural approach

I n the previous chapter we argued that, without a requisite total systems approach, and the appropriate appetite for complexity this requires, the effectiveness of a resilience system will always be heavily undermined. A risk-based resilience system demands, conceptually and practically, that the recipient organisation disruptively evolves its structures to embrace the capability and accept its implications on other systems. In essence to accept that resilience will be disruptive.

One way to accept this disruption it to seek to avoid a rolling operational debate focused on the purely technical differences between issues, incidents, crises, disasters and resilience. We propose that resilience risk systems, to add unique value to large, complex distributed organisations, have to transcend these legacy risk systems definitions. Resilience needs to be designed not as a synergy with existing capabilities but as a goal-directed strategy within the total triple business context of supply, value and reputation.

The evaluation of whether a resilience capability delivers into the value, supply and reputation chains of a business must be focused on a suite of

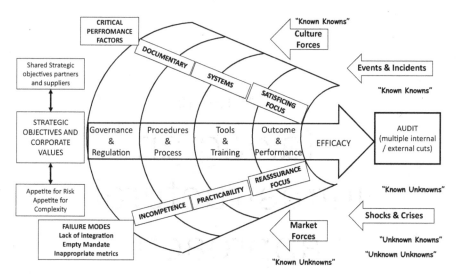

FIGURE 13.1 *Infrastructural support summary*

very few things in the end. These must not be compromised by trying to satisfying industry Standards or 'playing nicely' with all the other business interruption systems. It is important to accept that all of these will be disrupted to a greater or lesser degree by the presence of a resilience reasoning chain which itself has a complex infrastructural design to deliver business outcomes.

To make decisions around an organisation's tolerance for the complexity of its risk-based resilience reasoning system, we propose the eight-stage design process summarised in Figure 13.1.

1 STRATEGIC OBJECTIVES AND CORPORATE VALUES MUST DEFINE SYSTEM AIMS

A resilience risk reasoning system must be the natural offspring of a strategy and values exercise and formally incorporate these in its aims. All businesses are working with detailed strategic objectives reflecting track record and the desired gains described to shareholders. Current performance is always seen as needing to optimise to grow. A company's growth strategies are crafted and followed within a series of corporate values. This much we know.

It is a straightforward matter to read across from the strategy and the values of a company to set the high-level objectives of the resilience piece. Just as strategies turn into actions and values translate into behaviour (codes), resilience objectives need to do the same. Strategically aligned goals for resilience must be translated into measurable operational behaviours owned and monitored by the senior team. Resilience should be formally measured as a business performance and it should influence (future) strategy.

Any large, complex, distributed company strategy also depends, in part, on the strategic objectives of other companies. This is not confined to the world of competitors, which is of course important, but recognises that objectives are facilitated at some direct level by the output of other companies – the suppliers, service agents or target consumers. The behaviour of other companies in all ways that matter to corporate risk – legal, reputation capital, cost and efficiency to name a few – puts them in your supply chain of risk and resilience.

The resilience system that fails to examine critical external business strategies may not be making beds in a burning house. However, it is certainly failing to recognise sources of ignition. So, some articulation of the strategic objectives (and values) of critical partners is an essential part of the objectives, operating sphere and even ethics of your resilience system.

When the definition of resilience is so operationally abstract that it bears no resemblance to, or has no contact point with, this strategic context of the company it will bring no observable value return or, worse still, will create false confidence of protection for it. Infrastructural resilience should be a natural self-defence mechanism, facilitating/protecting the strategy, and also an enabler, to win in the marketplace through proportionate and appropriate measures to enhance business performance the presence of risk.

2 GOVERNANCE ISSUES MUST BE RESOLVED

A resilience system must be sufficiently coherent to contribute explicitly to the organisation's licence to operate by mandating its own authoritative and binding requirements. The external regulatory landscape is the invocation of a company's licence to operate. If you are a bank, if you are a pharmaceutical company, an oil company, an FMCG or a third sector group, there are rules. Corporate audit, finance, legal, HR and safety between them may soak up the majority of the heat. They are responding to external forces of the legislative kind (national and transnational) and also the practice-affirming kind (industry codes). If you don't wish to be prosecuted, or have your reputation capital destroyed, you play within the accepted rules. To do that you make sure that internal corporate structures are given the necessary jurisdiction.

Resilience needs to be one of those jurisdictions and this, as we have seen, is where the real fight for definition can get started. It is extremely rare for resilience to have stand-alone governance and any associated executive authority. Very commonly it is a governance orphan trying to make a home in several places at once, e.g. finance, corporate risk, enterprise risk, public relations, security, supply chain and so on.

Resilience needs a clear home in the governance landscape of a company, a coherent mandate and associated sanctions for non-compliance. It needs a well-defined and enforced position in the policy structure for the entire organisation.

3 STANDARD OPERATING PROCEDURES MUST ALIGN

Defining the impact of resilience across the existing procedures is a critical task. This is also the place where the complexity begins to increase. The governance cloud of the operational lens contains many different cuts on business interruption. These approaches have signed-off procedures associated with them. The interactions between these, and how to plan and check the effectiveness within a specific chain of command, must be coherent. When the procedures for resilience are written, these must be in a clear, conceptually obvious, relationship with these other requirements. It is a critical analytical task to ensure that the resilience procedures and all other relevant procedures are interlinked.

Too many textbooks and standards try too hard to envisage the sagacity and harmony of companies facing this task. The key to this is appetite for complexity. Standard operating procedures normally enshrine processes saying what people need to do. Processes also often contain threshold measurements to enable decision pathways. It is a critical exercise when introducing a resilience procedure to have extracted all the behaviours and decisions from the entire procedure suite and to look for redundancy, inconsistency, inefficiency and synergy.

The key to success in infrastructural resilience is an integrated system that is designed to be workable as a practical reality. Resilience is not an addition to that reality – it is a revision of it. The policy-ware, hard-ware, soft-ware, wet-ware must be intentionally coherent in the light of the cognitions and behaviours expected by the resilience construct and its procedure.

4 DESIGN TOOLS AND TRAINING HOLISTICALLY

Tools and training should be fit for purpose and convey empirical evidence that the resilience procedures and processes do penetrate the organisation. Resilience approaches develop a behavioural flavour when phrases like "proportionate to the risk" turn up. The people who are to execute resilience will need appropriate evaluation tools to judge what proportionate is. They need targeted training for the procedure set.

If your resilience tools are optimistically entitled a "roll out" but are only a communications package, or even just a document, this is not good. If your training is a self-administered online training tool, this is not good. Telling someone what to do does not empower them to do it. Resilience may be in a long line of other communiques from safety, HR, legal, corporate risk and annual performance appraisal. Sending resilience out into that desert ensures its near instantaneous death. Audit, the next time resilience is a priority, gets to play the undertaker.

A tool makes a task easier and its success auditable. A tool enables someone to seek the appropriate data from an authoritative and timely source, and it helps them to come to a recommended decision. Do you want people to assess risk to capital assets? Then they need a capital asset risk assessment tool from you. Such tools and the training to support them should be purpose built and fit for purpose. Too many systems perseverate around plan writing and audit. Consultants are frequently drafted in for this and off-the-shelf products may be purchased. Most of that effort and money is wasted in a cul-de-sac in expedience management.

Resilience will require you to actually build a comprehensive and bespoke toolkit for your organisation. Good tools and effective training are not the work of auditors who diversify – they are the work of tool designers and validated training designers from the Human Factors disciplines.

This increased complexity must be accepted as directly proportionate to the efficacy of the resulting system – a construct validity argument, not a face validity one.

5 MEASURE EFFICACY

When an organisation sets a sustainability goal on sourcing renewables, the efficacy of that effort is dictated not just by the proportion of renewables, but the costs of them and the uplift in social capital. Efficacy measures qualify intent and benefit and trade these off with cost. The design of that sort of measurement is easily within the skill of the organisation.

Resilience is a complex system, and its procedures, tools and training do make it possible to articulate what the behavioural evidence for system efficacy should look like. The outcomes have been pre-specified. Relative system performance should be measurable against some overall cost and disruption standard linked to the benefit of those outcomes. The design of that sort of measurement is not easily within the skill of the organisation. Very few professional groups can validate training and measure the long-term business penetration of behaviours. It is the work of an Occupational Psychologist or similar discipline. The confidence that people have in their hard-won resilience systems is essentially bogus when they design these metrics internally.

Resilience that is practical to do, founded on believable evidence, vouchsafed by credible professionals and proven to meet business objectives will be effective. These measures have to be in place – anything else might just be spreadsheets and pretending. The target of resilience is not, as we have said, reassurance that enough effort is being expended on resilience. It is the evidence that the effort creates business value.

6 CLOSE THE BUSINESS VALUE LOOP WITH AUDIT

The resilience system performance must be linked to a verifiable business value metric. Nothing as complex as a meaningful resilience risk reasoning system happens by magic. Although compromise might be essential to getting the task done, the task is not compromise. To be taken seriously in the long term you will need an evidence-based approach, you will need a systematic design with business chops and you will need to be absolutely convinced of the validity of what you are asking *all those other busy people* in your organisation to do for you. Frankly, people dodge that complexity bullet way too often by hiding behind terms like "signed off".

What you can do is push back against the design of your own resilience system, or the one you have inherited, and ask a simple resonant question: where is the tangible business benefit being measured and reported? Was money saved (or better used), were efficiency improvements made, have threats been cancelled or called out, were impacts mitigated, did the organisation perform better than before/than the competition?

A measurement system in your process must capture evidence that your system is, above all things, actually alive and working and not a paper concept. The effort in this measurement complexity will repay itself in a feedback loop with compliance. This is where a good relationship with insurance and with audit is an absolute boon. Spend some quality time with your insurers and re-insurers explaining the evidence to them. They will welcome the best practice sharing for one thing. For another it will affect their confidence in you and maybe your premium too.

Take your evidence to corporate audit and explain why it is necessary for people to perform well the tasks you are asking for. Give them the keys to understanding the risk–cost–benefit trade-off that your system brings. Explain why that would mean that it is massively more beneficial to your company than any 'react on the day' policy. Give them the testimonials of improvements, threat reduction, etc. above. Audit will thank you for making their job easier by helping them to understand what 'good looks like' in your world and being able to tangibly test it. They will then go out into your business and re-enforce your system exactly as it was designed. They will do this by the best of means – by putting authoritative audit pressure on people to deliver exactly the behavioural evidence that you want.

Linking resilience through business value to insurance and audit is a massive positive feedback loop. The benefit of clearly and unambiguously defining effective resilience at the business value level is that it causes your organisation to take it seriously.

7 ADDRESS PERFORMANCE FAILURE MODES

It is a critical design constraint to look for ways to build an effective system which nonetheless fails. In Human Factors terms, performance factors are an essential feature of any system. They dictate those critical factors inside your control which mediate the routine performance of the target behaviours. For an infrastructural design, three performance mediators are critical – documentary, systems and satisficing focus.

PERFORMANCE MEDIATORS

Documentary
So much of the intellectual control of the competences in this field rests on written guidance. It is critical to look at the sweep of the documents that hold up the argument. Are these integrated, consistent, of a high quality and with a declared shelf-life? The integrated nature of the procedures in the resilience system we are proposing is always subject to decay because multiple owners may update their procedures independently. One key tool is the use of something like a document fitness assessment similar to the ones we described in Chapter 11.

Systems

The applicability or interoperability of related parts of the whole
governance system – change over time. This happens when parts of the
system are changed and the impact of that is not worked through.
Alternatively, new systems are introduced, because of some exogenous
factor such as regulation change or a subject matter change, such as cyber-
security, and the impact on the quality of the resilience reasoning is not
worked through. There is no magic bullet for detecting this source of
decay, but a multi-disciplinary management committee for the whole
system is definitely the best bet.

Satisficing focus

Once a system is completed, it will have a satisficing focus. You can
identify it by asking how people satisfy this procedure, process, training
outcome, business measure, etc. Danger lies in a satisficing focus which is
purely driven by a high level set of Key Performance Indicators or by
asking whether things meet a highly generalised standard, like being up
to date, and so on.

If the satisficing focus is not linked to decision quality, behavioural
outcome, professional competence and strategic impact, then it is in
danger of being deeply buried and wholly ineffective at controlling
quality.

FAILURE MODES

In Human Factors, failure modes ask in what ways the normal operation
of a system can lead nonetheless to failure. The main failure modes for a
resilience system are not a surprise, they are: lack of mandate, poor
integration, inappropriate metrics incompetence and reassurance focus.

The lack of mandate, or an empty mandate, is where the organisation
says it wants to be resilient but it doesn't marshal any time, resource or
appetite for complexity to get there. Poor integration is where a team is

given the task of resilience but in isolation from the business in the ways we have already discussed. Inappropriate metrics come in the form of copy and paste KPIs at the wrong level of definition. Incompetence comes from not recognising that a manager trying to copy a standard, or something done in another company, or cherry-pick the best advice of a consultant to make it fit for size, to deliver the system is not being rational. Reassurance focus we have already covered at length; it is a failure mode when it becomes the dominant or only criterion for effectiveness.

8 INCORPORATE ENVIRONMENTAL FACTORS

Environmental factors, i.e. those factors which are critical to system performance but outside of the organisation's control, are hard to specify at the generic level because they depend on the organisation's operating context. They are shocks and crises hitting businesses at great cost and revealing little underlying adaptability – market forces and trends changing the fortunes of businesses where they have too little flexibility to diversify or modify their propositions; cultural forces, for example in attitudes to technologies, morality, environmentalism, etc., that play a deep role in company success and perception. These are a particular vulnerability in the VUCA environment where very different cultures specify very different tolerances for essentially the same behaviours, values or ethics.

Understanding and monitoring the environmental factors is an integration piece. It essentially aligns resilience with forces brought on largely by the reputation chain – and therefore requiring a direct link to horizon-scanning, issues management and crisis systems. It also seeks to align it with the value chain as an essential performance factor for the whole organisation.

TOWARDS AN INFRASTRUCTURAL APPROACH

In these eight ways (strategic alignment; resolved governance; aligned operating; holistic tools and training; efficacy measurement; audited business value; failure modes; and environmental factor mitigation), a resilience risk reasoning system can be well designed, elegant even. In all these eight ways, by omission or incompetence, it can be very poorly designed, doomed to fail even. The discussion in this chapter strikes back at the heart of three core questions for us. How do we build a meaningful risk construct? How do we build a meaningful resilience construct? What is the appetite for complexity of reasoning that a business has in so doing?

If it seems reasonable to argue that the systems approach we are espousing has now become far too complex, that is fair enough. However, the paucity of evidence that far simpler systems have the validity and the veracity to actually deliver on their mandate would be a stinging cautionary riposte. Large, distributed, complex organisations, particularly if they operate transnationally and in VUCA environments, can mandate what they like on paper. They can have appetites for complexity that are as delicate as moth wings. What does it mean in the end if your resilience system doesn't achieve anything except proving to yourselves and your friends that you can point to a system?

We would argue that resilience is not one of those things that can be bolted on to pre-existing governance or delivered by a concerted drive to get some plans in place. It needs to be infrastructural to the strategic business and, to achieve that, this eight-factor analytical approach has to be the work of a resourced, switched-on and professionally supported team.

CONCLUSIONS FROM THIS CHAPTER

This chapter has focused on designing resilience as a system in a triple context – that of being taken seriously in a business and not a hollow shell of documents and ideas; that of being defined with a strict relationship to all other similar or affected systems that are already in a mature organisation; that of being able to deliver a demonstrable business value.

We concluded that only an inherently more complex approach to this challenge would satisfy a sensible set of Human Factors, operational effectiveness and business value criteria without debilitating compromises. The only positioning of risk-based resilience that we believe will work to support the value, supply and reputation chains of a large complex business is for it to be in a formal and infrastructural relationship with the business strategy.

To achieve this, it needs to be a policy system, have integrated procedures and manage a (sophisticated and coherent) process which adds measurable value to the business metrics that keep these other chains justified in the eyes of the strategic business.

Although these considerations do add to the complexity of the design, we propose that they are essential for the efficacy of its outcomes. This means that the appetite for complexity in a business that requires a risk-based resilience system cannot ever be low. As the first design constraint this remains the greatest.

Summing up
Part 3

RATIONALE FOR COMPLEXITY

This section begins with some core rationale questions that you may be asking yourself at this juncture. Isn't this too much? Is there really the case for this new and more powerful kind of resilience system? Do organisations really need elaborate, detailed and time-consuming structures to protect them from the possibility of what are very rare events? Isn't this just making an industry for its own sake? For those of that persuasion consider this comparison.

On 11 October 1997, at the height of the Mercedes A-class debacle, Jurgen Schrempp the CEO of Daimler (who owned Mercedes) – who had been very slow to respond to allegations about the safety of the car and publicly criticised for his silence – apologised nationally; an apology that analysts predict reached 45 million people in the days before social media. He was commended in the national press for that contrition, and it was to be the public relations turning point of the crisis for Mercedes.

On 20 September 2016 the Volkswagen Audi Group began showing some contrition after a two-day lambasting for emissions cheating. Chief Executive Martin Wenterkorn ordered an external investigation and said that he was "deeply sorry". On 22 September VW now admitted there were 11 million cars worldwide fitted with its defeat devices. Winterkorn said that he was "endlessly sorry". On 23 September, he resigned, or, depending on how you read this things, was fired.

On 2 November 2017 Juergen Hubbert, head of Mercedes cars during the A-class crisis, in an interview with *Automotive News Europe* reflecting on the crisis 20 years on said:

> Today I am not sure whether you would be able to manage this successfully a second time. With social media, emotions enter the public discussion, and they frequently stand in the way of objective information and the solution to problems.
>
> http://europe.autonews.com/article/20171102/ANE/171
> 109997/mercedes-a-class-moose-test-crisis-recalled

The world of the 1990s was less globalised, less digitised and slower moving with fewer new paradigms based on aggressive disruptors. Back then, a passive approach to resilience, with some notable exceptions in the textbooks, may have been adaptive in its own way. Today's more aggressively pacey and aware world seems to make a worst case scenario feel more likely for the non-resilient business.

Reacting on the day in today's world can lead to loss operations, lost value and lost reputation and these can, with dizzying speed, give way to repercussive blame and a loss of trust. This is almost immediately reflected in the share price. This is almost an expected norm. It is certainly a feared one. A key thing to note is that a lot of the systems thinking around risk and resilience, and many of the prevailing attitudes and beliefs about it, actually dates from the 1990s and early 2000s.

We may need to have a complete rethink. Something more complex, to suit our more complex world, might be needed.

WHAT DOES AN EFFECTIVE RESILIENCE SYSTEM LOOK LIKE?

We began this third part of the book by speaking about the need for a distributed reasoning system approach to the design of resilience in large, complex and distributed organisations. By system we meant to convey a reasonably well-accepted definition of that term – one that refers to objects which are familiar in industry: artefacts like Standard Operating Procedure; behaviours like measuring performance; and tangible outcomes such as strategic decisions. By distributed we meant to convey geographical and temporal complexity.

Current resilience-type systems in these contexts, we noted, can be a response to the application of one, or more, industry Standards. More commonly they can be a collation, or indeed confabulation, of a host of historical risk control devices loosely compartmentalised into differing governance strands and reporting lines. What they always tend to be however, inescapably, is aspirationally complex upon inspection. Away from the easy rhetorical devices that encapsulate them, they are multi-component, multi-attribute, multi-stakeholder objects in a linked narrative, however occluded, with the many business systems with which they interact or upon which they impact.

Our examination of the relationship between resilience-type systems and industry Standards shows that the latter are not the silver bullet argument that, in isolation, their comprehensive authoring processes might lead us to expect. A hierarchical content analysis approach can be a very insightful method to expose both their underlying behavioural complexity and a potential business performance model that might adequately reduce that to a set of principles which could audit system health. The unintended commonality of these Standards encourages us to believe there is an underlying set of constructs. This way a system can be shrewdly cognisant of the challenges of best practices from Standards but remain an elegant solution to their potentially overwhelming combined demands.

WHAT ROLE DOES BUSINESS CONTINUITY MANAGEMENT STILL HAVE TO PLAY?

Business Continuity Management had to be considered in its own right in this discussion because it was, and in some settings remains, the dominant resilience-type risk reasoning system in industry. An observation of the factors that predict a systematic failure of this approach to protect businesses, more than in reassurance terms, highlights certain pathologies. For example, how unclear definitions, born of the need to react to threats, leads to the over-elaboration of an administrative demand focused on document creation. An outcome which distances itself from business process and metrics leaving it adrift from strategy. Leaving it to report impoverished key indicators based around an immature risk model.

A consideration of how BCM might succeed was also an enlightening discussion. In short, it might succeed if it evolved to take on more of the qualities of a mature approach to resilience. These included more authoritative governance and better tools and metrics design. Supported by greater senior attention, a real budget and a link to business decision making in the long term, a BCM approach could fare very well. We noted, however, that these conditions rarely accrue and such systems perseverate eventually on providing reassurance in and of themselves.

WHAT ABOUT OTHER RISK SYSTEMS?

Just evolving away from some of the key pathologies of a poor application of BCM is an insufficient argument to position a risk-based resilience system. To be better designed it has to tackle head-on the dominant question of its relationship with, not just BCM, but all legacy risk systems already found in organisations. This is a proposition which can quickly become quite obfuscated. Organisations can be shown to prefer paths of least resistance, such as definition by exclusion, hierarchical integration or partial hybridisation to seek greater face-validity. We note that, as none of these approaches gives an intellectually or pragmatically satisfactory outcome, they should be rejected.

THE NEED FOR INFRASTRUCTURE

In their place is an infrastructural argument that demands a resilience system be a *prima facie* strategic business system. Designed as such, it must function as such in an integrated way. It must actively support the value chain, supply chain and reputation chain of an organisation. To do this it must be, in both appearance and functionality, very much like these. It must have a strategically relevant position, an impactful governance (where it speaks directly and coherently to all legacy risk systems including cancelling some of them) and a concrete set of tools and metrics. These must be constructed to produce business relevant outcomes.

Furthermore, all of the metrics generated and reasoned upon in resilience systems must create a transparent efficacy index for the effort associated with running the system. This means that it will close out on a value creation argument – one, for example, which could convince Insurance and Audit of its business relevance. Care must be taken to situate the business objectives of the resilience system in a framework where it can be tested for when it begins to stagnate or fail. Finally, the impact of external factors outside of business control must be actively monitored for their potential to become system-destructive free radicals.

If a resilience system was to be designed with these very high performance standards in play, it would deliver a comprehensive value proposition to a large, complex and distributed organisation. It would also, by dint of being locked into real business value assessment, evaluate its own performance as an output.

Widely and currently, we note, the key determinant of the desire to have such a system is not this formidable long-term strategic benefits package.

Rather it is the pragmatic, and highly informal, cost–benefit analysis the receiving organisation undertakes when it decides whether, or not, it has the appetite for complexity (and therefore disruption) that the introduction of such a system would doubtless create.

A QUESTION OF SATISFICING

The mechanism to specify a resilience system is therefore a satisficing question. Satisficing is an interesting word – interesting because people often challenge it by saying, don't you mean satisfying? The two are related, of course, but in Decision Science satisficing has a formal meaning which suits our purpose very well. Suits it because of a specific nuance. It is a term attributed to Nobel-laureate Herbert Simon (1956) and refers to:

> A decision-making strategy that aims for a satisfactory or adequate result, rather than the optimal solution. This is usually because the optimal solution would necessitate needless expenditure of time, energy and resources.

What the very detailed treatments in this part of the book have tried to show is that designing a risk-based reasoning system for resilience in a large, distributed and complex organisation is a serious challenge to an organisation's desire for low-impact satisficing – one that legacy systems have, to varying degrees in our observation, failed to meet. It's a challenge that would need to be constantly guided by a process of recognising the trade-offs in an intelligent complexity reduction process, as opposed to rushing to an inarticulate simplification. To accept at all, in a large, distributed organisation, the aims of risk-based resilience systems is to accept that the complexity in question is formidable: that is just a fact.

Thus, the resilience system, as a consequence, has to be designed to be a distributed multi-attribute, multi-stakeholder system which is fluent in a range of simultaneous risk dialects. This way it can seamlessly service different strata in the organisation without aggressive aggregation. It must be highly engaged with the mature systems of the target business and their overall processes and outcomes. This way it can speak coherently to decisions that have to be made there to effect risk reduction or acceptance. Furthermore, the Human Factors argument has to be coherent. The expectation of operators has to rest upon a fiercely meaningful cognitive and behavioural, policy, procedure and process.

This complexity, and indeed the involved process of intelligently reducing it, is a battle of sorts to find the appropriate satisficing agenda. This is an agenda that, pursued too aggressively and too culturally, allows the fallacious reasoning of various complexity intolerant adages in business such as: 'let's not make great the enemy of good', or, 'don't build a Rolls Royce when a Mini will do'. Fallacious because they set an expectation which is based on preference not evidence. An appropriate satisficing agenda, pursued at the right level, actually addresses the two most significant challenges of any reasoning system, and particularly one for risk and resilience – elegance and fitness.

SYSTEM BENEFIT

Elegance of design and fitness for purpose allow complexity reduction, which is satisficing on the basis of system benefit. A meaningful reasoning chain supports actions and decisions to evidentially promote efficacy, offset risk, enhance social capital and add business value. Satisficing is not simplification; it cannot be seen as the same as intolerance for detail. It cannot manifest itself as the sort of mend-and-make do apology that professionals do offer in this space – for example, when they justify why a coherent measurement system is rejected out of hand in favour of one done with post it pads and voting instead.

This is not to suggest, for systems satisficing, that one is free from the challenge to avoid impracticability. The design must continue to function in the long term without the imprimatur of being an audit priority or the consequence of a major shake-up following and embarrassing crisis. The right design will satisfice inasmuch as it creates a stand-alone result which is highly practicable, replicable and brings a direct return in value for the organisation.

The same is true for documentary satisficing, i.e. the quality of justification and guidance, and this must avoid incoherence. You cannot prove that a policy works. Policies guide thinking and mandate behaviour – they do not "work". They satisfice inasmuch as their documentary basis is sound and contains strategic, practical and ethical coherence.

For evidential satisficing the audit mechanism must at all times avoid the faux reassurance of too high level a reference point – such as meaning impoverished KPIs. This responsibility rests very heavily on the audit design process, as it does on the intensity of its application. They satisfice inasmuch as they generate believable independent evidence of effectiveness that long-term behaviours and cognitions have been affected.

IN DEFENCE OF COMPLEXITY

We have concluded that resilience risk reasoning must be a (satisficing) system. In order for that system to be well designed, elegant and fit for purpose, a business might attempt a very robust opening conversation about appetite. To what degree has your business (maybe just the leadership) fully accepted what the Business Resilience of today actually needs to achieve? Does it recognise that it operates in an openly hostile world of trial by social media? Does it recognise that for this external reason, and, in fact, for many internal reasons presented by a complex VUCA context, it has to operate ambiguously? Does it accept that it needs to be formally linked to, and actively qualified from, business decision making? Does it accept that it has to be actively informed, at the cultural level, what risks constitute entrepreneurial, acceptable etc., at what times?

MODERN, EFFECTIVE RESILIENCE

Has the business environment been prepared to do modern resilience? Are the aims of the business aligned to the aims of its resilience process and vice versa? Has this been informed by a cost–benefit and volatility analysis? Are senior mangers holding resilience to account for demonstrating that it can protect today's highly volatile triple-value (supply, value, reputation)?

The modern resilience debate, and therefore the risk with it since they are inseparable, in this sense, is on a trajectory much like the one we observed for modern quality and safety. Both of those constructs have long been re-formed into "cultural" arguments. Creating 'a resilience culture' is perhaps a long way off for some businesses at this stage, but they will be perfectly comfortable with 'a safety culture'. The culture of the organisation is critical to the expectation, and the performance, of any resilience system it cares to specify.

To take an example, supposing a modern resilience countermeasure has, as almost all of them should, cost implications. What does the culture of your organisation say about adding business cost to increase resilience? This may cut right across the boardroom bravado that perennially (in audit season) says something is indispensable but then refuses to pay for it.

SATISFICING SUMMED UP

In summing up the satisficing arguments, appetite, business fit and cultural alignment you are helping yourself to reason creatively around whether your system will be a wasted effort. The acid test for that is simply the opposite position from the one we are arguing. We have given you the tools to spot a complexity-intolerant, business-irrelevant, culturally isolated system, and below are samples of them.

- knee-jerk simplifications in every element;
- a 'just do it' approach from gung-ho board members;

- the absence of real funding;
- or even real staff time;
- roles that have been tacked on to other busy job descriptions;
- the prominent belief that the end-game is a document;
- the lack of integration into any wider business process or strategic metric;
- the inappropriately robust measurement platform resulting in little more than agreement scales operating a high, medium, low mentality;
- a high-level audit based on stratospherically generic KPIs.

These are all to be expected and to be assiduously resisted. The reason we think these attitudes of yesteryear can be avoided today is because all of these factors are internal and controllable from within the business. If these simplification-hungry pathologies are controlled, the system has a chance to reflect the complexity of the organisation it is vying to protect. It will do this through creating a reasoning chain which interlinks with and supports the value chain, the supply chain and the reputation chain of the business.

In summary we are saying that an effective infrastructural resilience risk reasoning system will do that when you see:

- Alignment with corporate values and strategic objectives is demonstrable.
- Satisfying of regulatory and governance requirements.
- Alignment to the behaviours and decisions of all other pertinent standard operating procedures.
- Training is well designed and professionally validated (beyond the usual face validity).
- The outcomes which make the system effective to run should be measurable and measured.
- The business outcomes which mean the system adds or protects value must be measured.
- Failure modes must be explored and actively defused.

- Outside environmental factors must be understood in line with the use the rest of the business has for this kind of data.
- An audit which has been co-designed with the system to reflect its behavioural performance.

Once that (design) decision has been made, the critical questions become cognitive and behavioural. How does the organisation now get people to hold appropriate perceptions of this system and the time, data and effort it requires? How does the organisation support busy people to behave in a compliant and efficacious manner to apply the constructs meaningfully to their business decision making? How does the organisation commit assiduously to testing the material business outcome of the system to evaluate and evolve it?

That is to say:

A risk-based resilience reasoning system must be a strategic model of the real-time complexity of the business it is trying to protect.

BIBLIOGRAPHY

Specht, M., 2017. Mercedes A class moose-test crisis recalled. *Automotive News Europe*. Available at: http://europe.autonews.com/article/20171102/ANE/171109997/mercedes-a-class-moose-test-crisis-recalled (access date 16/01/18)

PART 4

Risk-based resilience reasoning chain

Introduction
to Part 4

MAKING THE REASONING
CHAIN WORK

This book splits into four parts. Part 1 deals with the construct of risk (language, systems, measurement). Part 2 deals with a risk-based resilience construct (design, challenges, reasoning). Part 3 deals with systems to support this (governance, process, efficacy).

Now, in Part 4, we need to address their combination. We need to understand how the more elaborate intellectual and functional architecture for risk and resilience reasoning we are discussing would support and complement the three chains in a large, complex, distributed business: the value chain, the reputation chain and the supply chain. To understand how we meaningfully integrate a fourth strand to their helix arrangement. To understand the value proposition for the design of a reasoning chain.

In the introduction we said, to answer these questions, that it is imperative that businesses go on a journey of design. We are some way into that journey already and this part of the book will seek to draw it to a close. Before we do that, it may be worth a recap.

THINKING IN CONSTRUCTS

Parts 1 and 2 were focused on how our three objects of interest – risk, resilience and reasoning – do classically operate today, and how they could better operate as (more) rational constructs – that is to say, objects which have been put together via some kind of deliberate controlling cognitive and behavioural narrative. A narrative founded on an architecture of academically validated understanding. Even if your organisation doesn't have the intellectual appetite to perform this exercise themselves they still, passively, have taken part in something like it. After all, the risk and resilience systems that you prefer to use have to have been constructed by someone.

Thus, our argument wrestled with these accepted extant meanings for risk, resilience and reasoning. It offered the tools to help the user to question. Question the validity of visible industry-standard uses of these constructs. Question the, frequently barely expedient, approaches which certain definitions tend to foster in order to be able to say that we "manage" risk or "create" resilience. These were approaches which we were heavily critical of in terms of their academic support, their derivative nature and, most damningly, the absence of any evidence base for their long-term efficacy.

USE EVIDENCE-BASED DESIGN

The solution, a design-led analysis for enhanced construct definition and a more evidence-based approach towards business efficacy, relied on intelligence from users. Users who could make up their own mind, from a suite of available options or from creating entirely new ones, how these constructs should be defined and applied in their specific organisations. A design solution that asks them to embrace and understand, rather than fear, the cost and the complexity of building a fit for purpose resilience risk reasoning system. Our top-line conclusions were conveniently, if accidentally, tenfold:

1 Risk should be considered not more or less than: *the optimisation of profit within ethical parameters.*

2 The validity of risk reasoning: *is always predicated upon the quality of the knowledge – of all types – being used.*

3 Operationally strategic risk: *must be semantically coherent and able to abstract genuinely meaningful behaviours from an industrial system.*

4 Operationally strategic risk: *must be measured in a scientifically valid way to give outcomes which have a demonstrable link to business materiality.*

5 Business resilience should be considered no more or less than: *the optimisation of operations within the appetite for risk.*

6 Effective distributed reasoning: *is in a direct relationship with system validity expressed as appropriate complexity and effective sophistication.*

7 The purpose of a measurement and management system for risk and resilience: *remains a question of stabilising a realised business value.*

8 When it comes to measurement: *if used, the probability component of any risk construct must always be applied rigorously and accurately, a practice which will require detailed scientific training to achieve and expertise to execute.*

9 Irrespective of your industry or your available effort and time: *always use an appropriate set of measurement scales to create reasoning data.*

10 Irrespective of your occupational background or the advice of others: *always apply the appropriate Statistics and Mathematics to produce meaningful complexity reduction.*

We concluded that risk and resilience – to be efficacious constructs for industrial reasoning in a distributed system – must form part of a formal reasoning chain. The prize from designing an effective risk and resilience system is always, and only, good reasoning itself.

THINKING IN SYSTEMS

Part 3 of the journey of design has been a question of appropriate systems thinking. When organisations are functionally or geographically highly distributed, this tends to greatly increase the complexity of any risk and resilience system. This is especially where attempts are made to standardise that system in the worldview of the organisation's head office culture.

CRITIQUE EXISTING MODELS

Thus, we called into question the veracity of the extant, and ubiquitous, models for resilience and risk one can observe in industry to date. These models are often uncritically viewed through a lens borrowed from high-risk organisation, civil contingency or military applications. The practices of these types of organisation are often uncritically accepted as best practices. This is despite their highly significant physical and cultural differences from modern industrial supply chains. This typical command and control approach seems, emotionally and structurally, accepted without question. This is despite its problem-focused character and its bias towards extraordinary reasoning in times of crisis.

We raised a critique of the silver bullet argument in this space, how (sometimes derivative, sometimes novel) industry Standards might be applied to risk and resilience systems. We noted a compelling lack of research evidence to support their efficacy. We recognised the ethnographic value in their systematic approach to wisdom sharing. We discerned, with a test case examining eight of them, that hierarchical content analysis and performance-shaping factor extraction were both very promising techniques to release that wisdom at a more practical design level. This releases it from a controlling narrative of applying a Standard as a system in its own right. This transforms it into a more intellectually subversive narrative of extracting principle components as building blocks for a user-defined context specific design.

In that discussion we also tackled the pressing issue of the presence of numerous legacy and forerunner systems to resilience reasoning that will be found in mature organisations. We examined two key challenges that these raise. The first, a cardinal theme of this book, is the trade-off between complexity and efficacy. The success and failure modes of systems like Business Continuity Management observed from an ethnographic perspective provided ample evidence of the need to address this as a primary design constraint.

The second challenge is avoiding attempts to situate a reasoning chain approach into the existing architecture of functional systems, rather than elevate it to the strategic decision-making arena. The latter is always likely to be a failure of hasty syncretism. The reasoning chain for risk-based resilience is a disruptor of all such systems. Its purpose is to evolve strategic reasoning at the infrastructural level, in the interests of protecting and enhancing business value, as integrated business tools not as estranged audit tools.

USE DELIBERATE SYSTEMS DESIGN

The systems design solution space here relies on businesses resisting the expedient cut-and-paste of any inappropriate and unvalidated models. Instead, it is wholly necessary that they perform their own active contextualisation of resilience and risk constructs, their intended meaning for, and intended integration with, the normative supply, reputation and value chains of a very particular business – a task for which they may require much deeper expert support. The fact that the complexity of this resilience system should, in certain key ways, reflect the complexity of the organisation it is trying to protect was clear.

Thus, the systems design itself must be predicated upon facing the challenges of an appropriate and expert complexity reduction. This is not, we must reiterate, to create simplifications so that they can be communicated more easily to senior, external or inexpert audiences. This is in support of a more disciplined form of business decision making.

This is in support of identifying effective behavioural controls. It is the outcomes of these processes, and not risk scores, that should really be being communicated in any case.

PROTECT SYSTEMS THROUGH SOFTWARE

This systematic complexity 'realisation and reduction' challenge introduces the case for standardising fit-for-purpose organisational practices into supporting software. This is nothing more or less than what organisations already do to standardise and streamline other mission-critical processes such as finance or quality. It is also particularly important because – when sophisticated, efficient and appealing software systems house the resilience risk reasoning process – the organisation can quality control the reasoning framework.

We should further note that automating key parts of a more complex analysis and reporting burden is an easy win on two key fronts. First, it seeks to make the process more appealing to its audiences. Second, it makes it far easier for them to now legitimately communicate the superior results. This commitment to discipline and quality prevents resilience effort from collapsing back into expedience over efficacy, and creates smoother technology transfer as an additional benefit. Both of the key points in the two paragraphs above ought to be targets for the design at the starting point in any case.

ENGAGING WITH REALITY

The focus of Part 4 has to be to bring an end-game in sight. Throughout this part of the book therefore we will want to continue to emphasise the necessity of formulating outcomes. These will have to meet the standards we have now laid out to form an authoritative and negotiated system as the only effective means of reasoning rationally. The best way we can exemplify this sort of system is to show you one.

Our final detailed case study will formally explain a complex template of ideas that have been successfully deployed in a large, complex, distributed organisation in a VUCA environment. The reason we say these are templates is to emphasise one final time going into these closing arguments that our book is intended to equip you to take your own journey of design. To help you recognise the need for and create the shape of the particular and unique design that will be required in your organisation.

This case study (chapters 14, 15) contains all the successful cognitive and behavioural strategies you will need to design and run a resilience system in any large, complex, multinational supply chain. It will showcase worked examples of the more mature and applied, reasoning constructs for risk and resilience we have discussed thus far. Examples will include enhanced meta-risk-based reasoning and bespoke supply chain risk types, such as common mode risk and performance-shaping factor judgements to predict outcomes. We will also provide evidence to demonstrate our own cardinal reference point for systems efficacy – a direct business materiality outcome modelling. This will contain impact scenarios, cost–benefit assessment, links to profit, turnover and volume and cost of control.

FROM THEORY TO END-GAME

This case study will also serve as the bridge to exemplify how, particularly through the support of a software environment, we can join the design components exemplified in Parts 1–3 of the book – that is (research) validity in the constructs, (operational) veracity in the data and decision paths and (business) verisimilitude in the system model.

Holding the costs, complexities and benefits of this real-life system in tension, we will use it to illustrate a fully working version of the reasoning chain concept. With that evidence in play, we will be able to say we are at the end of our journey of design.

We will then round the argument off by going back to where it all began and must begin again still. We will suggest that organisations cannot really design their risk and resilience systems to be in any way like this one, without first deconstructing their strategic goals for using the constructs in the first place (Chapter 16). Combining risk and resilience reasonably (i.e. rationally) like this relies on the users first creating a systematic justification of their organisational goals for reasoning such as this in the first place. That assessment needs to address the barriers to the effective business application of the outcomes of these reasoning constructs in advance.

This end-game requires the user to demonstrate an adaptive tolerance for ambiguity and a declarable tolerance for risk, both achieved through the filter of an active appetite for complexity. This requires users to functionally understand exactly how risk and resilience constructs are to be used and viewed within their organisational culture. Used to inform different beliefs at different levels, to promote different behaviours in different places and to support decision making in the centre. To close that argument, we will introduce one final analytical approach to support this deconstruction. A taxonomy to help systems owners evaluate, in its entirety, the operational goals that risk and resilience constructs are serving in their business.

GET TO THE END OF THE JOURNEY

Enabled by all of these arguments and examples you, the readers, will now have what we promised you at the outset of this book. You will have the tools and guidance to be able to fully specify a risk-based resilience reasoning system that is appropriate to your large, complex, distributed organisation. A risk-based resilience reasoning system that liberates you to rationally make critical decisions on the governance, processes, tools (including software), training and metrics that support your business – a reasoning chain. One that you can apply. One that you can continue to guarantee the working health of.

Your reasoning chain will be a system internally validated by its direct links to decision support, behavioural control and material business benefit

– either through loss prevention or capitalised opportunity creation. It will be a system that is materially linked to your business outcomes and expressed in their recognisable forms.

We will conclude the journey of the book (about that journey of design) by surveying once more in summary those two landscapes, risk and resilience, and the valley that joins them together, reasoning, one final time (Chapter 18).

CHAPTER 14

A reasoning chain example

In the very first case study of this book we dealt with a very common kind of applied industrial risk reasoning challenge. It concerned the risk brought about by large-scale change management in a single manufacturing facility. From that case study we drew several important conclusions about the advantages of taking a journey of design which broke away, on significant points (of semantics, abstraction, measurement and so on), from the received best practices.

However, given our focus on large-scale distributed reasoning systems operating across VUCA environments, you may be feeling a little short-changed. However complex the first case study was, it was just in one place. Where is our evidence that – in the normal operating environment of our, oft-mentioned, large, distributed, complex organisations in a VUCA environment – it is possible not only to manage resilience through risk reasoning, but to turn them into decision support for business material outcomes?

Having read the book so far, you might already be able to guess at the specifications of the system that would meet this requirement.

Or, in shorthand, specify a reasoning chain that could support the value, supply and reputation chains of such a proposition. Here is a summary of the six critical questions you might expect the analysis tools which make up that system to address:

1 Where is my critical operations and hardware network located?
2 What do I already know about risk in the critical locations?
3 What are my strategic priority Stock Keeping Units (SKUs)?
4 Who supplies my critical brands, and are they resilient?
5 Who manufactures my critical brands, and are they resilient?
6 Does my portfolio contain discrete or harmonised sources of risk and resilience?

To reflect on the sort of reasoning system which could integrate the answers to those six questions requires us to dive into a much deeper case study . . .

INTRODUCTION TO THE CASE STUDY

In 2013, whilst the Director of Resilience for Unilever, I was approached by a team from one of the company's largest and most significant global supply chains. Unilever was a nearly 50 billion euro company at this point. The category of manufacture and the portfolio of brands under consideration were globally pivotal to that value in the order of billions. However, this supply chain in question had been under considerable stress for several years. Contrary to Unilever's stated policy, some of the manufacturing units had to have standing operational crisis management teams. This is because crises of supply were almost a weekly occurrence somewhere in their "local operating world". We say local, but it spanned four continents.

This was an operation which was struggling for external control, struggling in fact to de-risk its supply chain and render it more resilient even in the very short term. Frequent escalations and warnings of the unsustainability of this situation had made the company's global supply chain leaders acutely aware of this. It was a high-risk operation, they could see that, so they did three things:

1 They continued to capitalise market growth and therefore increase production demands and push innovations along the funnel; business is unrelenting.
2 They put faith in much longer-term solutions, such as the building of a new flagship manufacturing site in another country in that geographical cluster. Although this was well underway it was still years in the future. Consequently, the operational teams did not see this as the solution it pertained to be.
3 They asked the team to adopt the newly designed approach to Category Resilience.

What you are about to see is a detailed walk-through of that approach, to protect Unilever's confidentiality, fictional data are being used. The walk-through will achieve several things simultaneously:

- It will be a real case from one of the world's largest manufacturing companies operating in a highly distributed way.
- It will consider the operation of a global supply chain in a clearly VUCA environment – South America.
- It will showcase a single bespoke integrated software system for applied measurement and reasoning which housed the entire approach. The system is called DescartesR.

The aim of this case study is not only to reflect the journey taken by part of Unilever to address those six resilience questions at the beginning of this chapter. It is also to attempt to close out the entire argument of the book. An argument which, remember, is not about building the academically or operationally perfect industrial resilience system.

It is about how you go about reconciling the appetite for complexity. This has to be commensurate with the risks being tackled, to reflect the actual complexity of the decisions being taken and to manage that argument in a way which relates directly to the value, supply and reputation decision making of the business.

It is about how you go about satisficing the definition, measurement, judgement and analysis complexity. This has to be elegant and fit for purpose. Where there are heuristic judgements, this is not a problem, if they are as rational and transparent as they can be. Where it is possible, there should also be factual data of a material and trans-material kind – the former applying useful statistics of the business materiality, the latter recognising the decision-making housing for its manipulation in time and space.

THE CASE STUDY

This case study reflects how an FMCG (Fast Moving Consumer Goods) supply chain is an even more highly complex and interdependent system than a mere engineering or business analysis of it might reveal. It required systematic risk modelling which mapped to that complexity, rather than risk KPIs that explain it away. Once again, to protect commercial confidentiality, the specific data is fictionalised whilst the magnitudes may be reflective where this is important.

This case is an involved, multi-stage, multi-agency and end-to-end risk reasoning system. That is to say, risk is evaluated all the way from its root source (frequently outside of the business) to an agreed business case (and agreed budget) to instigate controlling countermeasures. This in turn opens the door to supported decision making.

A WORD ON Q&A STRUCTURE

To support your reading experience, we will structure our summary of the argument to describe both the system and the process in tandem. We'll do this by using a Q&A format to simplify. You may recognise the questions. Naturally that structure is a little false. Underscoring what we have already said in Part 2, the real processes we are describing are already in a holistic infrastructure (policy, procedure, process, tools, training and audit). The performance factors and the failure modes were also dealt with in solid detail by the use of a resilience manual. Space precludes us from describing either for you here, but they are infrastructural to the design you are about to see.

A WORD ON PROCESS

The master process for resilience should not surprise you. It is as simple as the splash screen from the software shows (Figure 14.1).

The process is: assess exposure; understand priority; build countermeasures; develop business case for sign-off; and decide to follow through. The scale, of course, comes from the size and complexity of the distributed supply chain of a major category for Unilever, or indeed any other large distributed organisation. A large component of the risk comes from the VUCA environment.

SEVEN RESILIENCE QUESTIONS SHOWING A CONTROLLED PROCESS

1 WHERE ARE MY CRITICAL OPERATIONS AND HARDWARE LOCATED?

Global business categories usually work across several geographies. Importantly these geographies can be very different for the 'source' and the 'make' parts of their supply chain. The geographical and political conditions where you, your agent, or your supplier find raw materials will be wholly different from the geography and politics of the place you actually manufacture things from them.

FIGURE 14.1 *Process elements from the Descartes Reasoning system*

At this point we are interested in the Category critical hardware and operations for the 'make' aspect of the supply chain. For a business like Unilever these operations are much more likely to be wholly owned and operated by the company. Key factors which affect their operation need to be prioritised to help focus the initial resilience-modelling efforts. For the 'source' part, it becomes less likely that the company owns this aspect of the supply chain, and thus it comes later in the analysis.

This case study focuses on an analysis of the resilience of a particular category supply chain. Space precludes us showing you the other tools which interlinked several resilience forms – Category, Country, Criticality and Corporate – in the same DescartesR system. It is important to note that the Category assessment you are seeing can, as is clear below, access country-specific data and reason with it. Where this data is not there already, it is incumbent upon them to create it. The resilience of any supply chain operation cannot logically be independent from the resilience of the countries in which it sits. Anyone in the world who needed parts for their Toyota cars will have noticed this after Fukoshima.

The first Category tool is therefore a Critical Asset Profiling questionnaire. The business data this questionnaire draws up, you may recognise, is the kind that is often sought by Business Continuity Management approaches. It covers facilities (e.g. by type and strategic importance), employee numbers (with criticality), SKU production, presence of infrastructure (such as data hubs, etc.) and so on.

The result is a structured profile which will become an invaluable decision support tool when reasoning later about countermeasures. Some (fictional) data is shown (Figure 14.2).

Output 1
Is a list of countries and critical hardware locations broken down by their collective Critical Asset Profiles. Notice in the screenshot to the right here that it already contains some detailed analysis of the business criticality of the assets. This is essential to inform later reasoning.

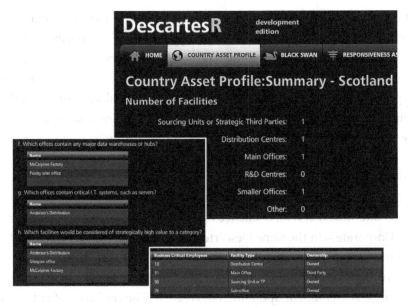

FIGURE 14.2 *Cutaway from the Critical Asset Profile (Business Criticality Section)*

2 WHAT DO I ALREADY KNOW ABOUT RISK IN MY CRITICAL LOCATIONS?

In addition to harvesting, or creating, the relevant Country Asset Profiles, the Category supply chain leaders need to either gather or create the outputs from two other tools in the system. These together complete the risk profile of the geographies in question.

Black Swan Risk

The first tool is a Black Swan Risk Profile. This uses a fourfold understanding of country-specific risk sources that might affect a supply chain. These are: epidemiology, meteorology, geo-political and geo-physical. As a side-note in 2018, when this book is nearing completion, we'd probably (in the light of Volkswagen and others) add a fifth type of Black Swan event of increasing importance in the globally digitised world: "ethical".

This assessment attempts to model the operational shock and strain sources for a particular supply chain geography. Whilst these may be very low-probability, very highly impactful, very difficult-to-forecast events, it is still essential to make a professional judgement to try and forecast at least the vulnerability.

To assess Black Swan Risks, recourse is made to commercially available data on the country in question. This is fed into the tool, including trends. However, that assessment is then qualified by an informed assessment of the true vulnerability of the company to that events stream. Sometimes this is dead centre with the analysis. Other times the company has unique management in play. This variable adjustment factor recognises that companies which have been around the block a few times in a territory might very well already be aware of a risk portfolio for the region. They may be seasoned to it and managing it rather well. We'll see more of this logic in later tools as well.

Nineteen data points in all are researched per country (from security and crime, to fire and flood, to community robustness). A cutaway of the final analysis is displayed as follows (fictional data shown).

Output 2: Black Swan Analysis

Current resilience assessment

The second geographical risk profiling tool is designed to assess endemic resilience. As we mentioned a moment ago, a company may have been operating in an environment, even an unstable VUCA environment, for a long time. They may have learned over that time how to survive and thrive. There is a need therefore to test that endemic resilience level prior to hastily planning countermeasure interventions to reduce risk. This is a critical cultural referencing tool which bridges that gap we discussed earlier in relation to VUCA environments. The central strategic thinking location may be in a head office that is situated in a wholly different geography. The ethos and values of the company may be culturally at odds with some of the locations in question.

FIGURE 14.3 *Cutaway from the Black Swan Risk Tool*

The test for endemic resilience we call Responsiveness Assessment –
named after the similar Supply Chain design concept. Critically,
of course, the data has to be provided by a team local to the
environment.

The tool for this assessment is called the Responsiveness Assessment
Tornado. So called because, unlike the Black Swan bar chart output
above, this tool priority orders scores into a tornado diagram. This data
in this case is based on a bespoke supply chain questionnaire designed
specifically for this FMCG environment. It asks thirteen questions –
for example, looking at the relative ease with which a key SKU could
be substituted with a similar (or even identical) SKU from another
part of the global business.

Importantly, the responsiveness assessment calls for a judgement from experts of both "the now" status of the business and "the future". This not only recognises our earlier point about risk metrics needing to avoid being too static, but it also helps give a cue to the business about how solvable a block to resilience might be. The results of the thirteen questions are rolled up into a tornado diagram (Figure 14.4; fictional data shown).

Output 3: the responsiveness assessment tornado

Please see Figure 14.4.

3 WHAT ARE MY CATEGORY STRATEGIC PRIORITY SKUS?

Although this question appears here, sharp observers might note that it could have been the very first question in this system. Indeed, this is often the seed question for a lot of supply chain risk reasoning. The establishment of a critical portfolio is a very centring exercise for a complex business. This explains why it is a frequent question around the annual strategy planning table.

All large manufacturing businesses, like the one in question, have a SKU portfolio, i.e. all the different unique things they make and sell. Portfolio is the right word to describe this state of affairs. Although businesses make a lot of things they, clearly, have higher and lower performing ranges by product and by geography. As well as this, they will have marketing plans in play for current and future priorities. Typically, one can see 50–60% of the profit of the critical portfolio coming from maybe 10% or less of its SKUs. Of course in a large, complex FMCG, that 10% may amount to 100–150 SKUs. Typically, sets of those SKUs will be housed under formats, e.g. brands, or the core technologies that create the product value, or both.

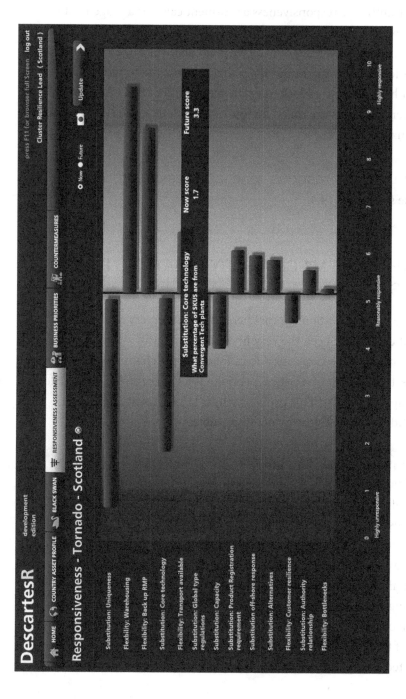

FIGURE 14.4 *The Responsiveness Assessment Tool Output*

Any evidently high value portfolio also monitors other business statistics and aspirations, such as innovation and volume targets. Also, if the operation is highly centralised on cost, then the key SKUs will likely be manufactured in very few places. If there is significant growth, under-production or capacity pressure in these sites, SKUs may be manufactured by licensed third parties. All of these factors are highly risk-relevant.

What we are saying at this point is twofold. First, we want to recognise the complexities in this question, whilst sparing you too much detail about them. Second, however, we want to point out that the answers should be native reasoning to a complex business. Nothing in the question: *what is my critical portfolio (and why)?* is a unique ask or additional analysis just because you are asking it in order to reason about risk. This thinking should *already* be there. This is a key principle we want to underscore at this early point:

A solid risk and resilience analysis system should be extracting existing high-utility business data more than it is generating the need for new data.

Answering this criticality question is simply part one of a two-part consideration for a business. Put simply it asks: what do you want to protect (what is the list of critical SKUs present and future)? We should note with great interest that any SKUs which don't make that final cut will be protected either by endemic safety nets, or by none at all. This is a deliberate manifestation of risk tolerance.

Part two of the SKU portfolio consideration for a business is establishing the value of it. SKU criticality estimation is not solely based on just financial value, as we have seen. However, arguing to spend money to protect a portfolio will be greatly helped by knowing its value. The investment in protection (resilience), when it comes to a business sign-off, will be a cost–benefit analysis.

That said, in a real business the value question has a subtler answer than one might first think. Thus, portfolio value is assessed in our approach in three key ways:

1 What is it worth (Profit, Turnover and Volume are the accepted value metrics)?
2 How is it distributed (some target level of customer provision)?
3 How tolerable (under conditions of incident or crisis) is a drop in that market provision?

Notice that point three is not only a critical question to answer, but it now changes the portfolio value. If the market provision is less in a crisis, then investing in crisis prevention has to be calibrated on that value at risk, not on the neutral value of the portfolio. Risk in this case is beginning to work with a banded severity argument, and this is critical for supporting later business reasoning.

Notice too that the derivation of this portfolio has become a serious piece of business analysis. In a medium to large company this would have to be the work of a team of specialists. In the interests of brevity, we won't outline the detailed process they would have to follow, but suffice to say it involves workshop, canvassing, expert voting, prioritisation, value estimation, business metric collection and perhaps even seeking additional expert commentary – for example, to consider SKUs that have historically high performance only in particular countries. This is not a high–medium–low spreadsheet exercise conducted in a single meeting.

The quality of this portfolio will not only determine the quality of the risk assessment, but all manner of other things, like data burden and workload. These have to be actively managed in the risk assessment contract. This is tolerance for complexity in action.

On the upside of that workload argument lies this key fact. Any modern competitive business that does not have the data to answer these questions, or perhaps even the answers themselves, has an operationally poorly performing business. Note the high level of strategic focus that the output of this analysis (fictional data shown) already creates. There is no clearer point of focus for a business decision maker than a set of business data analysed for an impact scenario based on hard cash.

Output 4: the portfolio value statement

Set Service Levels - Scotland

Material code	SKU		Resilience GP	Resilience T/O	Resilience Volum
134587	Format 1 Halo		255,637	446,398	22,795
9874632	Format 2 Halo		215,516	649,753	31,319
4555599887	Format 3 Halo		268,789	740,974	40,911

GP	T/O	Volume
433,283	756,606	38,635
267,722	807,146	38,906
426,649	1,176,150	64,938
746,120	1,098,092	547,713
415,121	1,158,719	237,925

Dispatch Rate %	% Crisis DR	% Incident DR
88	48	70
97	74	87
95	39	87
95	67	78

Resilience Profit	Total	38,299,500	Crisis	26,805,437	
Resilience Turnover	Total	82,896,401	Crisis	57,440,482	
Resilience Volume	Total	8,999,360	Crisis	6,407,578	

FIGURE 14.5 *Typical data in the portfolio value statement*

4 WHO SUPPLIES MY CRITICAL BRANDS AND ARE THEY STABLE?

The portfolio exercise above is an involved data analysis exercise using expert judgement around real business metrics. All of the metrics have an important contribution to make to the mental model of risk (or the match between it and the model of the business) in the eventual business decision maker's mind. Portfolio is a validity question.

The supplier stability question, however, it became clear, was not at all like that. It was a matter of real-time expert judgement in the live operation. It was a *who knows* question, not a *what is known* question. It was an example indeed of that naturalistic decision-making skill we highlighted in the reasoning chapter.

What we found during development was the data that surrounded suppliers, although critical to operations, was uninformative for risk purposes. The knowledge of supplier fitness we required could only be captured from asking a panel of experts in the operations some pretty fundamental questions. A working model of a supplier was a highly ethnographic object in a business. It was an expert judgement, not a data-driven exercise *per se*.

Prioritising suppliers is an exercise which leant itself to a multi-attribute questionnaire. We deployed a parallel system that had been designed at a separate time for prioritisation exercises called DescartesNeo. Working with an expert team, we created a heuristic judgement set taking advantage of the power of the DescartesNeo system to deliver a rich picture to support reasoning.

A sample of the high-level topics is shown (fictional data). Notice that in line with the prioritisation grammar is the visualisation of a plot for further reasoning. The multi-attribute questionnaire rolls up into two key variables – supplier performance and the flexibility of supply (Figure 14.6). Notice also, like the responsiveness assessment, that these judgements are being recorded for a present and future argument.

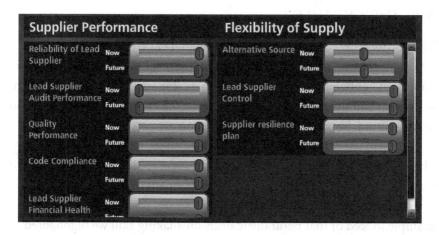

FIGURE 14.6 *Example of supplier performance scale output*

A key advantage of the DescartesNeo assessment platform is found in the fact that these assessments are made by a panel of experts. Resolution of the differences in scores taken into account (a key step in the use of expert judgement in risk reasoning) and the rolled-up assessment of various prioritisation cuts are now available in the DescartesR platform as a completed item. This process is designed to be as long or as short as needed. It should be a group scoring exercise or it can be an individual expert. An individual user, scoring perhaps thirty key suppliers, would expect that analysis to take around 2 hours in the first instance. Updates over time would take minutes. The owner of a group scoring exercise would need to budget a half a day of their time to reconcile differences in scores and settle on a definitive position.

Output 5: summary of supplier vulnerabilities prioritisation

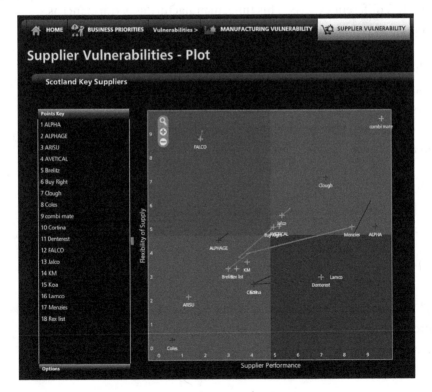

FIGURE 14.7 *Visualisation of comparative supplier performance*

Notice too the ability of this analysis to prioritise and highlight problems. The spread on the two scales is clearly high. In the real case certain critical suppliers were in highly vulnerable positions on this analysis. As such, it served as a formal way to focus the business attention on some of the unsustainable features of this supply chain design that were the root causes of such regular recourse to crisis management. It formally validated the risk burden of the operation.

5 WHO MANUFACTURES MY CRITICAL BRANDS AND ARE THEY STABLE?

A mirror exercise to the supplier fitness indexing shown above is now required to establish the stability the manufacturing base. DescartesNeo is again used. A heuristic expert judgement questionnaire remains the tool of choice. Of course this is a different questionnaire. It was designed, by and for, different experts. This time, manufacturing performance is compared to manufacturer resilience.

These attributes remain that same blend of objective questions (such as Capital Expenditure) and subjective ones (such as beliefs around Human Resource management). The result is a sister analysis to the one above. The same tool and approach generates a different set of reasoning inputs in a standardised format for decision makers to evaluate.

Output 6: summary of manufacturing fitness prioritisation
Please see Figure 14.8.

6 IS MY PORTFOLIO UNIQUE OR HARMONISED?

This is another of those questions that could have appeared earlier in the process when the portfolio was being identified. It appears here because the process we are explaining is, as we have indicated already, actually a little more iterative than we are leading you to believe with this Q&A device.

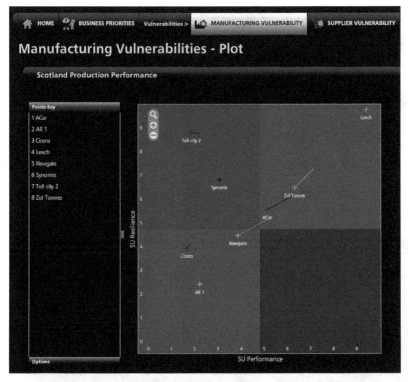

FIGURE 14.8 *Visualisation of manufacturer performance*

Profiling key uniqueness and harmonisation drivers is a critical exercise. They are a key determinant of the impact of business disruption to a Category. When something cannot be made or supplied because it is highly unique, consumers make other choices and the company can very quickly lose volume and even market share. When something is highly harmonised across a production chain this can be advantageous, but it also brings considerable problems of supply chain flexibility. Thus, these bespoke analyses are really two sides of the same coin.

Output 7: uniqueness and harmonisation results
Please see Figure 14.9.

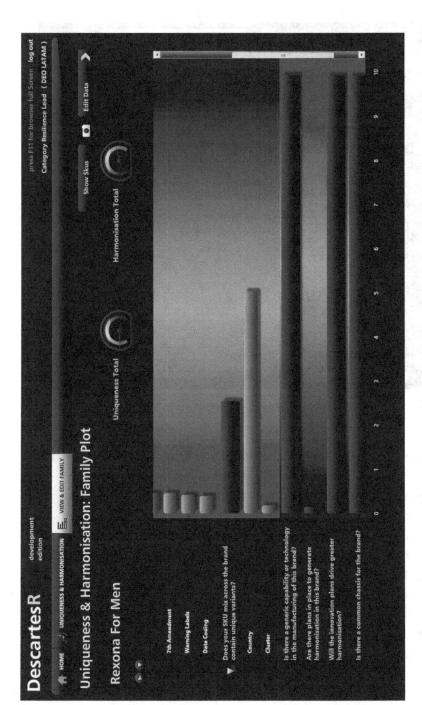

FIGURE 14.9 *Visualising key risk sources – uniqueness and harmonisation*

Similar in format to the Responsiveness Assessment, uniqueness and harmonisation are two expert questionnaires which have been designed, in this case, to focus on FMCG manufacture.

Similar in design to DescartesNeo assessments, the factors (shown in grey) roll up into attributes (shown in brown). This way, reasoning can take place at different levels of detail at different times.

7 DOES MY PORTFOLIO SUFFER FROM COMMON MODE RISKS?

The Common Mode Risk Assessment is both a recap and a mop-up exercise in this risk assessment. A common mode risk is a source of disruption, threat or uncertainty that is germane to the whole operation. As the name suggests, it is a common mode that the business could find itself in which would disrupt or support the total risk control prospectus.

Many of the tools used by this time will have been flagging up candidate common mode risks. For example, the Black Swan Risk Assessment might highlight an energy crisis or a currency devaluation. The Supplier Fitness Profile might highlight a chronically under-performing portfolio supplier. What the Common Mode Risk Assessment does is apply a structured questionnaire to identify all the remaining (commonplace) common modes that have not been picked up in these other analyses. For example, examining the materiality of a small amount of raw material that is nonetheless common to the majority of the SKUs and has only one supplier.

Output 8: common mode risk summary
Please see Figure 14.10.

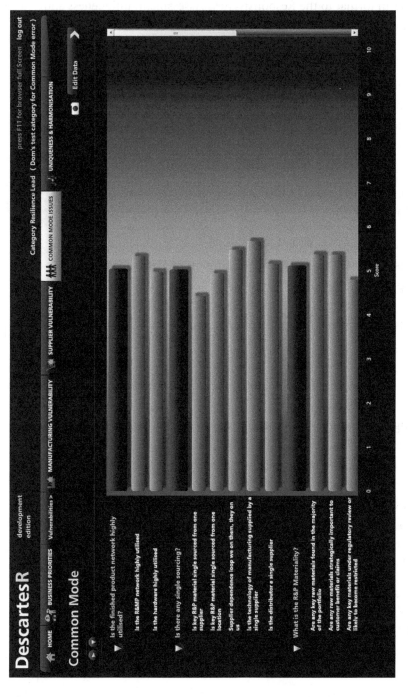

FIGURE 14.10 *Visualising key risk sources – common mode*

SUMMARISING THE CASE STUDY SO FAR

Although this is, necessarily, a whirlwind tour of tools and process, what you have seen is a resilience risk reasoning system for a large supply chain in distributed system operating in a VUCA environment integrated into a software solution. Or, in shorthand, a reasoning chain.

Table 14.1 provides a summary of all the questions and the analysis tools which can make up that system

See whether you can detect, in the eight tools that we have in this walk-through, our satisficing argument.

1 Objectivity: the tools vary to fit with the purposefulness of the question (can it be answered logically or only as an expert judgement).

TABLE 14.1 Resilience risk reasoning system: questions and analysis tools

1	Where are my critical operations and hardware located?	Critical Asset Profiling questionnaire
2	What do I already know about risk in my critical locations?	Black Swan Risk Analysis Responsiveness Assessment questionnaire
3	What are my Category Strategic Priority SKUs?	SKU prioritisation exercise and valuation
4	Who supplies my critical brands and are they stable?	Supplier Fitness Index evaluation
5	Who manufactures my critical brands and are they stable?	Manufacturing Fitness Index evaluation
6	Is my portfolio unique or harmonised?	Uniqueness and harmonisation driver assessment
7	Does my portfolio suffer from common mode risks?	Common Mode checklist tool

2 Modelling: they are able to model with real objective data (e.g. actual financial projections). When this is not possible they are able to mine for and blend in expert judgements.
3 Rationality: expert disagreement is resolved in a rational and transparent way (these are team tools).
4 Heuristics: in the absence of a comprehensive analytical model (because of time or feasibility) they use heuristic models.

The recurring theme in that summary is that of building a model. These are modelling tools, and this highlights a critical purpose of their design. It may not have escaped your attention that, in order to build these models, what has happened is that the resilience team has already set out on an involved reasoning exercise. A key deliverable of this sort of process is the enhanced reasoning (chain) that becomes a given of its use.

This commitment to a reasoning chain as a prerequisite of the analysis and its benefits cannot be emphasised enough. This is yet one more reason why the delivery of this process in a single online tool available to all players is a critical determinant of its successful transfer into operational practice.

Also clear is the benefit of the commitment to reasoning. By finding and evaluating the data required by these models, the team has greatly enhanced and shared its knowledge of the risk landscape faced by the supply chain. In this way they have already begun, by dint of the operational validity of the questions, to create its controlling narrative. From the perspective of the Human Factors of group reasoning and organisational decision making, the importance of this effect simply cannot be overstated. The key purpose, in fact, of these tools is all of the reasoning they create, not just the outputs they deliver.

It is only once that (total) reasoning is healthily underway that the outputs of these tools become compelling. The community that owns the reasoning chain not only believes in its outputs, but has evidenced this by deliberatively aligning them to the supply, value and reputation chains as a distinct part of the process.

CONCLUSIONS FROM THIS CHAPTER

What has happened in this case study is a much more sophisticated version of what happened before in the others. We have moved risk out of the abstract aether of trying to make it a thing that exists independently of a business materiality question. We have also completely ruled out making it into a simple list of things that don't tie up in the end.

Instead, discern how this case is both the genesis of, and therefore an expression of, the design rules set out in this book. By applying standards for semantics, abstraction, measurement and materiality, "risk" has taken a highly functional and radically meaningful shape for this industry. It is of course a complex shape – a blend of facts, data, judgements and heuristics. However, that is entirely scientific and necessary. The shape of this risk analysis now reflects the complexity of the system it is trying to protect.

By that same argument, the resilience proposition to address these risks has also taken shape. It, too, is complex but now it is representing a future state for that industry which is better able to manage specific and material risks. More than this, it is fundamentally more efficacious at stabilising and improving its real-time business value delivery. This is done through appropriately sophisticated reasoning linked to actual business objects. This linking, as much as possible, is through routine controls, not the extraordinary language of threat or crisis management.

The impact that resilience countermeasures will have on observable profit, turnover and volume outcomes is the critical output of this system, not the abstract language of priority risk. This richer, and more business-focused, resilience is, however, clearly predicated upon the quality of the risk reasoning. The quality of the risk reasoning has been built out of business behaviours and cognitions which are, above all, transparent and meaningful to the system host.

Risk and resilience reasoning in this system directly affects the actual decision making of the business. This will be in a range that goes from highly strategic to enormously tactical decisions fed forward into the routine operations on a needs basis. Most importantly, that decision making can therefore be shown to be material to the operation (normal and under crisis).

Thus, we have a proper resilience argument predicated on a meaningful risk argument supported by rational reasoning and housed in a system that is authored into the business reference grammar that the organisation already uses.

This is proof that a risk dialects approach can work in a large, distributed, complex system to deliver a consequential rather than cautionary resilience construct in business-as-usual terms.

Proof that it is not that hard to do this after all. The question is, what's keeping you from designing your own system aligned to your business reality using these same principles?

CHAPTER 15

The 'so what' moment

This chapter will be a second, shorter, consideration of the case study in the last chapter.

The evaluation activity we saw there, you will agree, was as comprehensive as the most exacting standards in this book would have called for. The risk and resilience, as constructs, were very well defined. They were clearly being fed by real business data. They were very clearly linked to relevant business decision points. The reasoning system at the centre of the design was not only enshrined in a totally self-contained software package, but this was purpose designed. Designed not by assuming the authority of a Standard or an off-the-shelf approach but in an Organisational Psychology-led multidisciplinary research exercise supporting supply chain subject matter experts.

Mediated by the software both supporting and housing the outcomes, detailed online and offline work by a specifically selected multidisciplinary team (itself an indication of an increased appetite for complexity) could be integrated. Orchestrating team and individual reasoning tasks in this way resulted in a logical process of interrogation of a well-defined supply chain risk set. Seven core questions addressed themselves to multiple interdependent layers of expert deduction.

The conclusions were never reduced to abstract judgements of likelihood and impact and associated serially remedial actions. Rather, these preferences, judgements, answers, values and confidence intervals, in multi-attribute combination, form the shape of a three-dimensional resilience risk reasoning analysis. The result was a set of evaluations predicated on holding a raft of detailed multidisciplinary subject matter knowledge in tension with discrete strategic decisions. To arrive at this tension point, it was a given that these strategic decisions have to become business outcomes. They have to be actionable, not aspirational.

FROM EVALUATION TO (BUSINESS) ANALYSIS

There is, therefore, still a final step to move from evaluation to analysis. It remains of critical importance that all this complexity – these cases, decisions, actions and trade-offs to protect the defined business value at the centre of the model – must be reduced back into a communicable stratagem. The findings have to be in the working language of the additional business decision makers who need to be involved post analysis. By that, in the large, distributed, complex organisation, we will be referring to senior leaders and budget holders.

This is a target audience for the analysis who would only be involved at the periphery of it, if at all. Thus, now that the complexity of it has been comprehensively and scientifically redacted by the expert team, this resilience stratagem must be rearranged to answer just one critical business question that this audience will pose: the 'so what' question.

A SINGLE COUNTERMEASURE WALK-THROUGH

In the language of the governance system at the centre of this resilience approach, the agreed terminus for all this reasoning behaviour was termed a resilience countermeasure. In fact, a large organisation trying to de-risk a supply chain of this complexity amid a portfolio of risks such as these would require a whole series of them. Although we have yet to examine their creation, the DescartesR system supports the systematic identification and detailed costing of these countermeasures. In fact, these are its endpoint. To close this case study, we will now discuss their essential elements by way of a short walk-through.

Professional judgement is required of the teams who use the DescartesR system and its associated category resilience approach. This is because countermeasure creation, somewhat of a blend of art and science, marks the beginning of handing the resilience and risk analysis back to the operational business – back to them as a set of business arguments. The resilience workshop which caps off this analysis process creates as many countermeasures as would be needed to de-risk the supply chain in question. As many as would be needed to restore, or protect, its value from incidents, crises and external environmental factors. In the actual case we've based the example upon, fifteen countermeasures were identified.

COUNTERMEASURE CREATION

Countermeasure creation is a professional team exercise made up of pure judgement. The DescartesR system cannot specify what countermeasures need to be in terms of their number, scope or cost limits. It only provides a structured reasoning pathway for authoring and costing them. This countermeasure development process, you'll no doubt realise, has been happening all the while in the background. Industrial thinkers are solution-centred thinkers and solutions will have been forming themselves all the way through the analyses we have described. In fact, the cost–benefit of the reasoning chain clearly depends on it.

The solution spaces to major risks, threats, shocks or stresses will have been rehearsed as people managed their way from the assessment to the evaluation. The final discipline the system needs to support is simply their expression in the form of countermeasures. To be valid these must dock with a business logic rather than just being an isolated action plan (however good). This is why countermeasure planning is still another structured process locked into the resilience system and not simply a set of tasks resulting from it.

This content of the countermeasures interrogation, so to speak, was designed by the supply chain experts themselves. Just like case study 1, this required an expert to facilitate that process. This content was then locked into the logical requirements of the countermeasure tools. These tools can be understood as a series of steps that lead you to being able to identify the strategic business decision you require. There are four of these, as follows:

1 Identification

To add a new countermeasure begins as a narrative exercise. In the system, three points of reference are required:

1 A name.
2 The description – usually more than a sentence but less than a paragraph.
3 The justification – a breakdown of the problem that it will solve and how effectively it will do so.

2 Interrogation

The tool now refers to a multiple choice expert questionnaire. Underneath the responses are further deeper questions depending on the answers. For example, the user is asked: does this countermeasure require securing a means of finished production? If the answer is yes, a number of supplementary questions begin to qualify that statement and move the user through the most appropriate countermeasure planning route. These questionnaires are hard-wired into the system but flexible enough to be meaningful.

3 Cost estimation (capital expenditure and on cost – or running cost)

As the countermeasure is now well described, it is time for the user to estimate its business cost. There are two methods in the system – one is objective and the other heuristic. The objective method is for countermeasures that are data rich. This is where detailed understanding of typical, or even actual, costs is available.

The heuristic system is for guessing the cost. Although guessing feels very uncomfortable, two things are clear. First, a business case without cost data will not fly. Second, although experts are normally very cautious about providing costs estimates without supporting data, they are rarely incapable of this. They are the experts and, if they don't know how to estimate cost themselves, they usually can identify someone who can.

A cost figure for each countermeasure is a non-negotiable. In fact, the system refuses to save the countermeasure without this data point. Sometimes you just have to control the quality of the data in a more forceful way like this. People take shortcuts when things are hard to do – it's only natural. The system has to prevent this when it is hostile to the credibility or utility of the desired outcome. Where the heuristic approach is used the uncertainty remains transparent. It is coded into the answer. The user is allowed to work with a rangefinder which sets best guess, highest and lowest costs and sets a confidence limit on those. Simple, but elegant, statistics.

4 Estimation of performance-shaping factors

This heuristic reasoning tool is designed specifically to defuse a particular tendency in industrial risk reasoning, which is this. When people are in situations where they are asked to write detailed action plans, that is what they do. What they do not tend to do is to monitor the quality of those plans. They do not tend to apply a tested set of business and Organisational Psychology filters to assess how successful they are likely to be.

Once again, although people have agreed to take part in a planning exercise, this can be extensive if the supply chain in question is large and complex. Thus, the performance-shaping factors have to be effective but pithy to use. Each is a short set of multiple choice, or in one case cost, variables which reduce to seven bespoke scales that are purpose designed to support better reasoning from subject matter experts. These are:

1 Complexity: the degree to which the countermeasure is technically difficult to do, as judged against a short checklist.
2 Set-up effort: a behaviourally anchored rating scale for the difficulty in establishing the countermeasure in the first instance.
3 Maintenance effort: another behaviourally anchored rating scale to assess how hard it would be to keep the effort going in the longer term.
4 Cost assessment: with the SKU total value impacted by this countermeasure and the cost of this countermeasure compared in the system, the user assesses the direct value for money.
5 Popularity: a categorical scale assessing the ease with which other relevant parts of the business will accept the countermeasure proposition.
6 Willingness to pay: an examination of whether the business can be counted upon to make this sort of investment.
7 Enterprise Support: not called this everywhere, very often in large businesses these are under service level agreement with outsourced parties. The degree to which indirect functions such as finance, IT, Facilities management etc. are implicated in the actions is assessed. Changing these can prove complicated.

Costed?	Prob of Success	Justification		
Y		To avoid sole supplier situations		
Y	Complexity		2	/ 8
Y	Set up effort		7.2	/ 10
Y	Maintenance effort		7.3	/ 10
Y	Cost assessment		3.5	/ 10
Y	Popularity		2	/ 3
Y	Willingness to pay		0	/ 2
Y	Enterprise Support		3	/ 5

FIGURE 15.1 *Performance-shaping factor summary*

ROLLING UP PERFORMANCE ASSESSMENT

B ecause these success factor estimates are mostly numerical, they can be analysed to generate a probability of success indicator. When these steps have all been completed, the countermeasures table is available.

With this in play, two further analysis outcomes are now possible. The first is a total plan cost to protect. The value of the portfolio can be compared to the countermeasure portfolio costs by switching countermeasures on and off. This analysis is a critical sanity check. As we have forced users to stipulate costs, they are often depressed by the total cost burden of the countermeasure portfolio. This is an essential benchmark exercise for them, one which you simply do not see in simpler systems that allow people to list actions without cost implications and without the capacity to see those actions as a total portfolio of intervention.

The other analysis that is available is one that is primarily aimed at senior communication, and this brings the probability of success variable out into the open. It is a standardised Boston box device that allows probability of

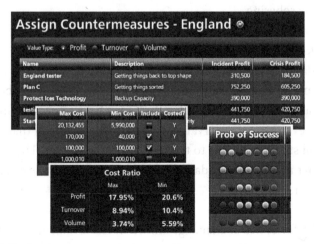

FIGURE 15.2 *Countermeasure analysis summary*

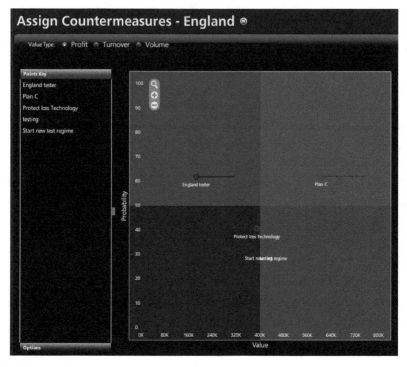

FIGURE 15.3 *Countermeasure success visualisation*

success to be compared to cost range for a countermeasure. Once again this is a benchmarking exercise for the proposing team, because these results can be sobering.

In the mock-up above it is likely that the most successful countermeasure recommendation would also be the most cost volatile. This does not necessarily mean that the team needs to go back to the drawing board. What it means is that the action plan itself may have to become more involved, or even more conservative. Crucially the source of that cost volatility will still be available to the team from the system. They can delve back into that more complex data causing this analysis at the click of a mouse pointer.

This capacity for cycles of challenge and rehearsal is enormously helpful for deliberation. As well as probability-and-cost, cost-and-value and value-

and-probability are also comparable. At different times these are more or less salient. Taken together they give a full 360-degree assessment of the interplay between cost, value protected and likely success. This is a critical sharpening device before the team authors their recommendations.

THE 'SO WHAT' MOMENT – GETTING TO STRATEGIC DECISIONS

A BOSCARD is a quintessential 'so what' tool. It is a programme management device, one like many that managers have at their disposal in planning and execution. The acronym breaks out as: B – Background; O – Objective; S – Scope; C – Constraints; A – Assumptions; R – Resource; D – Deliverable. At heart it is a narrative justification tool. The manager is expected to write a very few short paragraphs in defence of a course of action. Notice how, now we are at the appropriate point in the process for it, i.e. by design, tolerance for complexity argument can reassert itself.

Now that we have complete confidence in the rigour of the analysis that has led us here, the quintessence of complexity reduction in action, we can summarise with impunity.

A fictional, but typical, BOSCARD that might have come out of the supply chain resilience exercise we have been describing in this case study would look like that shown in Table 15.1.

In short, what a BOSCARD looks like is a miniature business plan. It is the sort of recommendation that can be considered, investigated further and approved or rejected by a senior leadership. It tells the business the implications of a resilience risk analysis by putting things back into a commercial context. The BOSCARD creates decision support.

The real final presentation of the conclusions of the case study we have been shadowing delivered a series of BOSCARDS that were genuinely as

TABLE 15.1 A fictional BOSCARD

Background

We have a single warehouse supplier – the Elm Group – for our entire razor product output. It is also the only validated warehouse to store razor products and there are no other existing alternatives in the market with the required dimensions that could be validated. In the case of a supplier disruption at this location, or unpredicted events, we have no alternative warehouse to operate. Thus, a disruption in the Elm Group business could stop Manuplant operations in total until a new warehouse is reconditioned. A process that would take at least 6 months.

Objective

Recondition part of current distribution centre to be able to operate with Razor products and commission it as a back-up site with a storage capacity of the minimum quantity required to operate the supply pipe.

Scope

All Razor SKUs manufactured at Manuplant. Portfolio value (minimum quantity to operate) 72 million euros.

Constraints

If activated and registered, may increase frequency of volume transportation to overflows of non-Razor product lines.

Assumptions

No significant uplift of Razor core technology or volume to new plant in Mexico.

No significant registered storage overflow in plan for new plant in Mexico.

Resource

Ex: TIMQ, RRHH, Engineering, SHE.

Capex: 2.2 million euros.

On-Cost: 0.15 million euros per year (warehouse capacity reduction effects).

Deliverable New Razor storage capacity online within six months.

---

pithy as the one above. The Regional Supply Chain Leadership team were then enabled to discuss the resilience of their Category Supply Chain. To give you just a flavour of that business discussion we can share three key headlines:

- 260,000 euros were needed to be expended immediately, and without challenge, to forestall forthcoming crises in a matter of weeks.
- 5.2 million (yes, million) euros was the recommended expenditure to remove just the priority sources of supply chain risk from the operation.
- A further 2 million euros was the recommended expenditure to place the supply chain into a proactive position vis-à-vis its critical long-term sources of disruption for the next five years.

These detailed recommendations were explained with depth and business clarity across 15 separate BOSCARDS, each of them a reasoned business case with costs. The high-level recommendation of all this work, hard as this might be to believe, was a single statistic – a single cost figure.

That statistic is the ultimate question of risk and resilience decanted into one business ratio. This was the (justified) cost to control the risks expressed as a percentage of the value of the SKU portfolio it would defend.

As one might expect, for business sensibility, this needs to be an extremely small percentage.

It also forms, for very busy senior executives, a quintessential expression (and test) of their appetite for risk.

CONCLUSIONS FROM THIS CHAPTER

It is more than possible to design an effective resilience and risk system for a large, complex, distributed organisation in a VUCA context. This much is plain. The appetite for complexity has to be significant – this is the real cost of rationality. The reasoning chain it creates has to be infrastructural, requiring multiple disciplines, team and individual reasoning on and offline and fusing heuristics with pragmatic measurement which can be held in tension.

The conclusions of such a process and systems thinking approach creates a bridge. This spans the space between the technical evaluation of risk and resilience constructs – designed specifically for the context – and a business case. A business case which is always about decisions and outcomes directly linked to that context.

The impact on the quality and integrity of the reasoning of the teams, individuals and leaders concerned vastly outstrips anything that could be offered by the classic approach to risk and resilience that one usually sees in these settings.

The output, resilience countermeasures, can be assessed for success factors, costs and value in exactly the same way a business case could be. In this way the dialect of resilience evidently meets, as it always should, the dialect of business decision making. Due to the comprehensive and elegant nature of this design being supported and executed by the exact experts who are its beneficiaries, it does so professionally and seamlessly.

CHAPTER 16

Deconstructing organisational goals for resilience

Knowing what we now know, it is time to bring the argument full circle. It's time to talk once more not about how organisations use the constructs, dialects, systems, meta-variables, measurements and so on of risk-based resilience reasoning, but why.

In Chapter 1 we introduced six typical examples of risk/resilience/ reasoning scenarios that anyone working in a large, complex, distributed organisation might face. We argued that the cocktail of definitions demonstrated by even these scenarios was, frankly, baffling. How could any organisation sensibly speak about a construct as confabulated as this? Yet, we recognised that all organisations can and do speak of a single risk (and/or resilience) construct in normal business in quite a routine way.

One way this confusing behaviour might be explained is by the idea that the risk construct has become as a sort of master clearing house for certain types reasoning. We attempted to build an understanding of how that could work by differentiating the dialects this language of risk seemed to be speaking. These aside, there was still a case to answer for the illogical and comparatively brutal simplicity with which its tasks are so commonly approached. We have already considered in some detail how this leads to profound analytical shortcomings.

Another explanation is that risk and resilience are not ends in themselves, but a common element of other goal-directed behaviours. Thus we see different coping mechanisms around complexity burden: a naïve realism – people don't realise the meanings are confused or inconsistent between contexts; a general incomprehension – that there is a science available behind risk measurement and reasoning; a blind trust in generalised applications supported by external Standards, guidance and best practice; and a drive for the reporting task of risk to inform only high-level discussions. We have already considered these topics in detail also.

What we have yet to do is to discuss risk-based resilience reasoning from the point of view of the operational goals it is supporting. The rationality here, too, at this macro level, is of great interest, not least because it sets these dialectic rules for your appetite for complexity.

So in this chapter we want to examine the links between the operational goals organisations have and their risk and resilience methodology options and choices. To do so we will centre that discussion around the use of a final analytical tool – risk methodology benchmarking. Having discussed the template this creates, we then take a final step back and discuss four maturity goals which we believe would be of great help for organisations to set themselves in order to centre, or even re-centre, their approach to risk-based resilience reasoning.

THE DUAL QUESTIONS OF CREDULITY AND EXPEDIENCE

Most organisations, we note, don't see resilience as core to their business. As such, they meet its largely cultural demands with a

forgivable expedience. Their aim is a kind of operational credulity.
The imperative to provide something to meet the (regulatory, stakeholder, industry association, standard-setter, commentator, shareholder, sector best-practice) demand is agreed. The task of meeting it is duly allocated. However, rarely is it allocated to managers who – on top of their other responsibilities – are formally trained to work with these constructs. The competences to run such a system are seen as a rather generally available skills set. The credulity argument just recognises risk and resilience as another management task.

Credulity becomes the key goal because of another cultural factor also. This is that rarely, from the project meeting upwards, are risk and resilience assessments warmly received by the organisation's other hard-pressed professionals. They are viewed at best as an inoculation process and at worst as a waste of time. Rarely too, at the board level, are risk and resilience seen as upstream mediators of strategy or business process design. They are viewed in the abstract as key performance indicators, a process often called "sign off". What is being signed off therefore is credulity – the organisation has taken a credible look at their responsibility.

THE TRIPLE BIND

One key performance factor we can therefore observe within this confabulated corporate coping mechanism to a culturally interpolated demand characteristic is the following. People in such organisations will be somewhat forced to speak of risk and resilience constructs they do not wholly own, certainly didn't design and perhaps don't fully grasp. It is not a surprise that they do so inexpertly. Nor is it a surprise that the organisation would have to be seen as complicit in this.

What we, in fact, see is a complex triple bind – the confabulated use of multiple constructs/dialects, the fundamentally cultural, rather than material, desire shaping the outcome, the demonstrably poor application of relevant science. This creates an appetite, not for the necessary complexity to approach this task within evidence-based standards and professional competence, but for a capitulation to credulity. The end-game is that the tasks themselves have been completed. A reluctant business will write formulaic narratives, not to satisfy a range of accurately defined business goals, but to satisfy one far more general diligence goal.

Even with the reported self-awareness that this methodology is conceptually quite weak therefore, practitioners show little appetite for reform. The pressure to crunch the annual register of risks, impacts and actions in its usual formats is huge. Whilst this may be all so very expedient (although commentators prefer 'pragmatic') in the short term, this can never be viewed as a positive use of resources in medium to long term.

That's because this goal is not actually about harnessing (business) science at all, it is about credulity in the face of expedience. This reasoning won't add any measurable value to an organisation, it will detract from it – at the very least in a pure effort and productivity sense. Loss in value is always the outcome when the desire for coherent and effective risk and resilience system is supplanted by the desire to limit the number of applied goals the methodology will be permitted to address. Loss is always the result if we seek business value as our outcome but capitulate to a (more powerful) desire to minimise any disruption brought on by the effort.

RISK, RESILIENCE AND REALITY – A TOOL TO AID GOAL DECONSTRUCTION

Whilst many practitioners and commentators would validate these introductory comments, we feel there is something quite pragmatic that is still missing from this debate. It reflects, but doesn't tackle, two key points of *status quo*. The first is that there are already comprehensive legacy systems running in most mature organisations. The goals of these, as we have pointed out, must be reassessed. The second is that it doesn't give businesses any fresh narrative that finally combines all the different risk and resilience dialects and goals in an intuitively useful way. A combination where, we would argue, the value-add and business-benefit discussion should be at its most rational and most prominent.

To squarely meet these two challenges, we want to propose a taxonomy. This is not the solution to the poor alignment of goals, but it is a tool which will help organisations clear the runway to have that key discussion.

This taxonomy goes back to the very opening argument of this book. If resilience is an operationalised form of risk-based reasoning, then how are people currently reasoning about risk and what are their (actual) operational goals for so doing? We propose that large, distributed and complex organisations can answer this question when they see themselves as operating with risk reasoning across a continuum of five interlinked goal sets. These are summarised in Table 16.1.

TABLE 16.1 Risk reasoning as a continuum of five interlinked goal sets

Risk Case:	TECHNICAL	GENERAL	GLOBAL	STRATEGIC	LICENCE
Risk definition	Micro risk	Project risk	Programme risk	Strategic risk	Business ethos risk
Knowledge extraction	Rescripting technical knowledge	Aggregating general descriptors	Forming reasoning constructs	Strategic impact analysis	Predictive forecast modelling
Control features	Measurement	Risk-by-risk action planning	Performance-shaping factors	Satisficing audit	Narrative diligence
Expert judgement	Domain dependent	Operational discipline	Organisational goal alignment	Strategy development	Controlling values and story
Business integration	Independent	Assurance process	Integrated in control decisions	Strategic course correction	Corporate policy driver

Equipped with an understanding of these five goal sets, organisations can rationally tabulate the goals around each. As the five cases form a continuum we shall just compare the base, middle and high cases to illustrate how to use the taxonomy.

TECHNICAL RISK

DEFINITION

The technical risk case is perhaps the bedrock of what most people feel to be risk assessment. Its definition requires not much more than a list of discrete, unique risks which are described as present- or future-tense events. These are generally channelling learning from historical failures, or driven by just plain old contemporary fears and concerns. These are usually scored on a variation of the probability and impact matrix. Probability is often naïve, for the reasons we have discussed at length. Although impact is deemed a measure, it is rarely more than a calibrator – frequently not better than high, medium and low expectation of loss or disruption of a fixed magnitude. These event definitions are sometimes strengthened with mitigation statements.

KNOWLEDGE EXTRACTION

In the technical case the knowledge that is being extracted from the business is therefore really just a rescripting of its own technical knowledge. For example, what sort of thing can typically go wrong with this or that key process? Operatives are asked, often without training or guidance, for their risk list, so it is not a surprise that to satisfy this demand characteristic they simply translate one of their own operational dialects into a risk event dialect. Technical expertise points, and even historical lessons learned, are reworked into risk event descriptions. This is done not as a disciplined reasoning exercise *per se*. It is in order to satisfy the desire for risks. Sometimes this may be grudgingly so.

CONTROL FEATURES

As these technical approaches tend to be administratively driven, i.e. they are normally part of a governance that calls for reassurance, control does not feature very highly in the assessment. This is so much so that one might argue that the measurement itself is the only control. Whilst this argument might see some push-back because these types of assessment are seen as the basis of corporate risk assurance, we would argue they are no such thing.

This is because technical assessment like this, for large organisations and programmes, tends to bring a proliferation of risks and this makes the data very dense. Technical risks, because they are so discrete, can be generated in their hundreds. This means that the data can only really be used if it is violently aggregated and translated. Ironically, we observe it is often transferred almost to the opposite end of its continuum in that process. Any of you working in a company which holds a 'top ten' risk register will attest to that.

EXPERT JUDGEMENT

The expert judgement that is brought to bear on assessing risks at this level is domain dependent. Very often individuals are scoring these risks in isolation from other technical risk owners. Often the assessment is done alone by being asked to fill in and send back a spreadsheet. Where this is a group exercise, the scoring can be subject to another source of bias because it is a group consensus process. Arguably a worse form of reasoning.

BUSINESS INTEGRATION

Most critically of all, the business integration of technical risks formulated and scored like this is negligible. They are not in a dialect that can be used for business decision making. This is because, as we have already argued, there is no hope for a link to the business – either decision making process or outcome formulation – in their definition. This is doubly the case because they are set up to be solved at source. This is normally reflected through a mitigation planning expectation which comes at the same time as the assessment. The degree to which the mitigation is a response to the methodology, rather than a genuine process, we'll leave to your own experience. Ours suggests it is extremely weak.

LICENCE

RISK DEFINITION

A t the opposite end of our continuum is a risk dialect which could not be much further removed from the technical case we have just described. This is the one which justifies an organisation's licence to operate. Putting this at the opposite end of the continuum should not be seen as an endorsement of its superiority. First, that is not how the continuum is set up to work – all risk dialects in it need to be independently and internally valid and efficacious. Second, there are ways in which licence risk is no more effective a dialect than technical risk.

This is because the licence case defines risk in large encompassing value statements. This type of thinking generates business ethos sorts of statements such as "we manage any risk which threatens the sustainability of our global operation"; or "we manage risk because safety is paramount"; or "the risks to the BRIC economies are an essential driver of our future share-price". It is very hard for this dialect to have a measurable business outcome.

KNOWLEDGE EXTRACTION

The knowledge that is extracted from a business by this form of reasoning is a kind of econometric modelling thinking. People are being asked to imagine impacts as large as "the green movement", or "our deep water horizon", or "a catastrophic supply chain failure". Sometimes aligned with commercially produced mega-trend, or global barometer-type data, these risks operate more like meta-narratives. The expertise is the opposite of technical – it is aimed squarely at strategic forecasting and/or senior briefing.

CONTROL FEATURES

The control feature of this formulation of risk is a surprising one because it takes the form of further narrative diligence. Driven, as this risk dialect and its associated appetite are, by codes of business principles or the desire to avoid a repeat of a major reputation crisis, control is formed as pure strategy. Just as the risk statements themselves surround ethos, control surrounds the actual controlling story of the company.

This formalised (and quite transparent) control is only actionable, in as much as it can be, by a controlling story being cascaded. This comes through the strategic communication channels and, once it reaches certain strata, key performance indicators at best, and case studies in public relations at worst, are the indices of its success.

EXPERT JUDGEMENT

The expert judgement needed to navigate this licence risk is variously found in corporate risk departments, corporate secretaries' portfolio or even internal audit. Very typically it sits half-way between finance and legal. Like all its defining features, the expert judgement is very high-level. It surrounds controlling values and story. It surrounds what a company wants to believe, and project, about itself. This they all do by designing the story they tell themselves in order to effect that.

Licence risk that is unwanted is pilloried in edict and in CEO platform opportunities. It takes a less than canny company to attempt this without first checking the back story. The best place to check this is in any pending court cases, active NGO campaigns and by looking for embarrassing stories of legally approvable cost savings that are ethically doubtful.

In the main this complex expression of risk comes about because campaigning NGOs and rival companies often exploit large-scale or highly public inconsistencies to their advantage. One could argue that licence is not really a kind of risk at all. That said, how companies deal with whatever it really is drives them to dub the activity risk assessment/management.

How companies mine their own operations for emerging forms of licence risk is actually, ironically, to insist on the widest possible use of, and then summary analysis, or as we have termed it violent aggregation, of technical risk. The two are highly joined. That is why, prosaic as it seems, licence belongs alongside technical in this section.

BUSINESS INTEGRATION

The integration of licence risk into the business is, like all of the sections above, a narrative approach. When lessons have been learned from experiences, or in the severe crisis case from one all-encompassing experience, the organisation writes about its business. What it writes depends, but the narratives find their way back to corporate policy either in formal governance or in standard operating.

GLOBAL

A far richer hunting ground for valid risk reasoning can be found at the midway point between the two dialects discussed so far. This we have termed global because, if your company only has the appetite to do risk assessment once and well, then a global approach makes the most sense. Our case study from Chapter 4 can be rightly thought of as an example of a global risk system. It is not global in the sense that the whole company is now covered, but in the sense that risk is being defined at the right level for a large, distributed company.

RISK DEFINITION

The risk definition in a global system, as we saw in that transformation case study, is naturally at the meta-risk level. Only twenty-two risks in all were needed to embrace the entire operational challenge of the transformation. This is never to suggest that there is no place for technical or domain risk in that process. Their place is the risk elicitation process where they can be weighed and combined on a business-wide footing through analyses like the perfect storm exercise.

KNOWLEDGE EXTRACTION

The knowledge extraction that takes place in a global risk case is necessarily multidisciplinary. A number of techniques, such as those we saw in the case study in Chapter 15, allow experts to augment, challenge and qualify global risk at the elicitation point. As our opening and closing case studies showed in different ways, a good meta-risk is a reasoning construct predicated on the quality of the (expert) knowledge that is folded into it. It is built in such a way as to cause expert groups to concur on a subject matter that is common to them all without destroying their expert contribution or reducing it to a technical level.

CONTROL FEATURES

The control features of a global risk case are always the pre-existing businesses performance shaping factors, i.e. natural business mechanisms. For example, design, budgeting, planning, decision making, etc. will be used to comprehend and mediate the connectivity of risk sets. This is what makes this risk dialect so naturally amenable to supporting business decisions and outcomes.

EXPERT JUDGEMENT

The expert judgement in the global case is best described as an organisational alignment process. The various reassessments, briefings and validation rounds at different levels in the organisation at each iteration (and after each intervention) make for a highly iterative and corrective kind of judgement process. The more often different experts are asked to look at a meta-risk which has been superimposed on a business case, the more effective the meta-risk has been in causing reasoning.

BUSINESS INTEGRATION

Lastly, the business integration of the global case is mediated by the fact that the meta-risk argument (sometimes the whole of it, sometimes causal chains within it and sometimes just discrete meta-risk levels) is a central input to routine operational decision making. That risk-based decision making does not differ at all from the normal. Experts are enabled by this risk argument, as we have said, to stay within their zone of expertise.

USING THIS ARGUMENT TO ASSESS OR DESIGN SYSTEMS

For those of our readers who are systems thinkers it is, of course, a short step from recognising this conceptual analysis to making it into a benchmarking tool. The outcome could be a radial diagram, like the one shown in Figure 16.1, which addresses the intersect of the five descriptive continuum across all of these dialects simultaneously. Across, in fact, what would be an organisation's entire spectrum of risk approaches. Here we now see the possibility that an operational risk portfolio can be formally considered and assessed as a multi-dialect construct for a whole organisation.

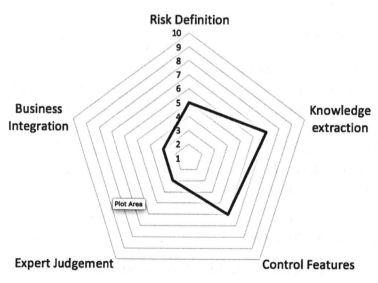

FIGURE 16.1 *Risk goals benchmarking*

A regular pentagon sitting somewhere around the 5 mark on each scale would, in our estimation, be a very effective holistic risk analysis system. For a large, complex, distributed organisation in a VUCA context, we would propose that aiming to build systems that maintain and draw operational business data from this "sweet spot" is the way that risk and resilience reasoning becomes a business engine. Tracking too far, in or out, on any single continuum would serve as a benchmark to highlight an inconsistency in the reasoning the organisation is using. Unless that is there were operational reasons for this.

WHY AREN'T RISK AND RESILIENCE BUSINESS ENGINES?

Is it worth stopping to note that three vital chains in any complex distributed businesses – value, supply, reputation – are accepted and validated because they are complex? Is it worth noting that they are mature, rationally monitored and heavily resourced business realities for all large organisations? Is it worth noting too, that these constructs didn't just turn up as fully formed overnight in a Standard or best practice? Their evolution was its own journey in industrial and organisational theory.

Could we also note in recent history a parallel with the arc of Health and Safety reasoning? It is well documented how this was initially frustrated by a low tolerance for complexity. We take heart from how well designed and well integrated it now is, and this despite the fact that, much like risk and resilience, safety remains an elusive social construction. In present businesses, even in far away and dangerous places, the fact that it is an accepted business goal is unassailable.

We believe, using something like the arguments in this book and the battery of assessment devices we have created along the way, that risk and resilience need to turn a corner like this. They need to be considered not as niche technical process but as a holistic business engine. The thing that determines their design, the key appetite, should certainly therefore be the appetite for complexity. A complexity that seeks to tightly couple risk and resilience to real business outcomes. To get to this position, the current appetite for credulity and expedience has to be forced into its proper place. At the moment it has supplanted and indeed prevented a wholly necessary discussion on complexity and business fit.

If this pursuit of credulity took a back seat for a while to allow the appetite for complexity, could we productively add value? Could we avoid resistance from a valued *status quo* of self-validating best practices? The answer is probably no. Not unless the modelling above, and the other approaches like it we have discussed were able to effect some significant maturity step-changes. These would need to be agreed by an informed (and enlightened) senior leadership. They would need to be incorporated into the competency framework of the responsible teams. These are as follows:

MATURITY GOAL 1 – INCREASE MEANINGFULNESS

If the management has wandered off down the postmodern labyrinth of delegated risk and resilience quite accidentally, it needs to snap out of this fog. The best thing to do is reassert the need to formally state, in business terms, the purpose of these activities. To what business goals do they align? The answer should outline a direct link to decision support and result in effective and manipulable behavioural controls. Every spreadsheet, indicator and audit has to align clearly with the pursuit of material business outcomes.

MATURITY GOAL 2 – SELL THE VALUE OF CLARITY

It is necessary to articulate, accurately and with enough evidence, what the clear benefits of risk and resilience (beyond a complicity with reassurance and audit culture) really are. The terms should not be obtuse and baffling; they should be clear business goals in the accepted business outcome language. Constructs still need to recognisably rational and scientific.

Metric benchmarks must still be pursued in a rational and business-focused manner. The clarity of the link to business must create the appetite for better reasoning.

MATURITY GOAL 3 – HARNESS INTELLECTUAL CAPITAL

Harnessing intellectual capital to design the system is essential. Large, complex organisations are bristling with clearly very clever people. These clever people should be supported and trained to go on a functional journey of design. We should imagine that, adequately supported, experts and teams who build entire global supply chains will be amenable to a rational, systems-led approach to build risk and resilience systems functionality that is fit for purpose if this was their mandate.

MATURITY GOAL 4 – DEAL WITH DISSENT

Creating a business engine is not a call for a new high benchmark of elite performance. Nor is it – in the pejorative parlance of managers who are somewhat entrenched in a desultory view of these things – "creating a Rolls Royce when a Mini would do". It is simply a call for demonstrably effective performance to be the defining business standard. Effectively, and with applied intellect, the organisation must design tools to manage this highly complex, volatile and business critical arena with sobriety. Fact.

This same sobriety is easily afforded to the other productive constructs that convey and measure value, supply coherence and reputation capital. Dealing with dissent will require business leaders to forcefully put down the "post-it pads will do" culture of risk and resilience planning. Rather they need to visibly recognise that a risk and resilience system is not a dry audit but a business-critical argument. They need to exact the same stringent performance standard by which other strategic decision support and control systems are judged.

Addressing these goals intentionally will move a business a very long way towards making risk and resilience direct engines of business benefit. This requires them to be accepted as a reasoning chain for that business – one which seamlessly interlinks with the other chains of value, supply and reputation.

The goal of risk and resilience reasoning is not to audit the value supply and reputation chains of a business in the interests of regulatory diligence or best practice, it is to augment them in the direct pursuit of their material business gains.

CONCLUSIONS FROM THIS CHAPTER

This chapter has discussed the necessity, in the light of our journey of design into what risk-based resilience reasoning systems are, to revisit the reasons that organisations have for using them. Examining organisational goals, both high-level and detailed, shows us how the organisation can be historically biased towards confusion. Shows how it can be historically satisfied with a kind of credulity born out of expedience to produce a system which does not stand up well to either scientific or, more importantly, business inspection.

The main goal for using risk-based resilience reasoning, we argue, has to embody the opposite case. It has to be the best available business science wedded to an enforceable business rationale based around a sufficiently complex set of constructs.

It is possible to clearly measure the health of candidate constructs – for example, control mechanisms or the use of expert knowledge – with a barometer-style tool. This arranges them in parsimonious continuum across five clear operational dialects, for example technical risk, licence to operate risk, etc. We would argue that this is not only possible, it is a business imperative.

Taking this rational approach greatly increases the likelihood of risk-based resilience reasoning becoming an engine of the business, a term coined to mean that it is linked intimately to strategic decision making and outcomes. To maximise this likelihood there are at least four maturity step changes needed at the goal-setting level. These cause the organisation to take a hard look at the meaningfulness, clarity, intelligence and consent around the system as an imperative of its design. These endorse the signal that the reasoning system is expected at all levels to be effective in enhancing direct business performance and delivering business value.

CHAPTER 17

Taking stock of the reasoning chain

L arge, modern, complex and distributed organisations have, amidst all their diversity, one thing in common. At the heart of their operational DNA lies a triple helix. This is made up of the value chain, the supply chain and the reputation chain. Very much like a DNA helix, changes to one affect the behaviours of the others sometimes subtly, at other times quite dramatically. The complex way in which modern supply, value and reputation are visibly and inextricably interlinked in our digitised age makes the imperative to monitor them a given.

Due to the broader and longer-term impact of the linked concepts of risk and resilience, certain critical forms of reasoning around this triple helix have also essentially shifted. Modern organisations no longer just want sustainable, flexible, profitable supply chains. They also want that supply chain to be risk assessed and resilient. They no longer just want a veneer of corporate social responsibility, they want a proactive issues management portfolio to defensively protect their brands. They no longer just want to maximise shareholder value. In the wake of Sarbanes Oxley and other reforms, they want unimpeachable financial transparency. Increasingly, their regulators, stakeholders and shareholders want these things too. These desires are now routinely expressed in the language of risk and resilience.

There the trouble starts, of course, because the implications of these desires on the integrity of that interconnected triple helix are complex. Even considered on a chain-by-chain basis, they are very unclear. For example, many of the behaviours that might make a supply chain less risky and more resilient, such as alternative sourcing, inherent redundancy and extra capacity, are also things that would make it more complex and more expensive. Would the Supply Chain Director agree with this definition of resilient? In certain ways, wouldn't the most cost-effective supply chains actually need to be the least resilient?

So it seems that, for each chain, we need to ask a more involved set of questions. What is the intended utility of the risk and resilience concepts? Are there differences of expression between the chains? How should these be measured and applied? What level of integration would we expect with normative business reasoning? How complex and expert should their assessment be in order to remain sympathetic to the goals of the chain? Where should the person who does the assessment be situated – inside the main team, or as an observer/auditor figure at one remove? Above all, how, and with what sort of authority should any outputs from this evaluation activity integrate meaningfully with the cycle of decision making?

So if, to continue the supply chain example, good practices in resilience start to look antagonistic to profitability, will they be resisted or supported? If the answer is that they will be supported, then clearly that can only be up to a point. Meaningful supply chain resilience would have to be brokered – it cannot be the only determinant of supply chain behaviour. Thus, agreement on appetite and tolerance will be needed. Where you draw that line that says how much resilience is needed must be a decision. Moreover, who owns that line and who bears the responsibility for the costs is also a consideration.

Once we have sorted all of this out for the supply chain, should we then turn to the value and reputation chains? Shall we discuss, for example, the merits of trading-off cost for ethical performance? This immediately doesn't feel sensible because astute observers would see how that impacts back onto the supply chain almost immediately. Thus, a chain-by-chain approach doesn't feel to align with the hard-won necessity to see the triple helix as interconnected.

Nonetheless, this is the observable path that industry has taken so far. They have pragmatically tackled the challenges of risk and resilience as a piecemeal set of assessment processes under the purview of each separate chain. This division of labour, even if the methodologies were consistent, which they are not, means that we are facing the complex DNA by ignoring it. We treat the chains of the triple helix as if they were really independent, even though we know with certainty they are not.

To go down this route estranges risk-based resilience reasoning outside of the known interconnectivity of these three systems. The integrity of such a risk argument quickly starts to break apart – flooded as it will be by the mixed imperatives of independently incontrovertible, priorities brought on by assessing the chains in this independent manner. The way that organisations have dealt with this inconsistency to date is as fascinating as it is confusing. They have turned, for a second time, to the concept of risk assessment to create its own separate controlling narrative.

RISK ASSESSMENT AS A 'MOBIUS STRIP'

Risk assessment itself has, ironically, become the accepted methodology to reduce the complexity thrown up by the presence of the need for so many risk assessments. The ascendance of the concepts of Enterprise Risk Management and the various forms of Business Continuity and Resilience are, in fact, the evidence of this reductionism. Evidence because they seek, albeit falteringly, to deliver a pan-business narrative around a total risk abstract. This interpolation only deepens when all risks activity terminates in one final and highly generalised corporate risk register.

The corporate overview attempts to foster a kind of last-word meta-expression, but our observation is that it tends to do this through the expedience of simplification rather than the coherence of complexity reduction. At the methodological heart of the expedient version of the exercise sits a requirement for each of the triple-helix organisations to essentially lobby with their discrete risk portfolios. This is in the hope that their risks – in a heavily summarised and stylised form to suit the dialect requirements of this new audience – will make some overall corporate cut. A cut that can be then by further summarised and shared with an oversight board, such as the Corporate Risk and Reputation Committee.

There is an irony to this peculiar Mobius strip arrangement. We see on the one side the proliferation of risks and control needs across the strata of a business. On the other (same) side we attempt their redaction, through aggregation or obviation, via the implied diligence of another risk assessment – a risk assessment of risk assessments in fact. The irony is that this has led not to the clarification of the efficacy of the risk concept but to the explosive expansion of the definition of the term risk. One that we can observe today is verging on the postmodern.

As the Mobius effect takes hold, organisations can use the concept and language of risk as a kind of free panacea. At one end of the spectrum – in corporate risk – it can defend their licence to operate, whilst at entirely the other end – in a safety management system – the same concept is expected to discretise the treatment of every minutiae of hazard. Thus, across entire landscapes, businesses now mandate risk assessments, keep registers, report to executive boards and have all these discretised practices separately audited.

Emerging from that behaviour set in the last decade is a new need that organisations have also settled on. This is the need to qualify the meaning of their meta-risk narratives by employing the highly related concept and language of resilience. This is a language which is used just as freely – because risk and resilience constructs are so heavily linked and because the same teams are frequently implicated. The long-term impact of this fractured and rationally incestuous application of both constructs on modern industrial thinking remains an uncertain science to say the least.

A REVISED MODEL – THE QUADRUPLE HELIX

It is illogical that the Mobius strip arrangement allows for a risk-resilience construct to hold so many different meanings simultaneously. The solution is simply that the current risk-resilience Mobius strip, to stretch the metaphor, should have its loop cut and its components rearranged into a chain. A chain allied to those well-understood chain metaphors of value, supply and reputation. Just as industry has learned to do with these, we need to be actually harnessing a descriptive and predictive power from this complementary activity. This has to have the same qualities as the inherent ways we have come to model the complexity of the triple helix itself.

So, instead of trying to wrap this bizarre Mobius strip in a cloud of thought around the elements of the triple helix, always multiply assessing them from different risk angles on the outside, we propose a rational alignment. The reasoning chain must allow assessment to take place from the inside. Furthermore, it has to be on the same terms using the same referents.

The unique added value of this proposition is the addition of a complexity reduction technique that both models the impact of uncertainty on the interaction of the chains and improves the clarity of the causal chains between them on that basis. A chain for reasoning, a chain to audit reasoning in fact. This can be achieved by inserting that fourth strand so that it is, culturally, professionally and objectively, on an equal footing with the other three.

To begin to close out our arguments, we would like to turn and describe how that could work.

A FIRST CHALLENGE: DIFFERENTIATE REASONING TYPES

It is true that at the heart of the pursuit of the current triple helix chains – by different segments and different specialist leaders –

lies reasoning. You can't demonstrate shareholder value, run Total Process Management or establish the Public Relations platforms for your business unless some group is getting their heads together, identifying the variables, considering the options, testing the decisions, learning from experience and reporting the results. And, yes, this behaviour is reasoning. So how can a reasoning chain add much to or be very much different from that?

What we can go on to observe are certain truths about this kind of mainstream industrial reasoning. It has very well-defined subject matters. It lies within the purview of specific professional disciplines. It calls upon particular expertise. It results in quite a bounded argument. The cognitive component (what needs to be thought about) and the behavioural component (what material is being manipulated) remain quite well exposed and evidence based – they are mechanistic even. The efficacy, and therefore the success or failure, of this type of reasoning is also quite bounded. This is because it stays tightly coupled to the definitions of its parent chains and their interrelated outcomes.

However, and it really is quite a big however, upon close inspection is it easy to see that current forms of risk and resilience reasoning are not at all like that. They do not, at present, enjoy a very well-defined subject matter. They do not, clearly and easily, lie within the purview of any specific discipline. Defining their expertise requirement proves highly troublesome. Their cognitive and behavioural components remain quite obscured because they are certainly not mechanistic – rather, they are borderline metaphysical social constructs.

As a consequence of this, the style of their outputs is necessarily quite self-fulfilling. Thus, it is very hard indeed for these concepts to prove themselves to be evidence based. These cannot, at present, be coupled to triple-helix definitions or outcomes other than in the very general and speculative terms currently being used.

This makes it all the more surprising that the call for something like this type of reasoning across all businesses has evolved in recent times to become so pervasive. So pervasive is it in fact that we have reached the point where it is regulated. This, astute observers will know, is also part of the great disconnect. Regulators and auditors are a completely different community to the people who actually do the planning and decision making within the triple-helix organisations. Also, key to our argument is that they speak a completely different dialect of risk.

Bypassing these problems, modern organisations found themselves in need of mechanisms to encompass this new set of non-absolute controlling narratives for business providence and success. Thus, in a relatively short space of time, much guidance, such as Standards, and much other advice under the blanket of best practice has sprung up. With it, the need for *reasoning about risk and resilience* as a language of its own had effectively been normalised. What hadn't been at all well understood was how to differentiate the kind of reasoning that would be effective to meet these requirements.

This has created a significant problem which we all have to face. When we isolate the industrial risk and resilience subject matter and examine the available guidance, best practices and the kind of language that tries to interpret the challenge to reason about these constructs, the evidence is unequivocal. The result so far has not been good reasoning at all. In fact, the result has been highly criticised, enormously limited and frequently very faulty reasoning. In the end this doesn't help anyone meet meaningful objectives. In some quarters this actually fosters resentment for the processes surrounding risk and resilience, making them into a set of burdens.

The question we all have to face is: what are we all to do about that? What are we to do to differentiate the largely very effective and well-understood reasoning types of the triple helix from the necessarily different ones of positive risk-based resilience?

LAYING OUT THE CASE FOR THE REASONING CHAIN

Our answer to that question is simple. To the existing triple helix we propose adding reasoning itself as a fourth strand on equal terms. Risk-based resilience has to stop trying to constantly qualify that complex triple-helix relationship from multiple directions and satisfying multiple audience who all speak irreconcilably different dialects. Instead, it has to join in as an operationally validated working partner bringing a unique contribution to and critique of the business reasoning. Three, needs to become four. Our reasons, as we have exemplified them so far, are complex but the facts are far simpler.

A regulatory, and therefore commercial, commitment to the desire for risk-based resilience means that the quality of operational reasoning around it has become a causal factor in an organisation's performance.

Our solution to this challenge is a simple one – dramatically improve the long-term quality of this reasoning. To arrive at a reasoning chain of sufficient quality in order to function alongside and comment upon those currently in the triple helix, those parts of organisations charged with risk assessing and resilience making need to do certain things. First and foremost, the overall scientific credibility of their systems must significantly improve. It has to be on a par with the quality of reasoning informing the helix. Second, certain governing standards should now be put in place.

An effective reasoning chain will be recognisable by an effective governance structure which calls for: superior constructs, improved practices, better application and a full commitment to infrastructural incorporation into the decision making within the existing triple-helix arrangement. Let's discuss those one at a time.

SUPERIOR CONSTRUCTS PREDICT GREATER INTEGRATION WITH BUSINESS MEANING

In Parts 1 and 2 of this book we decided that an elegantly constructed, meaningful and measurable approach to the basic constructs would have to link them in a far less *laissez faire* manner if they were to become drivers of business decision making.

THE RISK CONSTRUCT

For the risk construct we laid out the imperative of an enhanced evidence base to support or, where needed, challenge the legitimacy of normative practice. For example, this should particularly confront the unquestioning use of the sub-concept of probability in general and, given that it is wholly essential for our problem sets, conditional probability in particular.

Probability can be very easily demonstrated to be inherently counterintuitive and confusing, even to well-educated professionals. Besides this critical observation, we simply cannot escape the fact that the whole subject remains, academically, in constant dispute. This is a situation which is so serious it might contraindicate its use at all by non-experts. Furthermore, as we have demonstrated in our first FMCG case study, an appropriate design does not need a measurement of probability to be in the frontline of the construct.

We concluded that any definition of risk could immediately be far more rationally effected by following our strict four-point schema: agreed semantics, discernible (and stable) abstraction, validated measurement and proven materiality. These features of such a model would need to be discerned afresh for each and every organisational application.

The result of this would mean that business impacts have actually to be calibrated and compared using existing validated business metrics.

Individually defined risks have to be qualified for how they can affect the stability of other risks in the frame, up to and including the creation of meta-risks and risk-coherent scenarios fuelled by critical business constraints and decisions. Time, and particularly volatility over time, has to link clear risk outcome measures to the operational critical paths. The risk construct should always convey at least this level of sophistication and integration.

Supported by the right expertise, we recommend that organisations make all of these active choices, and exclusions when defining the core risk construct they will use.

THE RESILIENCE CONSTRUCT

There is an imperative not to assume that this is a natural and widely agreed referent that can easily be applied in any business. The discourse on resilience – in the academic community alone – is so replete with competing points of view as to be of little practical help beyond setting a general aspiration. Its use in industry can be shown to be approaching so wide a concept as to be of no discriminatory value when it comes to organisational outcomes.

Organisations are simply required to make a definition call and to stick to it. Methodologically, this starts as a choice between two clear alternatives. One is where the resilience definition is construed out of a legacy of impact mitigation, borne upon the erstwhile desires of businesses for continuity. The other is where it construed as a proactive business enabler, something which is as much promoting of success as it is protecting against loss. This is a key distinction which should be broached head-on. We can only recommend the latter choice as the most rational justification of the effort the system requires.

When the alternative has been chosen, the design questions do not end there. The interrelationship between this resilience construct and the remaining risk-bearing architecture of the organisation's mature systems has to be actively brokered. What do resilience outcomes have to offer crisis plans, emergency responses and disaster recovery of all kinds? Has an explicit interconnectivity been formed, avoided or fudged in a bizarre area diagram that tries to suggest a crisis timeline indicating when each approach has supremacy? The latter two states of affairs, or any such obfuscation, cannot be permitted to continue in our view.

We propose that organisations cannot continue to allow disinterest in objectifying the actual subject matter of resilience to remain a convenient consensus bordering on the postmodern. Rather, a firm, scientific and unequivocal definition must be agreed and owned. This must be visibly linked to the inputs and outputs of the normative business it aims to protect.

We have offered a template to allow organisations to introduce this discrimination. This should include at least the following. An exposition of the professional competencies to which they should relate. A call for a direct link to existing strategic drivers and live business measurements. The resolution of this dual question of the proportion of prevention and optimisation in the end-game. Clear decisions as to how it must tessellate fully with any other risk-based systems up to an including absorbing them completely.

The definition of resilience must remain in the working language, the reference grammar, of the business it deems to protect. The resilience construct should be at all times methodologically transparent and operationally meaningful.

Again, with credible expert support, organisations must seek to make this definition out of active and intelligent choices.

THE REASONING CONSTRUCT

Good inductive and deductive reasoning is never a given. Nor can it be treated as invisible in this context. Care is needed in approaching this subject because the reasoning with uncertainty field is a very much disputed area of science and philosophy. Many academic and applied controversies dog this construct. There is much contradictory evidence as to whether operatives in an industrial setting like the ones we have been discussing would either be naturally very good, or very bad, at reasoning with risk and resilience.

This said, broad evidence-based principles are discernible and widely, if not fully, agreed. Reasoning is the key construct that should explicitly join three concrete forms of the objects we are discussing – risk, resilience and business outcomes – and this is why framing choices is essential. Evidence shows that the use of abstract and technical framing, without appropriate training, counter-indicates effective human reasoning even among educated people. Evidence also shows that the antithesis, a semantically based natural reference grammar, is predicted to meet with good results without any training.

Sadly, most industrial risk and resilience reasoning is currently framed in an abstract technical form. For example, using probability estimates inserted into formulae to create apparently mathematical figures, plots and priority algorithms. Ironically, the alternative, a narrative approach, is often met with hostility because of its insufficiently scientific framing. The need for this framing is something that, on close inspection, might be a question of face validity with technical professions and little more.

The justification for whether people are expected to reason in the abstract or with the descriptive has to be explicit. If an abstract system is chosen, then appropriate training and quality checking must be added. If a narrative system is chosen, the material translation of its concerns to real business levers and outcomes remains imperative. If a hybrid is chosen, something quite interesting might result.

Whatever is chosen, we cannot emphasise enough that the use of a reasoning construct should optimise the efficacy and meaning of the operational effort needed to execute it. It should optimise the efficacy and productivity of the operation all told, in fact, but that may be a discussion for another season.

Real effort is required here, again supported by relevant expertise, to make active choices in the design of the reasoning principles that join risk to resilience and create business decisions.

A REFORMED CONSTRUCT SET

We have convincingly concluded that the use of the constructs of risk, resilience and reasoning in industry is ripe for intellectual and pragmatic reform. This is something that should be considered urgent, particularly in large, complex, distributed organisations operating in a high-value environment. In the immediate short term this reform necessitates that organisations should be foreswearing the received norms and striking out on their own specific journey of design.

This highly personal journey should be informed first by the widely available and relevant scientific disciplines, and second by the organisation's own particular expertise and context (adequately translated). In that sense the result is always a hybrid. Risk, resilience and reasoning have to be allowed to form into a complex causal chain that can actively reflect upon the triple helix of supply, value and reputation for the organisation concerned. This it must do in its native business reference grammars, both strategically and pragmatically.

Lastly, this reasoning chain must evade the obfuscation that so dogs this discipline via the use of the spurious language of business reassurance. It should firmly terminate in cost–benefit and decision-making outcomes that operatives recognise and value. It must do this before it attempts to speak in reassurance of external audiences. In fact, this quality sea-change to its focus, meaning and methods should now become that reassurance reference grammar itself.

It is only armed with a set of reformed constructs like those above that organisations can hope to avoid the postmodern vortex of thinking that so engulfs this area.

IMPROVED PRACTICES ARE IMPERATIVE TO ADDING VALUE

In Parts 1 and 2 we also explored in detail how many current assessment practices can be shown to be borderline meaningless. This is unless we define their function as being able to generate a reassurance dividend for a relatively low effort or disruption. This weakened design means that the current risk and resilience practices are of an uncertain quality. They are unlikely to have any demonstrable impact on business performance. The reasoning chain is a practical antithesis to this approach when it is allowed to question at least the epistemology, definitions and pragmatism in play.

EPISTEMOLOGY: WHAT DO THINGS MEAN?

The reasoning chain is allowed to ask certain epistemological questions. How does industry really come to know about and describe the phenomena it has decided to attach to this term, resilience? Where does the verifiable knowledge come from? Can we examine the whole rationality of the way that large, complex, distributed organisations in particular manage their discourse on risk assessment for the purposes of resilience? Currently that discourse appears quite naïve, where a *de facto* set of constructs drawn from standard protocols seems sufficient.

A true epistemology, we contest very firmly, must be in a cognitive behavioural framing. This can be described most lucidly at the intersect of operational logic, organisational psychology and statistical technique. Each of these is very clearly the work of different expert groups.

We believe the direct, deliberate and expert fusion of these disciplines is necessary to give risk-based resilience reasoning any real applied meaning. The omission of any one of these disciplines in a working model not only substantially weakens the logic – it also substantially weakens the likely efficacy of any decisions or outcomes founded on it.

DEFINITION: HOW ARE THINGS INTERPRETED BY REAL PEOPLE?

The reasoning chain asks questions that are definitional. It cannot escape our attention for long that the industry standard definitions for risk, resilience and reasoning, though we have shown these unequivocally to be scientifically impoverished, are widely and quite uncritically accepted. This is in the, largely unproven, belief that these will be in a fundamentally protective relationship with business value. A relationship in which the promise of which, at least, would indicate that something better than the intangible of reassurance was needed. We have to break this cycle of self-fulfilling prophecy.

There appear to be many short-term, predominantly cultural, priorities which nonetheless dominate the definition activity. Included here are: time pressures – creating an atmosphere of expediency; a lack of training in the necessary disciplines – leading to poor comprehension; and many interpolated factors from the history of accepted use of legacy systems – encouraging a low tolerance for (measurement and systemic) disruption or complexity.

We believe that organisations have to bring a strategic challenge to show that these short-sighted practices utilising poor definitions are now unacceptable. The definition activity must proceed solely from scientific principles to a localised expression of real objects and their manipulation.

STRATEGIC AND TECHNICAL PRINCIPLES FOR PRAGMATIC APPLICATION

This reasoning chain argument is clearly asking for some better practices with which few would, in isolation, really disagree – a stronger, scientifically based epistemology, so it is clear what the real, validated referents, and their combination rules, should be for a specific context. A more highly disciplined set of definitions, so it is clear what these are to mean is enforced in practice and across the available operating cultures.

We have to be clear that grounded and effective definition is, however, not going to be enough on its own. Long-term meaningful application is still a key concern. The meaningful interlinking of the constructs of resilience, risk and reasoning themselves with the triple-helix arrangement must bring a conceptual, cognitive and behavioural clarity to play. These must create a systematic objectification that operatives will recognise, value, be willing to work with and be affected by. This is a psychological task and it begins with acquiescence to disruption.

This process will be highly disruptive in at least two key ways. One, it will align with the irrefutable extant scientific critique of so-called best practices and abandon them. Two, it will steel itself to address the real complexity that these practices have so long obfuscated. For this to have an effect, a deeply pragmatic set of accommodations must now form a bridge. This bridge is needed to fill the gap between the rhetoric of the importance of risk and resilience and the demonstrable business efficacy of the systems which deliver them.

STRATEGIC PRINCIPLES FOR AN AUTHORITATIVE DESIGN

Such intentional disruption has to seek to forcefully apply the reformed constructs above to an impact point of business efficacy. Five pragmatic considerations will clear the runway with all key users and audiences:

1 Strategic positioning – the necessity to apply these constructs to connect and interact with normative strategic business decision making. This has to be accepted as potentially highly disruptive.
2 The governance proposition – the meta-rules by which an organisation might apply these constructs. These require detailed

consideration as they will be neither extant nor obvious from current practices and might face real resistance.

3 System integration considerations – the way in which the quality and integrity of their uses and outcomes is valued alongside other similar systems. This should be accepted as inherently complex.

4 Ready-to-use forms – such as a pre-existing Standard or an off-the-shelf capability from a consultancy offering. These must be viewed with circumspection.

5 Commensurate expertise – the team of operatives who own the risk and resilience space across a business must be breakaway experts in its application who are authorised and fully supported to deliver disruptive innovation.

The route to these positive outcomes is not an easy one. It requires an appetite for practical science rather than technical window dressing. It requires investment of significant time, resource and strategic intention. It is lined with intellectual and political controversy. It also happens to be the only intelligent alternative to deliver enhanced systems complexity.

These and other reasons extolled in this book are why there must be a commitment to design. This is not, as has so far lamentably been the case, the begrudging design of one assessment methodology among many to satisfy a tributary desire for compliance and reassurance. This is the design of the master system of pragmatic controls for the quadruple helix. The design, in fact, of a reasoning superstructure which will intentionally enhance the entire business prospectus of the triple helix in a meaningful and accountable way.

TECHNICAL PRINCIPLES FOR INTEGRATED AND EFFECTIVE DESIGN

The journey of design we have been speaking of in this book has been framing itself around a set of scientifically balanced principles. This is illustrated by the call for evidence-based framing for a start. From there, we have gone on at different points to exemplify other principles.

The application of coherent measurement scales. The derivation of appropriate and meaningful statistical models. The psychological benefit of the selection of effectiveness criteria for end users particularly and pragmatically suited to their own unique context. All of these must be, as we concluded again only a moment ago, supported by informed and effectively trained experts working in a multidisciplinary way.

However, it is fair to ask, once these intellectual imperatives have been accepted by an organisation, what then? What would the technical substance of this system actually look like? This is where we must return to the practical subject matter of this book and ask whether you can now recognise it more fully. Throughout we have introduced and framed all our technical arguments around as series of applied case studies. The technical substance of the design should resemble these. Now that the arguments are completed, we can briefly revisit these real examples and craft some more specific principles from them.

This is important because our case studies are real-world examples of better practices and therefore the credibility of our argument. They augment the philosophical and scientific case we are making with of a body of relevant applied research inside examples of the large, complex, distributed organisations which are our target audience. Organisations like yours.

Revisiting these case studies will serve to illustrate and summarise not only what is desirable, but what is possible. They make a valuable technical argument to support the new designs we are calling for. To facilitate this, let's look at the case studies in a slightly different order.

1 The deconstruction of risk and resilience Standards into a pan-organisational competence set for a major UK high street department chain.
2 The review of the decisions underpinning the positioning of a new resilience capability in a global FMCG.
3 The management of risk in a large transformation project for a global FMCG.

4 An examination of a heuristic approach to risk event measurement and discrimination drawn from an Air Traffic Management context.

5 The application of a resilience modelling approach and software for a major global brand in a VUCA environment.

6 A translation (from the same major brand exercise) examining the intersect between standardised business case authoring using justified resilience countermeasures.

A summary of high-level learning points might be helpful at this stage (Table 19.1).

DECONSTRUCTION IS ESSENTIAL

In Parts 3 and 4 of the book, we became concerned with choosing a systems design approach. With the help of our UK high street department chain, we searched for evidence-based templates from industry Standards. Although we noted the confidence of industry as a whole in the applicability of national and/or international Standards for risk and resilience, we felt this may be misplaced.

At this juncture in the scientific debate, the received wisdom of such approaches may be just that, a received wisdom. Furthermore, taking a helicopter view of the cross-organisational use of Standards and their guidance in any large, distributed organisation, we noted that these approaches have a tendency to proliferate behavioural demands on the whole business. The volume of compliance to new behaviours, when taken in total, seems unsustainable. This is particularly in the light of a controlling story about not adding complexity without value.

The wisdom-sharing communities who generate these schemata are without doubt qualified to bring their applied commentary. They are clearly collecting their views and developing consensus in an orderly and rational manner. However, the question of evidence dominates. There is, as yet, no formal evidence that the principles and guidance of any Standards can be applied to a live context in an efficacious manner. That is to say, in a way which is demonstrably, not perceptually, promoting of business value, supply chain integrity or reputational capital.

Holding these two ideas in some tension, we did not wish to totally discount that the, as yet unvalidated, wisdom of Standards might support design. Our test case examined the application of a hierarchical analysis technique from organisational psychology to assess key commonalities.

This proved a highly fruitful exercise. The wisdom across multiple Standards seems inherently reducible. Tens of components and hundreds of behaviours can be narrowed to meaningful descriptive meta-sets which could act as templates for better practice. Templates offering an attractive granularity across strategic, pragmatic and quality assurance variables. Of particular value is the fact that these could also form a basis for validation.

Technical principle 1 – use cognitive behavioural framing

Our first technical design principle is this therefore: only use specific and measurable cognitive and behavioural variables.

If an organisation wishes to use guidance and best practice, it should only do so after a process of deconstruction of the behavioural requirements as applied clearly to the desire of an organisation for self-understanding.

This process must generate rich and detailed questions to help people think around very specific risk and resilience constructs that can be married to their own context. This process must create a picture of the actual problem sets being faced. It must do this in the pragmatic language of the business. Direct and consequential business behaviours must be precisely specified as the outcome.

TABLE 19.1 Summary of high-level learning points

Case	Problem Application	Example of Reasoning Attributes	Example of Key Conclusions
Standards deconstruction	Extraction of core competencies Factor analysis of mediators of performance Understanding of behavioural burden	Showing how high-level factor model predicts strategic rationale Extraction and enumeration of behavioural factors Combination of performance-shaping factors	Standards are reducible to a highly complex and interdependent set of factors Factors are further reducible to elegant sets of a small number of performance indicators Assessment tools for related practices such as guidance writing
Resilience capability positioning	The relationship between a resilience construct and legacy systems for business interruption	Positioning by pragmatic exclusion Discerning the unique attributes of "new" resilience	Greater initial organisational acceptance of the resilience construct can be linked to lower disruption effects The efficacy of a resilience construct positioned in this way is questionable, as the definition outcome increases complexity
Manufacturing transformation	Discrete project risk management concerns Independence Static scoring Link to decision making Absence of control	Formation of meta-risks Chronological approach to risk tracking Linking to BAU hot spots	Interconnectivity of risks (volatility and amplification) is a key maturity feature Modelling reasoning is superior to measurement conclusion making

Heuristic risk event measurement	Managing low tolerance for complexity whilst increasing validity of risk scoring and reasoning	The introduction of a scaleable multi-attribute system of risk scoring The application of tolerance for risk as an algorithm for enhanced reasoning	A heuristic reasoning system can span both simple and complex measurement tasks within the same system The impact of readily available increased measurement rigour for relatively little increase in effort influences the appetite for risk judgement complexity positively
DescartesR supply chain reasoning tool	Large, complex supply chain in a VUCA environment facing multiple and repeated crises of operation	Seven key questions define the risk assessment and the de-risking opportunity space for a major brand	Objectivity using pre-existing business data is extremely valuable Modelling with complex risk constructs is more useful for complex interdependencies over time Well-crafted heuristics have a vital role to play to support risk reasoning
BOSCARDs and countermeasures	The translation of resilience reasoning system outcomes into discrete and costed business cases	Risk–cost–benefit analysis Reduction of complex risk and resilience data into coherent action plans	Linking of the outcomes of a resilience risk reasoning exercise and the business appetite for the cost and disruption of countermeasures embeds resilience into the strategic decision making of the supply and value chains

ACTIVELY RESOLVE THE RELATIONSHIP TO LEGACY SYSTEMS

Taking considerations of existing risk management systems, cultures and intentionality seriously, we concluded that, after appetite for complexity, the greatest mediator for success of a risk-based resilience reasoning system would be its positioning. This is as regards the holistic picture of operational risk control. With the help of our global FMCG, we noted that the optimal positioning ought to be as a higher-order strategic governance infrastructure to command and control this effort.

This positioning rejects the, less controversial, compromise of retro-fitting a new or evolved resilience approach into a pre-existing landscape without changing it. Rather, we concluded that disruptively reshaping that landscape is imperative to avoid self-defeating contradictions. The strategy for positioning can be summarised in an eight-stage model focusing on, for example, explicit strategic values, a direct link to Audit and paying far closer attention to environmental factors like markets, ethics and technology.

Where a disruptive approach is not possible because the desire is only to improve existing systems by an evolutionary, rather than a revolutionary, process, key target behaviours are imperative. System improvements must address transparency, authority and efficacy.

Our test case, exploring the current failure modes and critical success factors of the existing legacy/competitor systems, such as Business Continuity Management, led us to a taxonomy of design requirements. These demonstrated the imperative to direct this evolution at cultural, financial, operational and functional targets. These criteria safeguard against a merely rhetorical rebranding exercise. However, larger systemic considerations, not least the pervasive appetite for complexity, would still determine overall acceptance of any system.

Technical principle 2 – business outcome focus

Our second technical design principle is therefore: agreed and valid business outcomes must be the focus of this activity. It is simply unavoidably incumbent on the owners of a resilience risk reasoning system to fully explicate a strategic model of the real complexity of the business it is pertaining to protect. Only by being designed to promote business outcomes in a targeted, valid and measurable way can it hope to make a meaningful operational contribution.

USE TOOLS TO LOCK IN BUSINESS OUTCOMES AND CONTROL BEHAVIOUR

A key way to optimise, or at least stabilise, material business gains from a disruptive, infrastructural and complex approach to risk and resilience lies in the use of tools. Tools have at least three key roles to play. First, they can make the complexity burden more manageable through epitomising its process as an efficacious series of well-defined inputs and outputs. Second they can standardise and quality manage the reasoning process by encapsulating it whilst requiring it to be followed without compromise. Third, they can be designed to automate summary outputs for key audiences.

The positive impact of locking this process, measurement and conclusion making into a software system – to facilitate and standardise its execution and communication – cannot be overstated. The idea that of a reasoning system actually becoming a tangible, named and trusted system which users/beneficiaries can see is a hugely pragmatic facilitator of auditable best practice.

Scientifically it is also possible to design greater objectivity, more powerful modelling and superior rationality into a formal system. Not only can this be coded into the data structures and functions, but the methodology supported by the tool can be a prescriptive part of the processes.

In two case studies spanning the continuum of complexity tolerance, we demonstrated unequivocally that solid software tools are not only a key performance-shaping factor in system efficacy but also in system validation by users. We showed that well-designed tools that are computationally coherent can always supplant the desire for face validity which comes from adopting inferior mathematical housing without the requisite reasoning power.

We also showed that tools can encapsulate your reasoning design by releasing the full power of a well-crafted set of objective metrics coupled to a well-controlled set of decision heuristics. As a part of the solution to complexity intolerance, or time constraints, this process efficiency has much to commend it whilst safeguarding your intended rationality from the corrupting effects of shortcuts.

Technical principle 3 – build a formal system

Our third technical design principle is therefore: build a formal system. This is to safeguard the integrity of your design process by locking it procedurally, computationally and in terms of high-quality output capability into a software platform.

MOVE FROM COMPLEXITY TO PRAGMATISM

Accepting that a mature approach to constructs and a disruptive design was possible, we still had to address the challenge of how to deal with all this in a busy operational reality. We needed to explore the limits of this suitably complex and strategically placed formal system for risk-based resilience reasoning. A deconstruction of the organisation's existing goals for risk and resilience application remains the critical first step to test this appetite. Our test case here offered a template to maximise the insight of this process, for example by focusing on different types of knowledge extraction, control variables, business integration intention and so on. We noted that this led inexorably to a system design which was powerful at the cost of being complex.

To gain organisational penetration it was imperative to elaborate on the direct mechanisms by which these efforts will drive desirable business outcomes. We saw that this could be through facilitating a range of behaviours – from pragmatic cost savings, to risk contingency planning, to intentional culture change. This breakaway move meant turning risk and resilience systems into intentional business engines. This could only be done by linking them directly to the measurable performance of the value, supply and reputation chains.

The business engine concept also requires acceptance within the organisation that moving away from a reassurance-seeking agenda is desirable. The core activity should remain the overall drive of the business intention. This is not to suggest that simplified reassurance outcomes are no longer possible, just that they are no longer the focus. They become a by-product of the complexity-reduction reasoning embedded in a mature way into existing business systems.

To gain acceptance that this new approach is necessary, much work is necessary and much resistance must be faced down. Front-loading the argument with evidence of its meaningfulness, functionality and clear added value is an essential prerequisite. If it has been well designed, this task should not be imposing. These are imperative technology transfer success mediators. They have to focus on reducing dissent around the challenge to, or even loss of, legacy systems. Reducing it also around the increased complexity of a replacement multi-attribute, multidisciplinary, multi-stakeholder dialectic and the impact this has on time, cost disturbance and culture. The key success mediator is that the system wears its business relevance credentials in plain sight.

Technical principle 4 – business case must be the translator

One clear illustration of this is the necessity in our most mature resilience case study to be able to translate outcomes back into the language of a business case. The BOSCARD approach, although capitulating to a very stylised summary format, is an example of the necessity to re-translate complex resilience reasoning back into a consequential form.

Our fourth technical principle therefore is that the complexity of the risk-based resilience reasoning system cannot be an end in itself. It has to be a facilitator of a very demand-focused return to normal. When the work is done, it must translate back into the pragmatic and authoritative reference grammar of the normative business language.

CONCLUSIONS FROM THIS CHAPTER

As this is one of the closing chapters, the conclusions are already laid bare in the text. We are proposing that risk-based resilience reasoning be elevated to take an integrated position as a complementary fourth strand in the dominant supply, value and reputation chain systems of large organisations. This can be achieved when:

1 The key points of differentiation between business reasoning and risk-based reasoning are accepted and professionally codified.
2 A reformed set of intentional and expertly defined constructs for risk, resilience and reasoning are allowed to formally complement business reasoning.
3 Strategic and authoritative governance supports competent experts to integrate the two.
4 The technical outworking of the three conditions above satisfies five key criteria:
   a cognitively and behaviourally framed
   b allowed to disrupt legacy systems
   c dictated by valid business outcomes
   d locked into process controlling software
   e translated back into a business case output, not a risk one.

Based on the evidence of the scientific debates, the deconstruction of the extant approaches of organisations we have worked with and our own applied case studies – we think this is not only possible, but that it is essential. In our final chapter we will summarise how you might go about making this argument for the reasoning chain yourself.

CHAPTER 18

The reasoning chain

In the case studies throughout this book, particularly our last and most involved one, we have rolled up the evidence that the design principles we require can work. We have elucidated in detail, summarised in taxonomies and rarefied in checklists what we believe a risk-based resilience reasoning system for a large, complex and distributed organisation working in a VUCA context actually needs to look like. And we have explained how it needs to perform. You have all the principles to hand now.

You also have the key meta-principle, if you like. This is that a risk-based resilience reasoning system, to be scientifically valid and operationally effective, needs to be a complex and, above all, expert system. That's the crux of the matter. We would argue that the classic, extant, standardised and accepted so-called best practices are not that. They are something else far more compromised by a history of untenable ideas and constructs inexpertly atomised across a business in such a way that they never deliver a sufficiently clear narrative to highlight their invalidity. Their wastefulness, in fact.

We have given you a best-in-class example of a working alternative in a supply chain risk context. In the distinct interlocking processes of an involved expert system like DescartesR, or something like it that suits your sector, there are clear demands. Demands for experts to apply themselves to detailed pre-work in order to fully understand the landscapes of the problems they are facing. This is necessary if they hope to use the social constructs of risk and resilience to first conceptualise these and then to create solutions for them.

This conceptualisation and solution formation creates demands for involved business data conversion and collection. There then needs to be multiple detailed and formal multi-attribute evaluations of the implications of that data-rich picture. There needs to be a rule-based and systematic prioritisation approach which requires a reconciliation of the resulting insights across a group of experts. Often this needs professional workshops. Everything has to be concluded not in a risk narrative at all but in a formal set of agreed and costed business cases. Cases that are then validated by presentation to business leadership for approval and funding.

Lastly, there needs to be a commitment to the empirical method. Once the interventions are executed, the team needs to commit to re-evaluate the risk and resilience and iteratively thereafter, to ensure that positive changes have occurred and do persist.

In proving that all of this is achievable in a single expert system, we answer a meta-question which dominates this whole subject matter area. A meta-question that you, the reader, might have been asking yourself as you have gone through this book.

Is this complexity really necessary and worth all the effort?

Clearly, we believe the answer is yes.

WHY IS THE ANSWER YES?

We have said all along that the ultimate measure for risk-based reasoning system efficacy should be the demonstrable protection of business value and the verifiable optimisation of business performance. So it is time to ask you to face the facts. These don't come cheap. As lesser systems pandering to low tolerance for complexity and the expedience of reassurance do come cheap, we have consistently argued that they waste value in the end. With their heavily compromised structures, amateur application, tactical location, perennial focus, borderline meaningless measurements, endless aggregation compromises and therefore occluded reasoning, they are simply not rational.

The answer is yes, because organisations need reasoning power. To get at the shape of that we first had to clear the intellectual decks. This area has for so long been dominated by the shared wisdom of a self-referential set of best practices forged in the fires of pragmatic compromise that few people seem to question the intellectual integrity of these practices.

Our design journey concept invited you into a rational, scientific, pragmatic and evidence-based examination of their integrity as a whole for once, and in some detail. It was an examination of the integrity of "risk-based resilience reasoning" in industry itself. The logical end-point of that intellectual journey was to propose that the evident sophistication of a full-power reasoning system was the only real answer to the question. A multi-attribute, multi-level, multi-stakeholder expert system like DescartesR.

Our design journey concept invited you to qualify the time, resources and costs that the application of a system as powerful and involved as DescartesR, or some appropriate equivalent for other sectors, represents a clear business case. To do this, we argued that the compelling business case for the dominant, complex triple-helix argument itself was the justification for a risk-based resilience reasoning system. Only by being intentionally designed to strategically support the latter could the former make any sense.

Our design journey concept required intellectual and business logic combine to make a coherent, and above all rational, argument. Thus, the time and resources that should be expended to harness risk and resilience into a sophisticated reasoning chain should be two things. One, it should be an intentional process of trade-off, something we termed appetite for complexity. Two, that appetite should be entirely commensurate with the measurable value that the organisation expects to see from the activity and no other variable.

This risk-based resilience reasoning activity can only be effective if it forms a quadruple helix for a modern, large, complex and distributed organisation with supply, value and reputation. To close our discussion then, we would like to conclude by summarising, one final time for you, both the intellectual and the business rationale for our design "proposition".

IN DEFENCE OF THE INTELLECTUAL ARGUMENT

COHERENT RISK DEFINITION

This aligns with a definition of risk in its most business useful dialect, that of the providential reasoning level. That is to say, the risk assessments are using a process approach which, rather than describe speculative probabilities around isolated fears, describes pragmatic and verifiable operational phenomena. This greatly discourages the sort of coloured spreadsheet dialect of pedantry which, in its atomisation, is an enemy of rationality. Our risk sets are expert, they are rehearsed and confirmed by independent teams working on recognisably expert tasks and always moving between the correct reference grammars. The outcome is never a risk score or priority list per se. The outcome is the use of risk scoring rationality to create business risk arguments.

This approach measures risk in the necessary multiple contexts. This it does using a range of naturalistic, heuristic and formal statistical metrics.

More to the point, it never asks anyone to multiply the abstract probability of an isolated event by its independent impact on a notional idea of business. Risk is allowed to be in the currency of as many expressions as are needed to hold a genuine narrative in the right descriptive tension. This particularly includes some of the most attractive business descriptors that are unapologetically blunt and financial.

Probability, where it is being used, is represented in a psychologically rich way. It is conveyed by confidence bands, acceptability limits and reasoned cases. This is because it often has to be discerned in the absence of real data or in the presence of very little data. It even acts as a pure psychological summary term, such as in the case of performance-shaping factors of success. Thus, probability is being held in tension away from being a summary number or a data-reducing mean score. It is utilised as a power concept that can be in a simultaneously conditional and naturalistic language. It is applied to generate operational, psychological and statistical meanings.

ANALYSIS NOT SCORING

People are being placed in a risk analysis mindset, not a risk-scoring one. Risk scores are not the core of this exercise – they are the summary outcome of a clear audit trail of rationality. Where they are described in the rich architecture of exercises such as meta-risk, hot spot identification and particularly in BOSCARD-type outcomes, the risk burden of the assessment is being managed intellectually as an interdependent, time-based and volatile system of thought. It is created as an actionable proposition. The participants are being facilitated to think like this because a variety of interconnected risk expressions are being held in a business-meaningful, narrative tension. They are comparable only through simultaneously examining various assessments, evaluations and visualisations.

ASSURANCE IS NOT FORGOTTEN

This is based on a very explicit policy (although that was not described). The procedures that this requires also show a high degree of respect for the structures, processes and, most of all, expert credibility of the teams within the existing business operation. Although a degree of remove is required (risk process is never business as usual, risk outcomes are trans-material), people are being harnessed and supported to do what they already do well. They are simply being taught a new range of dialects within which to express it.

It also recognises the need for risk in other far more generalised dialects, such as risk assurance, as appropriate. In part this is because the very existence of this complex reasoning system is an assurance process in and of itself, a gold standard one if people stop to think about it. It is, in and of itself therefore, a diligence exercise, one that is actually completed with diligence. It demonstrably enhances the due diligence argument of the very high level of dialect required by a corporate risk assessment to speak to the well-being of an entire corporate organism. It does this by rejecting short-term paper tiger arguments which only reassure.

It therefore more demonstrably enhances corporate diligence by being defensible scientific best practice rationally applied. In doing this, because the process design incorporates corporate values and external environmental factors, it visibly embraces and stimulates the ethical dimension of risk – a critical element in a VUCA environment.

USE OF HUMAN INTELLECTUAL CAPITAL

It taps, as we have repeatedly stated, into the multidisciplinary expertise base of your human intellectual capital in a meaningful and goal-directed way. So it deploys their knowledge, skills and judgement in the decision making. It is not a man/woman with an abstract template and pestering e-mails. The reasoning it calls for aligns with how the rest of the professionals in the business already operate and deliver their own contributions to the value proposition. In this way it should never be thought of as "too complex" at all – rather it has a resonant complexity to release the most powerful asset your organisation possesses.

It seeks to predict and control behaviour from a position of amassed expert knowledge. Where knowledge is lacking (the known–unknown variety), research tools and applied heuristics seek to rationally fill the gaps. The 'unknown-unknowns' are approached in the only way possible, which is that space is given for problems to be examined and re-examined from multiple viewpoints by multidisciplinary groups. These teams of experts are given a licence to reason with risk without the (initial) burden of having to justify their activity through business correlates, such as time and cost.

IT IS BUSINESS SCIENCE

It is based on the science of operations utilising relevant experts trained in that science. It is not the abstract expertise of a risk, continuity or resilience expert trying to co-opt busy professionals to provide anodyne scores or data to support an action-planning approach. It enables people to meet their risk responsibilities whilst doing their day job at the same time. The key benefit of this business scientific framing is that expert can be a tremendous co-beneficiary of the process. It actually stimulates them in terms of collecting learning and sharing practices back into their operational roles. Stimulates them to do the business science that they are paid for.

It applies, rehearses and improves knowledge and judgement. It tackles the importance and the function of risk and resilience evaluation through applying coherent knowledge. All throughout the process, large banks of knowledge are being input as the feedstock for a rational evaluation. Where knowledge is lacking, specific heuristics are in play to allow teams to continue to reason within confidence bands and guesswork which is kept transparent through to the outcome. Tracking the outcomes of the process validates the speculative and increases knowledge.

IT IS NOT, SOLELY, IMPACT ACCEPTING

It blends a preventative and a mitigating approach to solutions. It is understood that cost–risk–benefits are to be the key drivers of action as expressed in a business case. This is not the defensive approach of impact acquiescence and contingency. In consequence, it is not above a restructuring of entire aspects of the business model if these prove to be risk creating, or if that risk burden is classified as unacceptable to leaders, stakeholders, regulators or shareholders.

So, it recognises that although the most cost-effective supply chains are often the least resilient, all cost-effective supply chains need resilience in the long term. Although the most profitable value chains are Machiavellian, all ethical value chains prosper on resilience. Although the most unassailable reputation chains are secretive, all reputation capital is publicly resilient. So the balance of prevention and reaction is logically redrawn as a narrative of appetite and, at the very least, internal transparency.

THE DECISIONS ARE BUSINESS TRANSPARENT

It is not based on the production of figures, lists or documents concerning fictive future states. Its outcomes are decisions in the form of a costed business case. That process is managing risk tolerance actively and through a deliberate feedback loop formalised in the normative rules of business sign-off.

To say that a risk countermeasure or resilience improvement will not be funded or approved is a *de facto* case of risk tolerance. Any senior team, or audit committee, who follows the trail of why things were, or were not, done is going to see risk tolerance in explicit action. Unlike the risks hanging on the imaginary washing line of the risk register, these have been integrated, in a transparent way, within the live business management process. They are in the same format and obey the same rules.

ALL OF THE BENEFITS ARE TIGHTLY GUARDED IN A COHERENT TOOL

The process embraces the need for an enabling tool to be designed specifically to safeguard all of these benefits from the attrition of later compromises in complexity appetite. The master outcome is a single piece of coherent software in a one-stop-shop. Moreover, wherever possible this process imports pre-existing business data (assets, SKU data, costs etc.) without the need for further manipulation. This greatly facilitates technology acceptance.

The tools help systematise and, to a certain degree, simplify the application of this data to the specific questions of resilience. This is because the analytics themselves have been designed by the organisation's resident experts. It even characterises a formal reporting mechanism to make communicating outputs at various levels within the host culture a lot simpler.

IT IS A COMPLETE DESIGN SOLUTION

Those thirteen reasons, you will agree, are, in effect, a grand tour of the journey of design found in this book. They are thirteen mechanisms by which a specific risk-based resilience reasoning system has been fashioned by the evidence to be a powerful support to the rationality of a business. To be a reasoning chain that strengthens an organisation's use of this conceptual hardware to support rather than just qualify its key business objectives.

IN DEFENCE OF THE BUSINESS LOGIC ARGUMENT

You'd be forgiven for thinking we had already just made the business logic argument, so integral to our design is a reflection of the business data structure and decision architectures. However, that design remains, as we have said, an argument of good social science, not of effective business. The real business logic of this design requires us to take a mature approach to the whole challenge of risk-based resilience systems decision making in all industry.

BUSINESS IS COMPLEX, ACCEPT IT

For any large organisation working in the contexts we are describing, the reality of resilience and risk is fiercely complex. Fact. The *reductio ad absurdum* of running a coloured spreadsheet which pertains to describe that complexity is in no way a true benchmark for how it should be simplified. As we have said before, it is patently stupid and obfuscates, rather than explains, the meaning and the flow of a risk construct for the organisation and its impact on resilience reasoning and their joint impact on value creation and business optimisation.

COMPLEXITY REDUCTION IS NEEDED

"Simplification" is always achievable in two ways. The first route is to be complexity intolerant. To demand, in effect, that things be simplified by a process which makes them simple. As we have argued, the driver for this behaviour is not rationality, it is intolerance. This is fed by a fear of communicating something complex that is not fully understood to an audience that doesn't have the tolerance for the ambiguity it will generate. Communication in a context where all of the professionals concerned in this dialogue are either fearful, or not willing to increase their expertise and change their mental models. Combined with a distrust of the social science expert community that could alleviate these worries, the result is a near-pathological level of complexity intolerance for this subject matter.

This complexity intolerance is instantly defeating of the idea that resilience and risk should be allowed to be complex, despite the fact that they are asked to be philosophically emergent properties of what are extremely complex businesses. Ignoring this, it requires them to be summarised in codes and colours within word limits and in a fixed number of PowerPoint slides presented in an extremely limited amount of time dedicated to sign off. At every point, this is fallacious reasoning. It's like expecting vitamin pills to perform the function of antibiotics.

Simplification is also achievable in a second, and clearly better, way. This is to do the required analytical work to reduce the complexity of the real variables in the situation through a deep comprehension of them. This form of simplicity is a skilled process to accept and summarise a complex system, not the *prima facie* rejection of its complexity. Once it has been complexity reduced in this expert approach, i.e. comprehended, then it can be summarised as a way to convey the key attributes of a deeper state of affairs.

LET EXPERTS BE EXPERT

Although systems like DescartesR are complex, evidently so, they don't wish away the real (and far greater) complexity of running massive multi-billion euro supply chains. They simply desire to face up to applying constructs which reduce the complexity of the risk and resilience propositions these convey. They do this best by asking the experts who design, run and therefore understand the whole complexity of the entire system to become fluent in a complimentary system of risk dialects. This then allows them to describe the necessity and the form of the system's resilience in the normative rationality of the target systems and the surrounding business model.

To do this effectively, a second group of experts must also be convinced; these are senior strategists. Senior buy-in to this more complexity-tolerant situation is achieved in two ways. First, and by no means an easy task, the senior attention is focused by the confidence they can have in the policy architecture. This is one of their own risk dialects.

Exposing the operational demand characteristics in this dialect, one that includes regulatory and external agency, helps senior groups to understand how risk-based resilience helps them to do their jobs. Jobs that require them to answer to shareholders, stakeholders and critics with, necessarily attenuated, arguments to show that they are awake at the helm. They do this by creating a credible risk and resilience narrative to justify operational decision making in a way that makes sense to the external context.

Second, senior buy-in is achieved through the output of the system being respectful of their decision-making architecture and expert judgement (veto even). That is why presenting a business case instrument at the end of this process is absolutely critical. It allows the authoritative senior business experts to assess the input of resilience and risk to that business in a way that is commensurate with their internal responsibilities and accountability.

Thus, a further net benefit of senior buy-in to such a process is that systems like DescartesR are designed to close the loop on the need for internal diligence and assurance mandates as well. They do this by creating a credible risk and resilience narrative to justify operational decision making in a way that makes sense to the internal and external context simultaneously.

ALLOCATE A BUDGET

There is very little to say here. This system is predicated on actual business costs, gains, losses and the long-term internal and external risks to those. The outcomes of such a process would be highly suspect if it did not contain a bill to be paid. That bill is justified by the net percentage (in our case) of the value of the supply chain being protected. The risk appetite calculation is mediated directly rather than indirectly by the live budgetary considerations in these tools.

DEMAND ORGANISATIONAL SYNERGY

The design of a system like DescartesR allows for a just-in-time reasoning set. In our case study, the organisation was already experiencing extreme duress at the intersection between its value and supply chains.

That certainly made getting permission to launch a large programme of resilience all the easier. However, even when the thumbscrews are not as tight, the process should be respectful of what the organisation needs to achieve.

This is reflected in the elegance of the design of the independent tools. There is nothing stopping an organisation using a part of this process, or a single tool, for other business purposes. There is nothing stopping them using a subset of tools to create and independently monitor key operational benchmarks. In fact, this net benefit has been specifically catered for in the design. This toolset is always useful to the business, not just when an audit of risk-based resilience is required.

MEASURE EFFICACY

A key take-home point is that although the data collection, workshops, discussions, measurement activities and so on are inescapably detailed, they are this way because they are of such a high quality. This at once gives a huge resilience benefit all by itself. As the operation in question rolls forward through time, these analyses can now be efficiently reused and updated. Once a comprehensive resilience analysis is in place, the effort required to maintain and update it drops back to less than that which would be required for the traditional yearly of the risk register audit.

A final point that we would, of course, argue is simple to make. This works. This evidence-led, research-based, operationally designed process works. It was greatly valued by the receiving organisation who went on to invest millions in the countermeasure set that it designed to protect their business. Operations don't do this on a whim.

In summary the design of this resilience risk system, or one like it, passes all of the strategic and technical business criteria we have set out throughout this book. This shows you, the reader, that this is not only desirable, not only possible, but effective also.

Rather than risk and resilience continuing to be the unitary language of violently aggregated probability and impact data forced through an uncritically accepted action planning system, it is now designed to be a fluent and effecting combination of multiple risk dialects being expertly spoken. We have demonstrated the costs and the efficacy of risk-based resilience reasoning as a systematic and scientifically valid pursuit, satisficing both the analytical and the communication needs of multiple relevant audiences.

In short, a reasoning chain that is a scientifically coherent, operationally elegant, business logical and fit for purpose system is entirely possible.

In short, its DNA can now be made up in equal parts from operational logic, organisational psychology and statistical technique.

What's keeping you?

A simple template for taking stock of your risk architecture

The template below is the basis of a helpful reckoner tool based on the conclusions of Part 1.

It allows you to build an assessment which can, in a very general sense, benchmark any risk system you are already using against the standards we have been describing.

To turn this template into a questionnaire, do something like the following:

1 Use question zero to generate an informative description.
   A well-designed risk system avoids pedantry, is biased towards providence but includes the three elements above it.
2 Prepare a questionnaire scale device, preferably operating a 1000-point scale. Excel and similar tools are quite good for this.
3 Attach the scale to each question and distribute the three anchor texts equally across the questions in the order they appear. These will now describe the span of the scale from low to high, and it is ready to use with individuals or as a facilitated group process.

4 To arrive at a final score, aggregate individual scores across questions 1–10 using a geometric mean calculation (because scoring high in all areas is necessitated for a well-rounded system design).

5 Take the following reckoner as a benchmark:
800–1000: World class
600–800: High-performing
400–600: Developing excellence
200–400: Adequate baseline (in need of improvement)
100–200: Inadequate.

6 Plot the individual question scores for 1–10 in a bar chart against the geometric mean score. This will provide as a basic gap analysis to help you plan system improvements.

RISK SYSTEM HEALTH ASSESSMENT TEMPLATE

QUESTION 0. DESCRIBING DIALECT

Allocate from a total of 100% the degree of emphasis your organisation places on speaking about risk in the following ways:

Ethical   Diligence   Assurance   Providence   Pedantry

QUESTION 1. SEMANTICS

Which of the following statement best defines the way risk functionally appears to your organisation?

Low anchor: One or more lists of discretised risk events.
Medium anchor: Thematic risk registers delivering an appropriate description of operational strands or groups.
High anchor: Meta-risks linked to strategic business process critical paths, decisions and outcomes.

QUESTION 2. ABSTRACTION

What form does the outcome of your risk exercise predominately take?

Low anchor: Events or actions that are mainly localised to a particular part or sector of the business.

Medium anchor: Business decisions with appropriate levels of escalation.

High anchor: Business case with cost–benefit analysis referred for sign-off.

QUESTION 3. MEASUREMENT 1 – DEFINITION

What type of measurement best describes the one that you typically use in your risk assessments?

Low anchor: Probability and impact classification leading to prioritisation.

Medium anchor: Linked business impact assessments including actions.

High anchor: Causal chain scenario description including volatility and business criticality indication.

QUESTION 4. MEASUREMENT 2 – SCALE USE

What type of scaling best describes the measurement instruments you typically use for risk assessment?

Low anchor: A low–medium-high severity or intensity estimate.

Medium anchor: An anchored 1–5 scale for severity or impact.

High anchor: A formal ratio level scale of validated business constructs.

QUESTION 5. MATERIALITY

What sort of description aligned to business outcomes does your risk exercise recognise?

> *Low anchor:* Risk magnitude advisory with local action planning to control or reduce key risks.
>
> *Medium anchor:* A business impact assessment of sets of risks with decision support.
>
> *High anchor:* Value creation or destruction statistics with business case, costs and benefits for remediation.

QUESTION 6. APPETITE FOR COMPLEXITY

How is the detail of your risk system best described with respect to its complexity?

> *Low anchor:* A "classical risk", i.e. rapid identification of risk events, probability and impact judgements followed by some kind of prioritisation mechanism.
>
> *Medium anchor:* A fit-for-purpose system which does its best to describe your particular operational realities using basic but meaningfully descriptive tools.
>
> *High anchor:* A complexity-reduction process whereby professionals are using validated methods from your industry to drive strategic outcomes.

QUESTION 7. PLANNED INTERCONNECTIVITY

Which of the following best describes how your system typically assesses risks?

> *Low anchor:* Assess risks one by one – treating them as largely independently identified events or outcomes.

Medium anchor: Assess risk by linking risk events or outcomes to your operational context – particularly its speed of movement, pace of change and planning timetables.

High anchor: Assess risk by allowing experts to link them to your operational context and to also specify connections between individual and groups risks in business outcome terms.

QUESTION 8. MODELLING RISK WITH TIME

Does your risk system use time as a factor when risks are being assessed?

Low anchor: Model with risks by measuring them at fixed intervals, such as quarterly or yearly.

Medium anchor: Model with risks over time by predicting and following some kind of trend possibility.

High anchor: Model with risks taking the passage of, programme and real, time fully into account in the measurement and prioritisation process.

QUESTION 9. OPERATIONAL APPLICATION

Does your risk system model with risks in a way which is linked to key business processes?

Low anchor: Look at risks in an exercise which is independent of the business processes.

Medium anchor: Assess risks with a view to understanding their impact on pre-identified business processes.

High anchor: Assess risk as a planned contribution of inputs, course corrections and decisions to existing business processes.

QUESTION 10. OPERATIONAL OUTCOME COMMUNICATION

What best describes the way your risk system communicates its results further up the organisation?

Low anchor: They are summarised as part of another risk exercise, such as corporate risk register.

Medium anchor: They are summarised as an expected briefing for relevant senior teams in a formal process.

High anchor: They are summarised as a complexity reduction exercise to explain the nature and mechanism of their business impact and the decision inputs this creates.

A simple template for taking stock of your resilience architecture

This template below is the basis of a helpful reckoner tool based on the conclusions of Parts 1–3. It allows you to build an assessment which can, in a very general sense, benchmark the quality of a resilience system you are already using against the standards we have been describing.

To turn this template into a questionnaire, do something like the following:

1 Prepare a questionnaire scale device, preferably operating a 1000-point scale. Excel and similar tools are quite good for this.
2 Attach the scale to each question distributing the anchor texts across the questions in the order they appear. These should span the full scale from low to high.

3 Aggregate scores across questions 1–5 using a geometric mean calculation (because scoring high in all areas is necessitated for a well-rounded system design).

4 Take the following reckoner as a benchmark:
800–1000: World class
600–800: High-performing
400–600: Developing excellence
200–400: Adequate baseline (for improvement)
100–200: Inadequate.

5 Plot the individual question scores for 1–5 in a bar chart against their geometric mean. This will provide a basic gap analysis to help you plan system improvements.

1 Objective: When you think about the core objectives of your resilience approach, what best describes their focus?

a) Low anchor: The system is designed for rounds of planning and the sign-off of a written plan is the success criteria.

b) Medium anchor: The system is designed around a business impact assessment for risk and aims to support business objectives to reduce risk exposure.

c) High anchor: The system is an independent business capability and informs decision making, risk reduction and course correction across the business strategy.

2 Reasoning: When you describe the purpose of reasoning about resilience in your organisation, what best encapsulates why you are doing it?

a) Low anchor: To generate contingency planning for the organisation to offset risk from threats, shocks and stress.

b) Medium anchor: To reduce the risks highlighted by a formal Business Impact Assessment and to measure positive business benefit from interventions.

c) High anchor: To create a business case for resilience counter-measures with cost and benefit analysis to generate value and propel success.

3 Metric design: When you examine the metrics that are being used to benchmark and track the success of resilience interventions and performance, how are they best described?

a) Low anchor: Risk mitigation plans have been filled in and responsibility allocated.

b) Medium anchor: An analysis of, or detailed commentary on, the threats and benefits to operability is shared with targeted groups.

c) High anchor: A value analysis of impacts or benefits which will optimise key business operability drivers is integrated within the strategy planning process.

4 Metric type: When you examine how the benchmark measurements for resilience improvement are made, what type of scaling best describes how this is done?

a) Low anchor: The measurements concern themselves with low, medium, high banding and priority scoring.

b) Medium anchor: The measurements are scaled using business metrics in a ratio form, e.g. cost of intervention, impact on turnover and volume or similar.

c) High anchor: The metrics are the same business case metrics that are used to assess the strategic impact of other mainstream interventions in the business plan.

5 Reasoning outcomes: When people are being asked to reason around resilience impacts, interventions or scenarios, what is the principle way they do this?

a) Low anchor: They are tracking abstract key performance indicators, such as risk reduction targets, which they manage through action planning.

b) *Medium anchor*: There are tracking abstract key performance indicators, but these have an accountability structure behind them which translates their efficacy into business terms.

c) *High anchor*: There are bespoke scales measuring appropriate resilience constructs which are linked to a narrative for the creation of a rational business case.

A template for taking stock of your policy and process/procedure architecture

The two templates below are the basis of a helpful reckoner tool based on the conclusions of Parts 1–3. They allow you to perform a basic scoring exercise which can, in a very general sense, benchmark the quality and heath of the policy and processes/procedures you are already using to deliver resilience.

They also link these to other known forms of risk management such as crisis response.

To use these templates, do something like the following:

1 Collect all the relevant policy and process/procedure documentation around resilience.

2 Familiarise yourself with the high-level categories in these questionnaires.
3 Read the documents in detail, noting evidence in margin notes around the high-level areas.
4 Alone, or with your team, allocate 0, 1, 2 against the pertinent questions.
5 Total the two questionnaires independently.
6 Take the following reckoner as a benchmark.
   Policy coherence
       21–26: World class
       15–20: High-performing
       10–15: Baseline (for improvement)
       >10: Inadequate.
   Process/procedure coherence
       36–42: World class
       27–35: High-performing
       19–26: Baseline (for improvement)
       <18: Inadequate.
7 Tabulate the scores against the questions and use a bar chart to give you a gap analysis (Tables A3.1, 2).

TABLE A3.1 Policy coherence

Policy Coherence		Yes (2)	Part (1)	No (0)	Total
Strong governance	1. Governance system attributes: The degree to which the policy is clearly in a systemic approach				
	1.1 The policy is formally stated as authoritative and binding				
	1.2 The policy refers to a single, coherent and transparent whole system of governance				
Senior Authority/ Support/ Involvement	2. Authority and endorsement: The degree to which the policy clearly articulates itself				
	2.1 Ownership and oversight of this policy is at a senior reporting level				
	2.2 Clear expectations of a "must" variety dominate the wording				
	2.3 There is explicit intolerance of low standards of alignment, quality or compliance				
Scope, Complexity and Value	3. Scope, complexity, values: The degree to which the policy reflects the organisation				
	3.1 The policy directly states the business intention/ business activity as a priority				
	3.2 The policy is tempered by "appropriate to" statements relating to size and/or complexity				
	3.3 The policy directly reflects the organisations core values in a meaningful way				

continued . . .

TABLE A3.1 Continued

Policy Coherence		Yes (2)	Part (1)	No (0)	Total
Roles and responsibilities	4. Roles and responsibilities: The degree to which the policy aligns to actual persons and roles 4.1 The policy unambiguously attaches responsibilities to real and existing roles in the organisation 4.2 The role of all responsible persons named in the policy is an explicit one with clear outcomes				
Intra-/inter-operability	5. Adequate integration: The policy is intra-operable with other polices and interoperable with outside agents 5.1 The policy makes specific reference to the relationship between itself and other live policies, standards and processes in the organisation 5.2 The policy stipulates the responsibilities in regard of outside organisations and third parties essential to its proper execution 5.3 The policy shows clear signs of internal and external stakeholder engagement processes				

		Obvious (–2)	Suspect (–1)	None (0)	Total
Demerit points	6. Demerit points: Remove points if the policy has a "too good to be true" nature				

continued . . .

TABLE A3.1 Continued

	Obvious (-2)	Suspect (-1)	None (0)	Total
6.1 The policy is suspiciously matter of fact or reads like a cut and paste from somewhere else				
6.2 The roles identified by the policy are non-roles: they only exist in relation to the policy and if someone takes them up				
6.3 The policy places itself alongside other policy but without a read-across in meaning				
Policy Coherence Grand Total (Total scores 1–5 minus total 6)	/26			

TABLE A3.2 Process/procedure coherence

Process/Procedure Coherence		Yes (2)	Part (1)	No (0)	Total
Leadership strategic awareness	1. Strategic and decisive leadership: The process clearly defines leadership location and decision authority				
	1.1 A clear focus on the authority of a trained leader or group to "command and control" situations through exercising authority over all other roles (e.g. safety, operations, logistics, communications etc.)				

continued . . .

TABLE A3.2 Continued

Process/Procedure Coherence		Yes (2)	Part (1)	No (0)	Total
	1.2 A clear focus on decision making that is authoritative, transparent and real time				
	1.3 Some evidence of techniques to avoid decision bias or prevarication through combining knowledge, judgement and intuition whilst managing pressure				
Fit, competent and adaptive	2. Adaptive and fit for purpose: The process shows clear signs of commitment to adaptation and learning built in				
	2.1 Clear steps to convert and exploit operational information into actionable plans especially to address critical dependencies and single points of failure				
	2.2 Commitment to an adaptive capacity through internal and external lesson learning and error sharing as part of mandated formal training				
	2.3 Risk management is detailed, structured and timely and identifies tools (e.g. techniques, templates, software, documents) that help people manage risk within the organisation's framework				
	2.4 Action is defined to help the organisation to anticipate, prepare for and respond to well-defined forms of crisis within a combination of risk treatment options (mitigation, acceptance, insurance etc.)				

continued ...

Process/Procedure Coherence		Yes (2)	Part (1)	No (0)	Total
	2.5 The risk management process understands and deals with legal and regulatory requirements, constraints and supports				
Multidisciplinary roles, responsibilities and communications	3. Planned, prepared, tested and communicated: All roles are tightly defined and understood by all players				
	3.1 The programme should be multidisciplinary (and expert) with clear role structures at the right (individual and team) levels for resilience, response and crisis that are well defined and trained				
	3.2 Recognition that communication is central and critical to crisis management success is expressed in robust, authoritative pre-existing structures and tools (inclusive of social media and formal reporting)				
	3.3 Crisis communications strategy, media, spokespersons and suchlike are in a 'head up ready to use' and generic form to utilise internal and external communications channels that have been regularly stress tested				
	3.4 Coordination and cooperation with other agencies has been determined ahead of time, negotiated and tested in advance within some kind of common or shared plans				

continued . . .

TABLE A3.2 Continued

Process/Procedure Coherence		Yes (2)	Part (1)	No (0)	Total
Planned, tested, resourced and costed	4. Risks benefits and good sense: All capability, plans and relationships need to work				
	4.1 Any capability must be supported by capital and resource with evidence that resourcing is regularly reviewed to resolve tensions, e.g. by balancing of just-in-time processes and just-in-case redundancy compared to "value-add" constraints				
	4.2 Where formal continuity, recovery or crisis plans are in place they need to be concise, thresholded, focused, flexible and action oriented in a way that is designed to speed effective response, not labour it				
	4.3 Process implementation can only be achieved through real-time training with all key players in roles where behaviour is structured into: detection, information gathering, planning, decision making, implementation and feedback				
	4.4 Training and exercises should be formal, targeted and include reflection on decision making and lesson learning				
	4.5 Seeking reliable behavioural evidence from key suppliers of their resilience programme is a prerequisite of your programme				

continued . . .

TABLE A3.2 Continued

Process/Procedure Coherence		Yes (2)	Part (1)	No (0)	Total
Situational intra-/inter-operability	5. Awareness and linking of process: All key crisis and risk systems should be linked to all other relevant systems and partners				
	5.1 Crisis management should be inextricably linked to early warning and response in issues and incidents and risk management systems				
	5.2 The interoperability of multiple responding agents should be tested and rehearsed including formalising relationship and responsibility with external partners and operators				
	5.3 For resilient operation the team needs to be highly informed about environment (internal and external), risks (events and opportunities) that compromise or influence resilience, and recognise opportunities and latent internal weaknesses or those beyond direct control				
	5.4 Systems must recognise that crises are by nature complex and require sustained adequate strategic and partnering effort including situation awareness process using channels and structures which pre-exist				
	Grand total (sum of 1–5)	/42			

Facilitation templates for taking stock of the best practice fit and strategic efficacy of your risk, crisis and resilience architecture

The two templates below are based around the deconstruction of international standards explained in the case study in Chapter 11. They are designed to form a helpful basis for two benchmarked conversations.

The first is on the alignment of your systems design. This examines key organisational performance factors, using a range of questions indicating whether your systems are effectively integrated into your organisation – a key mediator of success.

The second is on the behavioural effectiveness of your general systems in risk, crisis and resilience (RCR systems). This focuses on two core elements common to all Standards: the systems' strategic placement and their detailed purpose.

To use these templates, do something like the following:

1 Bring together the multidisciplinary group in your organisation responsible for the areas of supply chain and enterprise risk, resilience, business continuity and crisis management.
2 Use the templates as benchmark points to lead the group in a facilitated discussion about the alignment, performance and effectiveness of the current systems.
3 Use the templates as a basis to write up a gap analysis against best practice.

TABLE A4.1 System performance-shaping factors: a discussion facilitator

	High-performing	Medium-performing	Low-performing
1. Our strategic alignment	Our RCR system has valid senior sign-off on strategy WRT business and governance objectives	Our RCR system is signed off on strategy WRT governance objectives	Our RCR system isn't really signed off on strategy WRT to any business or governance objectives
2. Our command and control features	The command and control of any RCR incident is fully understood at strategic, operational and tactical levels and everyone is fully competent to execute their role	The command and control of any RCR incident is broadly understood at strategic, operational and tactical levels and everyone has an awareness of the role they need to play	The command and control of any RCR incident is broadly understood in some ways but would have to be worked out in practice
3. Our understanding of the scope of risks, incidents and crises	We have deep horizon scanning to anticipate, identify, monitor and evaluate the trends in critical strategic, financial, operational and reputational areas	We have horizon scanning to anticipate, identify, monitor and evaluate the trends for a broad catalogue of different risks	We have horizon scanning to anticipate, identify, monitor and evaluate the trends only for certain kinds of risks
4. Our analytical rigour	Our RCR systems clearly highlight the difference between identifying, scoring and comparing the value of risks (and groups of risks). These are analysed using numerical and non-numerical	Our RCR systems are based on identifying, scoring and comparing the value of risks (and groups of risks). These are analysed using sophisticated numerical measurements	Our RCR systems are based on identifying, scoring and comparing the value of risks (and groups of risks). These are analysed using averaged numerical measurements resulting in HML output

continued . . .

TABLE A4.1 Continued

	High-performing	Medium-performing	Low-performing
	measurements to avoid typical averaged judgements		
5. Our systematic risk appetite	The business impact risks covered by our RCR system have been clearly prioritised (using time and dependencies). This gives a clear, well-defined risk appetite defining minimum levels of acceptable service	The business impact risks covered by our RCR system have been prioritised to give us an understanding of risk appetite linked to acceptable service levels	The business impact risks covered by our RCR system have been prioritised, but not with an understanding of risk appetite linked to acceptable service levels
6. Our culture of performance monitoring	The risk controls dictated by our RCR system and any plans it produces are formally monitored, reviewed and reported in proportion to the risk severity	The risk controls dictated by our RCR system and any plans it produces are monitored and reviewed at least quarterly and reported	The risk controls dictated by our RCR system and any plans it produces are monitored and reviewed yearly
7. Our system's maturity monitoring	The maturity and performance of our RCR governance is formally assessed for failures, successes, training outcomes, legal and regulatory compliance and lesson learning	The maturity and performance of our RCR governance is formally reviewed as part of a wider governance exercise	The maturity and performance of our RCR governance is not formally reviewed in a meaningful way

8. Human capability	Our RCR system recognises deeply that crisis/risk management is a capability (not a plan or process) which needs to be organisationally validated in the fires of constant rehearsal, training and learning	Our RCR system recognises that crisis/risk management is a capability (not a plan or process) which needs to be kept healthy through regular exercises	Our RCR system recognises that crisis/risk management is a capability (not a plan or process) which requires some people to be trained to do it well
9. Validity-checking organisation and change	Our RCR system is subject to regular review (more frequent during periods of rapid change or where the risks being managed are themselves proving volatile) to maintain an agreed baseline of capability at all times	Our RCR system is subject to regular review (more frequent during periods of rapid change or where the risks being managed are themselves proving volatile)	Our RCR system is subject to routine review
10. Validation of cost and value add	Our RCR system is demonstrated to be fully cost effective in two key ways. First, we understand the full operational costs (time and resource) needed to deploy it. Second, we understand the business value that is being protected or added as a consequence of the investment	Our RCR system is believed to be cost effective as the operational costs (time and resource) needed to deploy it are understood	Our RCR system is believed to be cost effective inasmuch as the operational costs (time and resource) needed to deploy it are in the budget

TABLE A4.2 Alignment with placement and purpose factors: a discussion facilitator

Placement/purpose factor being measured	Benchmark statement (also printed on cards for the respondent)	Question to ask
1 Strategic	For an RCR system to be considered strategic it would have to be embedded in a governance formally approved by top management. This would be as something that creates and protects long-term value and be delivered within a system of accountability, direction and control. Top management would engage with, resource and underwrite this system.	To what degree do you think your RCR system is strategically well placed in these sorts of ways? Give examples
2 Operational Viability	The operational viability of an RCR system is determined by three key things. First, the authority of its lead agents to implement and maintain effective and respected systems. Second, the maturity of the model of the scope and complexity of the organisation. Third, the degree to which the controls it recommends are taken seriously in normal business decisions.	Can you give me concrete examples of how the operational viability of elements of your RCR system are being described here? Give examples
3 Intra-/interoperability	A high degree of intra-/interoperability is a sign of an effective and mature RCR system. This can be detected by several factors: coherent transparent links between the RCR policy and all other business policies; high degrees of integration between RCR systems and other organisational controls, processes, systems and skills; and management and reporting aspects of RCR enjoy equal status with all other business critical items	Are there any areas (policy, process integration, reporting) where your RCR system is particularly strong or weak in this regard? Give examples

4	Strategic value (direction)	An RCR system contributes to the strategic intent and direction of the organisation when its analyses evidently support the development of strategy and strategic decision making of senior leaders. They use its output to set at least some of the criteria whereby they control and audit risk-taking and exposure.	Can you give concrete examples to demonstrate that your RCR system supports senior reasoning and decision making in these sorts of ways? Give examples
5	Strategic value (appetite for complexity)	An RCR system is strategically coherent when it has an appropriate level of complexity. Thus, its documentation, processes and tools recognise the size, scope and complexity of the organisation. The scope and also the reach of the system appropriately match the size, nature and complexity of the organisation.	Would you agree that your RCR system has a) avoided over-simplification and b) accepted and communicated an appropriate level of complexity? Give examples
6	Support structure (fit for purpose & principles defined)	An RCR system is mature and effective when the support structures it stipulates are fit for purpose. This can be seen when it meets three standards. It encompasses the full range of risk control (i.e. prevent, prepare, mitigate, respond and recover). The processes and tools are forward looking and systematically matched to different parts of the risk management process (including a positive notion of risk). The overarching principles it articulates are transparent and sufficiently detailed to be obeyed easily in any crisis situation	When you think about your RCR system in these terms, in what ways would you need to improve the support structures it creates? Give examples

continued . . .

TABLE A4.2 Continued

Placement/purpose factor being measured	Benchmark statement (also printed on cards for the respondent)	Question to ask
7 Organisational impact perception	Successful RCS systems have an appropriate influence on the culture and behaviour of the organisation. They develop cultural and behavioural norms that promote trust in the effectiveness of the effort needed to execute their assessments and controls. They result in a rise in the perceived importance of the culture of risk management. This gives rise to the meaningful translation of "threat languages", e.g. cyber-threat quickly becomes coherent information management behaviours that people can model and report on	When you think about the impact that the perception of your RCR system has on your organisation, would you say this area is mature or requires more backing, promotion and activity? Give examples
8 Ethos and values	Good RCS systems have a defined and coherent purpose which reflects, supports and explicitly re-communicates the core purpose and values of the organisation. Where value shifts are needed from historical behaviours, these are tackled with honesty and authority. The process for managing RCR incidents and crises should be obviously commensurate with the values and objectives of the organisation	To what degree, if at all, do the ethos and values of your RCR system reflect a kind of "counter-culture" that leaves its operatives swimming against the tide at times? Give examples
9 Balance of risk and opportunity	Effective RCR systems help people balance risk and opportunity in a transparent, accountable and value-led way. The business impact tools, the plans and the benefits derived from the information shared should be recognised as a valid contribution to the organisation's capability to meaningfully and ethically balance risk	Does the risk and business impact modelling at the heart of your RCR system serve any business process or outcome other than RCR assurance? Give examples

INDEX

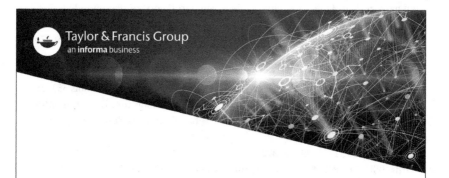